Mongrel Firebugs
and Men of Property

Mongrel Firebugs and Men of Property

Capitalism and Class Conflict in American History

Steve Fraser

VERSO

London • New York

First published by Verso 2019
© Steve Fraser 2019

1 3 5 7 9 10 8 6 4 2

Verso
UK: 6 Meard Street, London W1F 0EG
US: 20 Jay Street, Suite 1010, Brooklyn, NY 11201
versobooks.com

Verso is the imprint of New Left Books

ISBN-13: 978-1-78873-670-1
ISBN-13: 978-1-78873-671-8 (UK EBK)
ISBN-13: 978-1-78873-672-5 (US EBK)

British Library Cataloguing in Publication Data
A catalogue record for this book is available from the British Library

Library of Congress Cataloging-in-Publication Data
Names: Fraser, Steve, 1945- author.
Title: Mongrel firebugs and men of property : capitalism and class conflict
  in American history / Steve Fraser.
Description: London ; Brooklyn, NY : Verso, 2019.
Identifiers: LCCN 2019010273| ISBN 9781788736701 (pbk. : alk. paper)
  | ISBN 9781788736725 (US ebk.) | ISBN 9781788736718 (UK ebk.)
Subjects: LCSH: Capitalism—Political aspects—United States—History. |
  Social classes—United States—History. | Social stratification—United
  States—History. | United States—Economic conditions. | United
  States—Social conditions. | United States—History.
Classification: LCC HC110.C3 F73 2019 | DDC 330.973—dc23
LC record available at https://lccn.loc.gov/2019010273

Typeset in Sabon LT by Hewer Text UK Ltd, Edinburgh
Printed and bound by CPI Group (UK) Ltd, Croydon, CR0 4YY

Contents

Acknowledgements

I want to thank the editors of *Salmagundi*, *TomDispatch*, *Raritan*, *Salon*, and the *International Journal of Labour Research*, where many of these essays first appeared. Two of the essays were co-written with Joshua Freeman, for whose collaboration I'm grateful. Ben Mabie, Sarah Grey, Duncan Ranslem, and Jacob Stevens helped shepherd this project through Verso; thanks to all. The essays were written over a period of more than fifteen years, during which time they benefited from the advice of friends and a host of historians without whose work my own efforts would have been fruitless. I want to especially thank Paul Milkman, Rochelle Gurstein, and Corey Robin. My debt to my family is immeasurable.

Introduction

"Liberty produces wealth and that wealth destroys liberty." So said Henry Demarest Lloyd, widely read critic of America's newly risen plutocracy and leader of the antitrust movement during the country's first Gilded Age. The essays gathered together here comprise some evidence for the second half of that equation. Living in the age of the 1 percent and the 99 percent makes it even easier to detect its fundamental truth.

But it is the first element of that social mathematics which, more often than not, has epitomized the American mythos and anesthetized sensitivity to the grievous economic and political costs of capital accumulation. We are, after all, reputed to live in the land of the free, where that freedom has nourished a fabled cornucopia. So it is also the case that these essays are attempts to bring to the surface realities about the historical evolution of the country that its dedication to the liberty to accumulate have obscured or interred entirely.

Stories about what we now call "the homeland," its origins and unfolding, do not, conventionally, feature capitalism. Other tales about the country's history usually take priority. Favorites include, perhaps first and foremost, the New World as the incubator of liberty and democracy in the Western world. Others emphasize the nation's embrace of people from a global everywhere, America as the nation of nations. Another is heroic and tracks the conquest of frontiers, both physical and spiritual, a legendary odyssey requiring fortitude and audacity. Organically tied to that one is the apotheosis of America as the land of entrepreneurial genius, derring-do risk-taking, a business civilization resting on a human landscape of indigenous inventiveness. The last tale does indeed spill over into a celebration of capitalism, but less as a form of political economy, more as an epiphany of the self-made man, cleansed of the social abrasions that real capitalism inevitably trails in its wake.

All of these accounts carry their own truths. There is little question but that the country was in the vanguard of certain democratic forms and practices and that it incubated notions of civil liberties. "Huddled masses" did indeed flock here, and, no matter the various reasons they did so, their presence imparted a distinctive cosmopolitanism to the country's self-conception. Despite the presence of native peoples inhabiting societies ten thousand years old, there is too a truth to the flattering self-fascination with Americans as pathfinders, triumphing over all natural or man-made impediments. And it is a self-evident form of national narcissism that "we the people" have been astonishingly good, almost preternaturally gifted when it comes to entrepreneurial esprit.

No doubt, all of these accounts tend to leave out their more mordant undersides: the selective distribution of liberty and democracy and the frequent instances of their undermining; the chronic stigmatizing, stereotyping, and exclusion of the "huddled masses"; the pathfinder as exploiter, expropriator, and exterminator; the numbingly frequent collapses of entrepreneurial phantasms dragging down along with them lives and livelihoods; and the tithing of human labor and the insults to the human dignity of those legions who labored in the vineyards to make American capitalism the extraordinary world power it became.

Nonetheless, even those versions of these origin myths that allow for these taints and complaints retain a certain traction. Moreover, they all can be subsumed under the rubric of "American exception-alism." It's the story that functions as the meta-tale, the one that exempts the New World from the social antagonisms that had for centuries disfigured European civilization—the Old World—from which our freethinkers and freebooters, our instinctive democrats and immigrant refugees, our frontiersmen and adventurers were in flight. This was, and remains, a utopian fantasy, embedded in the heart of the heartland. Here social hierarchies and the fatal confron-tations they inevitably fostered would go to die, liquidated by the boundless prospects of self-advancement that a continental abun-dance of land and natural resources made possible.

If capitalism figures in at all, it is to forefront opportunity, entre-preneurial vigor, material abundance, and the seven-league boots of manifest destiny. Conflict may rear its unseemly face but only episodically, as a kind of alien or aberrant detour off the main road of America's exceptional career through the world. Instances of serious social discord, when they draw notice, get transcended, a course correction allowing the utopian project to resume.

The essays collected here work instead to raise the profile of capitalism in the national saga. Explicitly or by inference, they all challenge the consoling fantasy of American exceptionalism. They presume conflict. And by their nature they challenge the national framework which American exceptionalism inherently assumes. That is to say, the one nation so precious to the exceptionalism romance is seen here to be recurrently splitting into two nations, or if not "nations," then two or more social species which speak to each other—or fail to speak to each other—across a great divide and which every now and then threaten to rip wide open the fragile fabric of the national conceit. On the one hand, there is the demo-cratic or egalitarian boast; on the other, there is the capitalist reality.

Yet there is no denying the left side of Lloyd's equation. Liberty did produce wealth. Had it not, it is highly unlikely the faith and trust in the American dream would have gained the traction it did and lasted as long as it has. Moreover, that wealth exists not as an inanimate pile of things or their monetary equivalent, or not only as that. Freedom to venture forth, to transform organic or inorganic nature into vendible commodities, has also served as a spiritual elixir. Homely acts of commercial enterprise appeal also because the liberty to engage in them free of outside interference by political authorities or economic overlords armored with state powers makes them simultaneously acts of self-invention. They can seem to escape not only material privations but also all previously ascribed social positions, especially the humblest ones. This is the liberty that comes before capital accumulation and grows more robust in the process.

Freedom anchored in acts of self-reliance and the mastery of the market, of nature, of the libido, of other people can be intoxicating, functioning like an aphrodisiac. Even if its social reach recedes as capital accumulation becomes the exclusive terrain of only the mightiest conquistadors, the dream abides.

Lloyd was right, of course, that "wealth destroys liberty," which helps account for the enormous energy fueling the antitrust movement of his day, and for that matter the wide breadth of anticapitalist sentiment that darkened the flashy exterior of the Gilded Age. Nonetheless, precisely because of capitalism's fluidity, its systemic compulsion to sweep away established forms of economic enterprise and antiquated technologies, opportunities to refresh the dream periodically rise to the surface. This was true during and as a consequence of the maelstrom of cyclical booms and busts characteristic of the economy, beginning even before the Civil War and continuing with numbing regularity through to the Great Depression. Leveling the ground in this way crushed underfoot many a striving businessman (not to mention millions of working-class families) and turned bankrupted enterprises into trophies for hardier and more ruthless predators who could acquire these assets on the cheap. But in the aftermath, new terrain opened up for wannabe entrepreneurial heroes, nurturing the dream among many people, however unpromising their actual position on the ladder of social preferment.

Ambitions of this sort not only were alive and well during the original Gilded Age, but are again during what is now commonly characterized as our own second Gilded Age. The essays in this collection about the two Gilded Ages describe this phenomenon. In our own time and in earlier times, this is the soil in which free-market ideologies take root, where hostility to government generally, and to regulation in particular, bubbles to the surface of public life. Shaking off the straitjacket of any outside authority is part of the dream, at the core of the metaphysics of individualism.

Modern times reduces this prospect of everyman a speculator, an incipient bourgeois, to a pious hope for most whose actual chances of ascending out of a subordinate status of more or less well-rewarded proletarian dependency is close to nil. Yet the dream abides by shifting terrain. Mass consumption and the fantasies absorbed into the psychic bloodstream through the medium of consumer culture make space for internalized triumphs of self-invention, indeed for multiple acts that recreate the self over and over again. These soothe the wounds of real life insults to self-esteem and to precarious social position made so hurtful by the grand canyons of inequality that have become conspicuous over the last generation. The essay included here on "The Age of Acquiescence" dwells on this.

Paradise Lost

Still, "wealth destroys liberty." Beneath the gilded patina, notwithstanding the social leveling abundance promises and sometimes delivers, the lineaments of class and class conflict poke through the veil, disrupt the narrative placidity of American exceptionalism, and reconfigure that story so that capitalism takes center stage. That is the overriding drift of the essays assembled here.

Adam Smith's much celebrated (and often enough criticized) "invisible hand" has been treated as a kind of secular deity, a metaphor for a kind of economic deism. The operation of capitalism is often conceived as an exquisitely articulated clockwork mechanism set in motion by an unseen, offstage creator. Once set in motion by the presumably natural instinct to truck and barter, it would roll on as a self-regulating system whose every malfunction or disquieting social consequence would correct itself through the inherent genius of the laws of supply and demand, another import from the natural world into the human one. (This is far less a view of Smith's than of his epigones.)

Part I of this book presents essays that turn this inherently harmonious view of the capitalist universe upside down. It is in the nature of capitalism to reproduce maladies and calamities. They are, one might say, its second nature—and that has been as true in our own "exceptional" homeland as anywhere else.

A willingness to undertake risk, to venture into the unknown, is often cited as characteristic of capitalism generally, marked down as the reason for its superiority as compared to other economic forms that came earlier (and in the case of socialism, later). This celebration of risk is especially distinctive in the American context, mated to other qualities like frontier vigor and native inventiveness. However, in the unfolding of its career in the country's history, risk has played the part of the changeling. At one moment surfacing like a confidence man, manipulating and undermining the confidence upon which any capitalist economy depends; at another appearing in Napoleonic guise as a daring conqueror, admired by millions, yet demanding tribute from millions; or erupting as a savage beast despoiling the whole nation, as in the Great Depression.

Bernie Madoff's colossal Ponzi scheme and the hero-worship of Wall Street financiers in the closing decades of the last century and the traumatic near-collapse of the global financial system in 2008 are among the more conspicuous recent proofs that these toxic forms of risk continue to show their faces in our own times. The essay "The Three Faces of Risk"—the confidence man, the hero, the victim—explores these permutations more closely at various moments in the nation's past.

Risk enjoys a close kinship with debt, without which there could be no actually existing capitalism. The "art of the deal" is very frequently premised on debt. Donald Trump was for many years known as "the king of debt." The "subprime mortgages" that crashed the economy were a form of debt. It is also the case that debt underpins the mass-consumption economy, which is what, since World War II at least, has made Americans a "people of plenty." Without financing, that ardent desire to risk it all on some new venture may lie fallow.

So debt is part of capitalism's DNA. Sometimes, in fact, the deeper in debt the better; at least that has often been the case for high rollers, whose creditors stand to lose so much should their highly leveraged debtor go bust that they will work to keep him or her or it afloat. Again, Trump played that game for many years, intimidating the biggest banks. In these instances, the real leverage may be exercised by the otherwise beleaguered supplicant tottering on the edge of bankruptcy.

For ordinary folk, however, the shoe has often been decidedly on the other foot. "Another Day Older and Deeper in Debt" examines the way debt has functioned as a mechanism of primitive accumulation, extracting wealth from farmers, handicrafters, fishermen, storekeepers, small-town businesses, and an array of other petty producers swept into the orbit of merchant and finance capitalism. Whole ways of life, not to mention ways of making a living, succumbed to the relentless pressures of insupportable debt. The politics of debt accounted for some of the greatest social and political upheavals in American history, including nineteenth-century populism.

This dynamic was already familiar in colonial days, when debtors' prisons were common. Now and then a real grandee would end up there, unable to make good on risky speculations. In part for that reason, debtors' prisons were outlawed in state after state not long after the nation's founding. (The principal reason was that debt does indeed make the wheels of capitalism go round and round, so if you keep imprisoning those who venture but lose, the arteries of commerce are apt to get coagulated.) More recently, as deindustrialization has shrunk the incomes of working-class citizens, consumer debt has functioned as a treacherous replacement, temporarily buoying an economy that has for several generations relied on mass consumption.

When the Great Recession that followed the financial debacle of 2008 blew apart that bubble of debt, millions lost their homes and jobs as well as their capacity to make good on their mountains of consumer debt. The mercenary sympathy shown to big-time operators like Trump or Goldman Sachs does not extend so easily to working people, however. Consequently, imprisonment for debt has made a comeback of late. Consumers delinquent on payments to credit-card companies, car dealerships, or other retailers may find themselves in jail: debtors' prisons redux.

Jail time is still time, and capitalism assigns a high value to time, at least time spent at work. From the earliest days of the republic, businesses have found ways to turn a profit on jail time. "Locking Down an American Workforce" explores the rise and fall and rise again of for-profit prison labor. Prisoners were contracted out to private-sector enterprises all through the nineteenth century and beyond, working for a pittance and without even a ghost of a chance to resist. This was a state-supported system and one by no means confined to the South or to ex-slaves, although there the very worst abuses, including torture and death, were commonplace. The prison-industrial system flourished in the North as well, and among white convicts, especially those belonging to stigmatized ethnic groups. Once again today, we have grown gruesomely accustomed to mass incarceration as a feature of contemporary life. Two million are behind bars (only Rwanda has a higher per-capita prison population). Rikers Island in New York, where 10,000 inmates fester, is the largest penal colony in the world. Once again, many are rented out as hired hands for some of the country's biggest corporations. This is as well a racial scandal thanks to the overwhelming disproportion of African-American prisoners.

Incarceration rates so astronomical are evidence of another regularly recurring feature of capitalism: unemployment. Imprisoning people, building and expanding a prison-industrial complex, is one way to warehouse working people for whom there is no work. Nowadays, we take for granted that unemployment is a natural and normal, if lamentable, feature of modern economies. Our ancestors, however, did not share that assumption. Indeed, as capitalism spread into the American interior, absorbing various forms of precapitalist ways of life, people were shocked to find themselves without work. It was in some ways the most stunning proof that they had been transformed into dependent proletarians, stripped of the ability to sustain their own lives, supplicants of those who possessed the capital to put them to work. Another harsh truth emerged: even those without work could serve a purpose by constituting a reserve army of labor whose existence depressed wages and could undercut attempts by the employed to organize against their employers. "Uncle Sam Doesn't Want You" looks at the evolution of unemployment: the way it shattered lives in the periodic busts endemic to the economy, evoked popular resistance, and got normalized by policy-makers.

During the Great Recession following the crash of 2008, unemployment once again became pandemic. More recently, those numbers have dropped considerably. But it defies all past experience to imagine that this will endure, that somehow capitalism has overcome its innate tendency to implode cyclically. Improbably economists and pundits both liberal and conservative have been claiming that it would or already had for a century, most infamously before the Great Depression, and again before the Great Recession. But whether that flying pig ever gets off the ground, our contemporary dilemma poses the same question in a new way. Has the economy reached a stage—thanks to robotics, to automation generally, and to the global outsourcing of a vast array of jobs once done here in the United States—in which it will produce an ever-growing surplus of people without work? If so, where will they be warehoused? Will the proletariat of the future end up like its forebears in ancient Rome, a permanently superfluous population kept bemused by some high-tech version of bread and circuses?

Whether consigned to the dole permanently or only temporarily, unemployment has been naturalized. Economists even speak of a "natural rate of unemployment." If the ingenuity of the human mind can turn something so otherwise clearly a function of social organization and the distribution of power and property into something like the inexorable rising and setting of the sun, then "natural disasters" like devastating earthquakes or floods or fires or hurricanes have also, even more so, been seen as a function, if a cruel one, of Mother Nature. "Making Disaster Pay" provides a social autopsy on four of the most infamous calamities in US history: the Chicago fire, the Johnstown flood, the San Francisco earthquake, and Superstorm Sandy. In all of these cases, the origins of the disaster, its social impact, and the way recovery efforts were mobilized and distributed revealed the anatomy of a steeply hierarchical class system. There was nothing purely "natural" about the way these traumas unfolded. Moreover, disaster often provided capital a commercial opportunity. At the very least, upper classes usually escaped the worst of the devastation and any culpability for causing it. The appalling state of Puerto Rico many months after Hurricane Maria hit the island in 2017—close to five thousand people died rather than the sixty-four originally reported by the Trump regime—once again suggests how ocean waters and atmospheric winds, themselves made fiercer by the fossil-fuel-industry-driven impact of global warming, punish the weakest, the poorest, and the disempowered.

Capitalism Evolves

Natural disasters may reveal again and again the visible hand of class preferment and class discrimination that capitalism inescapably trails in its wake. However, these patterns of domination and subordination don't always show up in the same way. After all, capitalism changes and has its own history. Merchant capitalism, in which trade and the financing of trade (including the slave trade) were the principal profit-making activities, characterized the colonial and early national periods (in the New England and Middle Atlantic colonies, not the South). This was a system of value extraction some distance removed from the actual sites of production. Extractive capitalism throughout the nineteenth century tore right through the mineral-rich and forested landscape of the earth to realize value. The second half of the nineteenth century and the first half of the twentieth belonged to the reign of industrial capitalism. More recent decades on into the new century have witnessed the deliberate cannibalism of industrial capital at the behest and under the reign of finance capitalism.

Moreover, accumulation by merchant-bankers, landlords, mine owners, industrialists, financial speculators, and others was sometimes carried out through the family, the dynasty, the depersonalized corporation, or some combination of these social types. Political life, moral beliefs, psychological motivations, and class conflict looked different depending on whether the family enterprise or the limited partnership or the closely held dynastic empire or the publicly traded corporation was the vessel of capital accumulation.

Each form of economic organization has grown up alongside distinct kinds of work, ladders of class privilege, institutions through which the political and cultural hegemony of elites were deployed, historically specific methods and organizations for conducting business, and appropriate ideological rationales. And each has called forth acts of resistance to exploitation and oppression that were indigenous to the larger social system in which they were embedded.

The essays in Part 2 of this book cover a bit of this terrain. They span from the last third of the nineteenth century, popularly referred to as the Gilded Age, through the Great Depression and New Deal, and from there to what many now think of as the country's second Gilded Age but which I refer to as the Age of Acquiescence. On the surface, the transit from industrial to finance capitalism may seem to leave class relations, the distribution of wealth, the role of the state, the makeup and motivations of ruling elites, and much else besides untouched. The rich prevail and grow richer; government largely takes its lead from the business community; democracy lives on as an endangered political species; secular as well as religious intellectual circles hypothesize justifications for inequality.

There is an undeniable element of truth to this picture, but the import of Part 2 is that this is too flat and static a portrait. "Two Gilded Ages" acknowledges what the two have in common but argues instead that what distinguishes them is more important. One lived for and enjoyed the spoils of industrial production; the second battened on the financial waste products of industry. How ruling elites were composed, their family backgrounds, education, and careers varied widely; the first largely nouveaux riches with little political experience or even interest, the second more often to the manner born and deeply enmeshed in politics and the machinery of governing. During the first Gilded Age the work ethic constituted the nuclear core of American cultural belief and practice, presumed frugality and delayed gratification, frowned on debt, and feared libidinal excess; the moral and psychic economy of our Gilded Age couldn't be more opposite. The first Gilded Age was suspicious of and fended off the state while relying on it to coerce insubordinate people from farms and factories; it hated democracy. The second lives through the state, largely eschews violence (at home, that is), and learns to manipulate democratic forms rather than ignore and suppress them. Most fundamentally, the capitalism of the first Gilded Age rested on a process of primitive accumulation, absorbing and transforming precapitalist ways of life in town and country, both here at home and abroad. The second Gilded Age instead is characterized by a process of autocannibalism in which the values of a century of industrial capitalism are devoured by a politically empowered financial sector. For that reason, this new Gilded Age, notwithstanding its patina of luxe, is also rightly depicted as an age of austerity.

Of all the substantial differences between the two Gilded Ages, the most striking is the way working-class, as well as plenty of middle-class, people reacted to the prevailing order. The original Gilded Age engendered an extraordinary period of resistance to the advent of capitalism, an anticapitalist persuasion that crossed boundaries of class (and even race and gender); spread itself across rural and urban America; inspired artists, politicians, preachers, and journalists; built impressive mass movements; challenged the complacency and apologia offered up by capitalism's defenders; and envisioned a range of alternatives to the capitalist way of life. The second Gilded Age has managed precious little of this, and so I have called it an Age of Acquiescence in an essay that bears that title.

"The Age of Acquiescence" tries to figure out why. It's by no means an easily solved puzzle. The yawning disparities of wealth and income, the suborning of democracy by the politics of money,

chronic financial scandals and collapses, the downward mobility of
so many working-class people, the evisceration of the social safety
net—all of this and much more might have invited rage, outrage,
and mobilization. Rather, Americans demobilized. Surrender had
many accomplices. The essay points to the economic and social
impact of deindustrialization, first of all, and then to the systematic
disarming of the labor movement, to the self-consoling delusions of
consumer culture, to the advent of precarious forms of work, to the
Democratic Party's abandonment of its working-class constituents
and their anticapitalist traditions, and to the ideological and political onslaught of an ascendant conservative movement.

Transformations so momentous may seem inevitable in hindsight. In real time, however, the supplanting of resistance by acquiescence was hardly foreordained. In between the first and second
Gilded Ages, the popular as well as elite reactions to the Great
Depression of the 1930s suggest that although capitalism may
endure, it is vulnerable to the contingencies of history, in particular
to crises of its own making. "American Labor and the Great
Depression" treats the insurgency and mass organization of the
industrial working class during the 1930s as the culminating chapter in the story of popular resistance to capitalism, and one might
say the end of the long nineteenth century that might reasonably be
called America's age of resistance.

Moreover, the Great Depression was feared not only by those
occupying the mudsills but also by those at the pinnacles of
economic and political life. They were compelled to reckon with
what many thought might be capitalism's terminal breakdown.
Segments of American business, together with reform-minded
circles, mainly in the Democratic Party, were prepared to challenge
an ancien régime run by old-line capital-goods producers, their
allied investment banks, and their political enablers, clustered
largely (although by no means exclusively) in the Republican Party.
These new reform-minded elites formed an uneasy partnership with

the currents of popular rebellion. "Partnership" doesn't quite register the distinctly subordinate status of the labor movement within
this concert of interests. But together they created a capitalism with
features unfamiliar to earlier eras.

The New Deal, or the Keynesian social welfare and administrative state, was something new under the American capitalist sun. It
civilized the laissez-faire regime by regulating finance and industry,
by recognizing certain collective rights of the organized working
class, by establishing a minimum level of material survival, and by
licensing the state to intervene into the marketplace, using the levers
of fiscal and monetary policy to even out the wild oscillations of
economic boom and bust that threatened to undermine the social
order fatally. Although this outcome preserved the basic framework
of capitalism, it also required a sea change in the way ruling circles
behaved; in the scope and powers of the central government; in the
reigning ideology crafted to explain and justify the New Deal order
that was so at odds with the social Darwinism of an earlier epoch;
in the internal composition of the Democratic Party; and in the
degree to which capitalism was obliged to make more room for
democracy. Whatever the severe limitations of this new world, these
were not inconsiderable changes from what the country was accustomed to and they point to the malleability of capitalism.

However, as a social as well as economic order, the New Deal
was not only the outcome of previous history; as a historical formation, it enjoyed no immunity from its own pathologies. Perhaps the
best recent evidence of that is the dismantling of the New Deal
order over the past half-century. In the age of austerity, the welfare
state has been placed on hard rations. Deregulation became the
watchword of both major political parties during the last third of
the twentieth century. The collective rights of organized labor now
approach the vanishing point. Free-market ideology reigns not only
in the economic sphere, but across broad stretches of social life,
from education to the privatization of public services. Meritocracy

is our version of social Darwinism. Crony capitalism makes a mockery of democracy. Old ruling elites are challenged by newer ones, rooted in the recrudescence of dynastic as distinct from corporate capitalism. Oligarchs like Trump, the Koch brothers, the Walton family, Sheldon Adelson, Robert Mercer, and others don't subscribe to the social and political meliorism typical of the faceless corporate CEOs of the mid-twentieth century: still capitalism to be sure, but different with a vengeance.

The Return of the Titans

Part 3 tackles this new age of what I call "populist plutocracy." The New Deal order decomposed. That decay was abetted by elements profoundly hostile to its existence. But the line separating its own internal failures from the hostiles gathering outside the tent is not so easy to draw. "The Limousine Liberal's Family Tree" explores the origins of right-wing populism. From Henry Ford and Father Coughlin, running onward to Joseph McCarthy and George Wallace and culminating in the Tea Party, a current in American public life has fused a resentment of liberal, cosmopolitan elites, including bankers and members of the Fortune 500, with a fear of the lower orders, especially those of the wrong complexion and alien nativity. Richard Nixon's appeal to the "silent majority" was a successful and cynical attempt to channel this politics of resentment on behalf of established centers of power. The erosion of the Democratic Party's base in the white working and lower middle classes began then. The Democrats' subsequent capture by the ideology and policy prescriptions of neoliberalism and the edgier liberalism of identity politics consigned their onetime left-inflected populism to some dusty attic of archival mementos.

But history had its revenge on the strategic high command of the Republican Party as well. The "silent majority" gradually found its voice and, with growing fervor, raised it against its creators. By the first decade of the new century, the Republican establishment was engaged in a losing battle against its own homegrown insurgents, denouncing party hierarchs, fuming against bank bailouts that the party's officialdom approved, decrying their cultural and moral agnosticism when it came to matters of gay marriage or their incontinence when it came to banning immigrants. Those and a multitude of other grievances made the Grand Old Party less than grand and verging on incoherence.

Populism has a checkered history (not only in the United States but abroad as well, as recent developments in Europe suggest). Moreover, its relationship to capitalism has been an ambiguous one. Once there was William Jennings Bryan vowing that the masters of Wall Street would not get away with "crucifying mankind on a cross of gold." Now there is Donald Trump, who has ascended to the presidency by inveighing against the establishment—but is, in many ways, that establishment. "The Genie Grown Monstrous" tries to capture populism's strange career by comparing "The Donald" to the only figure in American history who was, like Trump, a plutocrat yet practiced in the arts of populist demagoguery. William Randolph Hearst, the great media mogul at the turn of the twentieth century, was—like Trump—adept at using the media as a vehicle of self-promotion. He—also like Trump—inherited a fortune, made a bigger one, and avidly pursued a career in politics, nourished dreams of becoming president, and did nearly become mayor of New York. Hearst, however, appealed to the waves of anticapitalist sentiment sweeping over the country at the turn of the twentieth century. So he embraced the antitrust movement, was a friend to immigrants, and defended labor unions. First and foremost a demagogue, Hearst had to tailor his demagogy to capture the prevailing winds.

Trump too is a demagogue. But he came onto the political scene at a moment when right-leaning populism was in the ascendancy. So he traffics in xenophobia and racism while hurling an occasional verbal thunderbolt at big business and postures as a friend of the working classes. As a human spectacle, he is practically *sui generis*. But he is also a type that has rather suddenly appeared on the stage of public life.

Trump inherited and now runs a dynasty. Dynastic capitalists like him, with just as little or no political experience but the same Napoleonic self-certainty that their own commercial successes and habits of command qualify them to preside over America, have invaded the political arena as senators and governors and now as president. Others like them who don't care to actually hold public office use the family patrimony to steer public policy—the Koch brothers, for example. "Playing God" looks at the rise and fall and rise again of this kind of family capitalism and the strategic ways in which it differs from corporate capitalism. It also suggests why it can exert a real appeal to ordinary people who have not a ghost of a chance of ever climbing to those heights, but admire the "family values," patriarchal machismo, and consoling myth of self-reliance that have always incubated inside the womb of the family enterprise.

Is Trump the nether end of Western civilization, stripped bare of its historic commitments to liberty and enlightenment and democracy? Probably not. Still, he became the most powerful man on earth on the five-hundredth anniversary of the Reformation and the centenary of the Bolshevik Revolution. Whatever one might judge to be the enduring significance of those events, when they happened, they seemed to open up new chapters in the story of human emancipation. If the "arc of the moral universe ... bends toward justice," as Martin Luther King Jr. believed, it has taken a nightmarish detour. "The Priest, the Commissar, and The Donald" appears here as an afterword, a chance to reflect briefly on that half-millennium and its interlinked tale of liberty and oppression.

The Enigma of Resistance

By its very nature, capitalism is conflict-ridden. Pious claims about its self-regulating character notwithstanding, the system pits people against one another; after all, competition is what is supposed to make the machinery hum. Even at that most elementary level, what's being limned is a world of winners and losers. Inevitably, such a world calls forth resistance. It shows up all over the geographical and social landscape. Its intensity varies: sometimes like a volcano exploding, sometimes like a volcano at rest, cooking beneath the surface. A deep mystery surrounds the appearance and disappearance of organized resistance. As I write, thousands of public-school teachers working in the deep red, deeply conservative, anti-labor-union states of West Virginia, Kentucky, Arizona, and Oklahoma are on strike on their own behalf and on behalf of the school systems that had been starved for funds and resources for a decade and more. These otherwise law-abiding "middle-class" professionals do so in defiance of their state's lawmakers and, in some cases, in defiance of the law itself. Only in hindsight might someone imagine such an upheaval.

All of the essays assembled here implicitly and often explicitly raise the specter of conflict, class conflict in particular. Why people resist power, why they acquiesce, and why sometimes they may believe they are resisting when they are in truth acquiescing are profoundly difficult questions to answer.

In 2011 I had occasion to attach these questions to specific moments in my own life. That year happened to be the hundredth anniversary of the Triangle Shirtwaist Factory Fire. I found myself doing a fair amount of speaking at public events commemorating the tragedy. It was also the year I traveled to Mississippi to reflect on my own time there as a civil rights activist during the summer of 1964.

Even in our United States of Amnesia, we remember the Triangle Fire, in which 146 young immigrant workers, most of them women, toiling in a garment factory burned and jumped to their deaths on a March day in New York City. The shock waves from the catastrophe reverberated around the country. A hundred thousand people filed by the mortuary on "Misery Lane." Four hundred thousand grieving, angry people marched behind a horse-drawn hearse in a solemn funeral procession. Laws were passed to prevent such things from happening again.

The Triangle Fire is a landmark moment in the prehistory of the New Deal of the 1930s, especially the legislation it inspired to civilize and democratize the workplace and rein in a savage capitalism. I refer specifically to the Wagner Act, legislating the right to organize and engage in collective bargaining; the Social Security Act, to protect the elderly, at least minimally, against the ravages of the free market; and the Fair Labor Standards Act, establishing a floor for wages and a ceiling for what had been endless hours of work, as well as an end to child labor.

But the fire itself was not the reason these reforms (and others) were achieved. The reason the fire turned into such a horrid disaster is what tells the tale. Many of the young women might have escaped immolation, but the exit door was locked by the factory's owners—in part because they wanted to prevent union organizers from getting in.

Triangle became part of an extraordinary resistance movement against industrial autocracy. That movement lasted about a hundred years, in a sequence that spanned the trade-union movement from 1870s to the 1970s. Just before and just after the Triangle factory burned, the garment workers of New York and dozens of other cities erupted in strikes and demonstrations: some citywide, some violent, some attacked by the police or privately employed thugs, some led by socialists or anarchists or syndicalists, some lasting an hour, some for months. These explosive events had been happening and would continue to happen for a long time in the coal mines, on the railroads, at steel mills and copper mines, in cotton fields, on prairie wheat plantations, in lettuce fields and grape arbors, by the docks, on ships at sea, in turpentine swamps and hard timber forests, along telegraph and telephone lines, in cigar-making tenement sweatshops and textile mills both North and South, on horse-drawn trolley tracks and subway tunnels—everywhere the capitalist production process planted itself.

Why shouldn't these events have happened, one might ask? Certainly, that was the assumption of many attending memorials a century later, listening to me and others. After all, we all know how bad things were. This was industrial capitalism's dark age. At the time of the fire, a hundred people died every single day in industrial accidents of one kind or another. America's proletariat lived amid appalling squalor and poverty, worked without letup, sent kids off to the factory floor at pathetically tender ages, got sick or maimed or killed at work, died young or, if old, lived in penury, were treated like something inanimate or subhuman, were subject to a thousand petty tyrannies and insults and humiliations by bosses and gauleiters of the shop floor, disappeared into the black box of the factory, a land removed from the land of the free, a place where the language of rights and liberties and democracy was written in a hieroglyphic no one in charge was eager to translate.

So of course this mass of the rightless and exploited rose up. But things aren't really that simple. Would you rebel? Weighed down by all this, exhausted, struggling just to keep yourself and your family alive, confronted at every turn by the coercions of the foreman, the boss, the police, the courts, sometimes even by the army, by the weight of public opinion that holds you in contempt and honors your tormentors, would you rise up? Would you risk your livelihood, not to mention life and limb? It is just as much a great mystery to ponder why the Grand Army of the Triangle—let's call it that—ever found the psychological and emotional strength, the organizational ingenuity, the social courage, to create itself and rebel as it is to ponder why for so very long people bent the knee.

Mulling over this deep mystery led me south and to my secret friend J. Edgar Hoover. I wasn't alive when the Triangle Army was in the field. But I did go to Mississippi in the summer of 1964, and because I did, I was privileged to slide through that elusive wormhole that carries people from acquiescence to resistance. The memory of that experience lodged in my soul. But it is not impervious to the erosions of time. I had come to a time in my life when I wanted to revisit, perhaps rekindle those days.

Memory, however, stood in the way. During what was then and still is called Freedom Summer, I had worked mainly in two towns: Columbus and Starkville. I wanted to return to specific places there to help me reconstruct events and, if possible, track down people I'd known. Especially, I wanted to locate local comrades in the struggle to win, first of all, the elementary right to vote, to win that and thereby help bury American apartheid. That was a long time ago, and as departure day approached, I worried that I'd be wandering about in terra incognita without much of a map.

And then, the day before I left, I remembered something: my FBI file. I had gotten hold of it years earlier (the highly redacted version available under the Freedom of Information Act, that is). Sure enough, J. Edgar Hoover and his lieutenants had compiled a meticulous record of all my run-ins with the law (not to mention extensively tracking my law-abiding life as a political activist) before, during, and after Mississippi. There it all was: arrest dates, addresses of the places I'd lived and worked, meeting places in barbershops and cafés deep in the hollows of the black community, sites of beatings and the Southern version of drive-by shootings. There were the Klan names of the Starkville sheriff, health commissioner, and mayor; names of friendly black preachers and black preachers we were told would be friendly but weren't; names of white storekeepers and gas-station owners who weren't likely to be friendly and weren't. I left the next day feeling armed—by J. Edgar Hoover, of all people.

Like the Triangle Fire, the civil rights movement remains alive in popular memory. More so! Because today people remember the fire but not the Triangle Army, while in the case of the revolution against the racial caste system, they actually remember the movement. It is inscribed in searing images we're all familiar with, in the sorrows and exaltations of its music, in the lingua franca of political speech-ifying, in the iconography of a national holiday—perversely, even in Glenn Beck's lachrymose sacrilege at the Lincoln Memorial in Washington. If ever in the national experience there was evidence of the capacity of people to move out from under generations of oppression, exploitation, and submission, out of the perennial midnight of all-sided coercions and fears and crushing condescension, to free themselves of self-contempt, fatalism, and helplessness, this was that testimony. To one degree or another, in one way or another, most people alive today know that. I can't, nor need I, do more than acknowledge that astounding act of collective triumph.

Except, perhaps, to register a few homely observations about the way it played out in the dirt roads, jails, courthouses, moonshine shacks, churches, and green fields of Columbus and Starkville. Thanks to Hoover, I was able to track down the spot in Starkville where something happened I've carried with me ever since.

Lomax's Café was a dilapidated one-room shack probably put up not long after the Civil War, set down in the sandy depression off the main road running through Starkville. It was nestled in one of the town's black neighborhoods, a heavily wooded enclave traversed by dirt roads. The houses were just as frail and just as aged as Lomax's place, some with backyard vegetable gardens and a pig or some chickens, and here and there a rickety church. There were dozens and dozens of Lomax's cafés throughout the black South, inviting places where people drifted in and out during the day and gathered at night to eat fresh-made pork rinds saturated in hot sauce and drink corn liquor from countryside stills (Mississippi was a "dry" state back then) and be together.

It was a natural place for our local freedom movement to assemble, to plan efforts to try to register to vote, to discuss putting together a Starkville branch of the Mississippi Freedom Democratic Party (MFDP), which at the end of the summer would challenge the legitimacy of the all-white state delegation to the Democratic Party presidential nominating convention in Atlantic City. We would also go over "smaller" matters, like what to do about the daily harassment (insults, firings, threats, false arrests) that affected anybody bold enough to associate with me and my fellow student volunteer assigned to Starkville, an African-American undergraduate from California. Or we just gathered at Lomax's because its lopsided front door; the savory aromas of coffee, moonshine, and hot sauce; the makeshift counter put together from nearby logs; and the cool darkness inside even on the most sweltering summer days made it feel like a haven, a sanctuary, its fragile shingles somehow capable of protecting us against a very hostile white world just across Route 82.

Above all, we gathered at Lomax's Café because Frank Lomax let us—not just let us but welcomed us, despite all the completely self-evident risks he was taking. When I stood on the site of Lomax's place back in 2011 (the shack is gone, the roads paved, but in so many ways not much has changed, especially the poverty) I could see Frank's face: very dark and round, a scar across his forehead, cheeks grizzled with gray, small-boned, smiley in a sardonic sort of way, a gentle face beneath its weathering. Frank knew the dangers he was courting far better than me and my California comrade; how could he not, having grown up black in Mississippi? But he took them, made himself a target.

One day at twilight we collected at Lomax's. It was fairly late in the summer and we had convened a meeting of our fledgling MFDP group—as we had several times before—this time to plan for the Atlantic City convention. We had made enough progress in Starkville that sending a delegation to a statewide meeting of our new party actually seemed possible. For that reason, fellow Council of Federated Organizations (COFO) workers had come down from Columbus, a bigger town, site of a bigger project, and only a half-hour away. (COFO—which sponsored the Freedom Summer—consisted of the Student Nonviolent Coordinating Committee, the Congress of Racial Equality, the National Association for the Advancement of Colored People, and the Southern Christian Leadership Conference.) They joined us and fifteen people from the black community of Starkville.

And then the police joined us as well. That, too, wasn't unusual. Just a few days before we'd arrived home late at night to be greeted by a police car, lights out in the rural pitch black (there were no streetlights in the black backwater of Starkville), filled to overflowing with one officer and a half-dozen vigilantes. No questions were asked. We jumped out of the car, dashed through the surrounding woods—I fell into a pig bog along the way, which everybody but me thought was very funny—and finally holed up in a friendly house where every window and door had someone stationed at it with a gun, waiting for the law officer and his "deputies" to attack, which they didn't. Nonviolent resistance was suspended for the night. I was scared that night, as on other nights, and my first and last thought was flight, not fight.

When the police showed up a few nights later at Lomax's, we were, therefore, not shocked. We had all grown accustomed to an omnipresent undercurrent of menace from a summer's worth of jailings, beatings, being followed or chased, everyday nastiness, even one or two shootings that missed. But on this occasion the police turned out in unusual force. Two carloads of local policemen and state Highway Patrol officers pulled up outside Lomax's. They had dogs, clubs, and guns. We were in a wooded cul-de-sac—no one outside could witness whatever they did next. Flight or fight?

Well, neither, actually. We were outside the café and they came at us looking nasty, the dogs growling near our knees and thighs.

Instinctively we arranged ourselves in a circle, clasped hands, and sang. It was not an unusual thing to do—at least not in those uncommon times. We sang the soulful lyrics of spirituals that had become the combative anthems of the movement: Jesus at the barricades.

Two things happened. Like an electric current running around our charmed circle, the fear that I think I can safely say possessed us all at that moment was alchemized and became instead a power in all of us to prevail together. This wasn't something ethereal, other-worldly; on the contrary, it was uncannily sensual, erotic even. The world—this darkening abandoned mote in time, humid with menace—all of a sudden looked different because our collective eyesight had improved into a kind of X-ray vision. We could see and act inside the body of fear, confront it, peer into a more civilized world beyond it, only because each of us found that strange superpower in our living relationship to each other.

So we sang and we waited. Then the second thing happened. The second thing was nothing. The police left. That was truly uncommon, and another lesson in the psychodynamics of resistance and acquiescence. Tyranny, whether industrial or racial or grounded in some other form of subordination, often enough resorts to blunt instruments when challenged—but it doesn't rest on that. It depends instead on an anterior atmosphere of intimidation and fatalistic resignation that this is the way life is, that there are no alternatives. Dread and awe in the face of power, obedience to its mystery even when it's out of sight, becomes the custom of the country. In Mississippi people on both side of the racial divide breathed that belief—their cultural oxygen, so to speak—day in and day out. The Starkville police had every right, every longstanding reason to anticipate that we would back down, as that had almost always been the way things were. To suddenly be faced in the flesh with the repudiation of those axioms of everyday life can be so shocking, so disarming, if only for a moment, that it may paralyze the will to act.

Through that fractured will can slip the new world. Just for an instant, that was what happened at Lomax's Café that August night.

"The past is not dead, it's not even past." So said William Faulkner, who of course was from those parts. Memories of the way things were, however remote from the realities of those dead times, provide the nuclear energy powering animosities about the way things turned out. Partisans of the Tea Party and other movements on the right draw their remarkable energy from resentment about a lost way of life and all its imagined consolations; that, and a thirst for revenge.

However, being anchored in the past is not necessarily a bad thing or a right-wing thing. The Grand Army of the Triangle rebelled against capitalism in part because it was eviscerating older ways of work and ways of life which, whatever their multiple inequities and iniquities, contained a stinging moral critique of the new capitalism—that it was not only immoral but, scarier than that, amoral in the bone. So too, the civil rights revolution was steeped in folk Afro-Christianity. But the Triangle Army and the civil rights army could imagine a future fundamentally different than the racial feudalism and savage capitalism under which they lived. From that reservoir of visionary emotion came the will to resist.

Our own ironic predicament is not so different. Can we imagine something other than the restoration of the New Deal? Is there no exit?

Part 1

Snakes in the Garden: American Capitalism and Its Distempers

1. The Three Faces of Risk: An Excursion into the Cultural History of Wall Street

Speculation is a risky business; risk comes with the territory, so to speak. Wall Street, as we all know, is a privileged, high-visibility site on which people risk their fortunes, their material as well as their psychic well-being. What goes on there has fascinated Americans (and eventually people around the world) virtually since the birth of the nation, like some great spectacle, a carnival of chance. Some have played the game themselves—that number has grown tremendously in the last quarter-century—while millions more have participated vicariously: seduced or revolted, but in one way or another engaged.

Just what people have made of this risky business, the meaning they've given it for their own lives and the life of the country, has actually varied a lot. Speculating on the future—that seems to sum up what even the most cautious investor is trying to do—arouses all

This chapter originated as a seminar paper delivered at the Center for Critical Analysis of Contemporary Culture at Rutgers University in 2004.

sorts of passions, desires, fears, and expectations. Risk wears many faces, many masks. Three are particularly instructive: (1) Risk as allure and danger. It wears the face of the confidence man. (2) Risk as Napoleonic romance. It wears the face of the conquistador. (3) Risk as social pathology. It wears the face of the oppressed and despoiled.

A few preliminary observations might be useful.

Risk is not the same as chance, at least not on Wall Street. Of course, there have always been people who approached the Street as they might a casino. They've gambled with the gods, come armed with arcane "systems" that have aligned the movements of the stock market with various unrelated phenomena. There was a famous astrological one in the 1920s that made market predictions based on interstellar perambulations. The astrologer, Evangeline Adams, held court in her studio above Carnegie Hall; her clients included European royalty and movie idol Mary Pickford. Another "system" predicted bearish downturns in any month containing the letter R. Another tracked sunspots. Yet another derived its picks from a code assembled out of comic-book dialogue.

But there is an underlying premise to most speculations on the stock exchange that they are somehow, even if only remotely, tied to tangible, measurable developments in the real-world economy. Risk, from this vantage point, seems more prosaic, more about the comprehensible than the inscrutable. It might even be said that a constitutive illusion of the stock market, especially in the twentieth century, has been that, in that arena at least, the risky gets subordinated to the rational, is subjected to lawful processes—albeit laws that seem to live in a chronic state of amendment. For most people, most of the time, speculating on the Street has seemed a hybrid activity, part luck, part skill, with the quotient of each varying according to time and circumstance. Even if sometimes only delusional, people enter the arena (or watch it from afar) believing its pure chance, its utter capriciousness, can be domesticated with liberal applications of empirical information, mathematical insight, and so on.

Second, when people think of Wall Street and its history, they naturally conjure up wild escapades, meteoric ascents, disastrous crash-and-burn scenarios. This has been especially true over the last two decades or so, punctuated by airborne stock-market fantasies followed by a market meltdown and a tidal wave of financial scandal. Risk, even unconscionable risk, would seem to be Wall Street's middle name. But for long stretches of time Wall Street has worn the face of prudential calculation, of the soberest aversion to reckless risk-taking. This ethos apparently informed the world of J. P. Morgan and later Wall Street establishment figures. How much this image of responsible trusteeship ever corresponded to reality is another matter, but to ignore its salience is to miss one of the fundamental cultural ambivalences that define the contours of Wall Street's cultural history.

In this connection, I want to raise a hypothesis about the dialectic of risk in the nineteenth century: that it becomes at one and the same time more familiar, more integrated into the American character structure and moral physiognomy, absorbed into the rationalist mythos of Progress and out from under the shadow of economic parasitism and moral transgression—less and less alien—and yet more and more fearsome in a secular sense, so that the same array of secular forces responsible for its growing presence and acceptance is mobilized to keep it under control, to ward off its catastrophic consequences.

Each of these three faces may be treated as a distinct miniature. However, in real life, they cross-fertilize, bleed into each other, take on traits from kindred faces, and share a cultural heritage: all are born out of a market society in which there is an inherent tendency for "all that's solid to melt into air."

The Confidence Man

The confidence man is endemic to market society. That's first of all because market society rests on confidence: confidence that strangers can be relied upon to live up to agreements made often at long distance and extending over long periods of time; confidence, too, that contractual relationships bind people together on the basis of mutual self-interest. The confidence man trades in that confidence, takes advantage of it. We are all familiar with his basic traits. He's charming, glib, seductive, even charismatic, perhaps sexy. He's a trickster. What's most important is that his trick depends on the willing collaboration of his victim or mark. The mark indulges in an act of faith born out of his/her own cupidity: that there is a way to fast money that skirts the rigors of the work ethic. *Cupidity* is a loaded word. The mark's motivation can be far more ingenuous, idealistic even, amounting to a buoyant optimism about the future. Still even the most innocent approach the confidence man with a certain foreboding; something feels not quite right, something feels illicit, something echoes danger, but that same something is very hard to resist.

Confidence men appear particularly at the frontier zones of market society, at those times and places where the unknown beckons even as it frightens. Capitalism, in its surges of "creative destruction," is always producing and reproducing new frontier zones, new fields of such expansive opportunity they are almost impossible to map, boundless and therefore ripe raw material for the commercial imagination as well as the criminal imagination of the confidence man. For this reason, confidence men show up all through the history of Wall Street. To the degree that speculators on the Street live in a limbo-like state of permanent impermanence—a weird, alluring, and menacing landscape without end or resting place—capitalism and its financial networks always extend an open invitation to the confidence man.

During certain moments in American history, however, confidence men seem to breed like rabbits—or at least the level of popular preoccupation with their presence rises noticeably. Both the 1920s and the 1990s were such periods. Strikingly, they coincide with high levels of technological innovation, indeed with a kind of techno-futurism that promises not just a new product but a whole new way of life. For the Jazz Age that was that best represented by the radio; more recently by the internet. In such eras mere matters of dollars and cents get transmogrified, become strange forms of commercial exaltation, draw on subterranean energies not normally part of trucking and bartering, leap beyond the quotidian. Thus there was a kind of boozy eroticism that linked the stock market to the flapper and the speakeasy during the twenties, an emotional brew memorialized in the novels and stories of F. Scott Fitzgerald. At a more mundane level it made the name of Charles Ponzi infamous. So, too, day traders and stock-market hustlers like the ones captured in the film *Boiler Room* or the best-selling novel *Bombardiers* registered the nineties' messianic faith in the utopian commercial promise of frontier science and the spiritualized (re-enchanted) free market. Both were, by any measure, times of high confidence and the disillusioning collapse of that confidence. A kind of giddiness pervaded the air, an atmosphere full of excitement, of living large and dangerously—the oxygen on which the confidence man thrives.

Jacksonian America, however, is where it all began. If it's right to say that confidence men crop up on the frontiers of market society, then it's arguably the case that all of America represented such a frontier zone in the antebellum years. Market society began its own long march through the corridors of American life, unsettling all previously existing social relations, family lineages, venerable institutions, and honored traditions, fixed identities of person and place. Its upheavals were felt on the land, in towns, and in the city. The country underwent a veritable orgy of speculation: in new lands, in the canals and turnpikes and railroads of the transportation revolution, in the whole infrastructure of a waterborne mercantile economy, in new towns and cities that seemed to spring up overnight (at least in the imaginations of their promoters). For people with either

no or limited contact with the marketplace, its impersonal relationships, its indifference to custom and nonmonetary values and moral
prohibitions, the world began to feel suddenly stranger, fluid, promising yet uncertain. Jacksonian America overflowed with confidence
about the future of the country. Yet it was obsessed with the confidence man. In a word, it experienced a great crisis of confidence.

Some observers took the measure of this new risk-prone world
and pronounced it good. Washington Irving, for example, who for
a long time deplored the new spirit of avaricious self-seeking, later
discovered its metaphysical justification. Mere trade might be
grubby and pedestrian, but speculation was its "romance ... It
renders the stock-jobber a magician and the [stock] exchange a
region of enchantment." Irving himself became a propagandist for
the Western imperial schemes of John Jacob Astor and a speculator
in railroads and land, where he lost heavily. In his own way, Ralph
Waldo Emerson agreed with Irving. While he resented the new
order of things that deferred to wealth and nothing else, he drew a
connection between the popular passion for speculative risk-taking
and what he considered the American genius for enterprise, innovation, and great projects. Even Horace Greeley, who could turn
apoplectic about the depravity of gambling, nonetheless found it in
him to offer up apologia for speculation as inherent in the national
character and expressive of a democratic social order, a form of
equal opportunity open to the bold. Ordinary folk like Jeremiah
Church saw things the same way. He noted in his diary that in
America "Everyman is a speculator from a wood-sawyer to a
President, as far as his means will go, and credit also."

In one way or another, they all expressed what was quickly
becoming a national faith, reiterated endlessly in newspaper editori-
als, political stump speeches, a burgeoning self-help literature, and
so on: that what really distinguished the American character was its
audacity, its eagerness to venture into the unknown, its inspiring
confidence that what lay out there was bound to work out well, not

only for the individual seeking his fortune but for a nation growing more muscular and with its eyes on glory.

Confidence this outsized was ripe for the picking. The harvesting might be relatively benign. Americans came to celebrate a certain native capacity for commercial guile, captured in the figure of the peddler "Yankee Jonathan" (who looked a bit like Uncle Sam—lean, angular, sly but friendly), who was charming, full of folktales and good humor, had a way with country wives, and knew how to strike a sharp bargain, but stopped this side of the felonious. A more malignant figure, however, began to command attention. Confidence men were abroad in the land concocting and hawking agricultural arcadias, gossamer towns and paper cities, bone-dry canals to nowhere, railroad lines consisting of "two streaks of rust."

Charles Dickens (who traveled to the United States at this time and disliked most of what he saw, especially the rampant commercial avidity of New York) provided one of the most searing and hilarious depictions of the fatuity and hypocrisy that lurked just beneath this romance of risk. Martin Chuzzlewit, the hapless ingénue hero of the novel of the same name, is seduced by the huckstering riffs of New York land promoters—an irresistible rhetorical blend of highfalutin democratic egalitarianism and unblinkered covetousness—even before he gets off the boat from England. Here's just a bit of this spiel deployed by the "General" (the confidence man who will entice Martin to invest in the aptly named Eden Land Corporation). Martin asks if there's really anything in this for the buyers and, puffing himself impressively, the General replies:

> For the buyers, sir? ... Well! you come from an old country, from a country, sir, that has piled up golden calves as high as Babel and worshipped 'em for ages. We are a new country, sir; man is in a more primeval state here, sir; we have not the excuse of having lapsed in the slow course of time into degenerate practices; we

have no false gods; man, sir, here, is man in all his dignity. We fought for that or nothing ... Here am I, sir ... with all my gray hairs, sir, and a moral sense. Would I, with my principles, invest capital in this speculation if I didn't think it full of hopes and chances for my brother man? ... What are the great United States for, sir ... if not for the regeneration of man? But it is nat'ral for you to make such an enqueery for you come from England and you do not know my country.[1]

Soon enough, shown a map depicting "banks, churches, cathedrals, market-places, factories, hotels, stores, mansions, wharves; an exchange, a theater, public buildings of all kinds," Martin takes the plunge and invests his meager capital in the Eden Land Corporation— only to discover, after schlepping out to some remote corner of Illinois, that Eden turns out to be nothing more than a hellish, fetid swamp where Martin nearly loses his life, not to mention his life savings.

Wall Street was hardly at the center of this upheaval. Dealings on the recently created New York Stock and Exchange Board involved a tiny number of people. It was out in the countryside where the new obsession with speculating on a rising market took root. The era is well known for that, for wagering on the commercial future of new lands and the farms and towns that were supposed to spring up there, wagering that became so out of control it ended in a devastating depression that lasted from 1837 into the early forties.

Wall Street did indeed emerge, however, as one site where people wrestled with this more widespread crisis of confidence, with their mixed emotions about risk. Urban life generally fascinated people as a realm of mystery and transgression. George Foster, who became perhaps the best-known chronicler of the urban demimonde in the

---

1 Charles Dickens, *Martin Chuzzlewit* (New York: New American Library, 1965), pp. 316–17, 376–77.

antebellum years, produced sketches of urban life—*New York by Gas-Light*—which included ventures onto the Street. Foster and others painted it in lurid colors, saw it essentially as a site of depravity, but were alert enough to the cross-currents of popular emotions to recognize how alluring it was to so many. The dream of instant wealth was of course part of that allure, but so too the attraction to Wall Street's inscrutable doings, its flirtation with the illicit, its crossing over the boundaries of conventional morality. Foster and other amateur anthropologists of the urban experience provided the reader a sneaky thrill. They likened the Street to the valley of riches depicted in *Sinbad the Sailor*, "where millions of diamonds lay glistening like fiery snow, but which was guarded on all sides by poisonous serpents, whose bite was death and whose contact was pollution." It seemed "a place of deep and dangerous mystery, a region of dens and caves and labyrinths full of perils." For Foster, the Street was above all a boulevard of masquerade and hidden realities, a zone of tempting transgression—risk as romance and danger. By the 1870s Wall Street had become a regular stop for tourists to the city, described in all the travel guides not only because of its growing economic throw-weight but because it was becoming an increasingly conspicuous arena in which what might be called a "risk society" acted out its encounters with chance.

A criminal case we would consider so ordinary today it's unlikely it would get into the newspapers at all became a cause célèbre in 1849. A confidence man operating in New York, one William Thompson, gulled his victims into believing that if they lent him some valuable belonging—a gold watch, say—he would let them in on a sure thing. The details are not important. His pitch—very common in this line of work—stressed that what was important was not the monetary value of whatever they were loaning him, but rather that it would function as a token of their confidence in him, which in turn would give him confidence in them. Wonderful when you think about it. Anyway, Thompson was arrested. He became

famous overnight as the Confidence Man, talked about in newspapers all across the country: a celebrity who enjoyed his sudden
notoriety and exhibit A about how fascinated people had become
with the phenomenon of the confidence man, how anxious they
were even while they indulged in their new passion for
speculation.

One newspaper account is worth inspecting a bit more closely
because it lets us see why, when some people turned their gaze to
Wall Street, they saw there the face of the Confidence Man. James
Gordon Bennett was the publisher of the *New York Herald*, a
pioneer of sensationalist journalism, a precursor of William
Randolph Hearst. Bennett used the occasion of Thompson's arrest
to triangulate the Street. He was vivid and direct: Thompson was a
petty swindler. But

> those palazzas, with all their costly furniture and all their splen-
> did equipages, have been the produce of the same genius in their
> proprietors, which has made the "Confidence Man" immortal
> and a prisoner at "the Tombs." His genius has been employed on
> a small scale in Broadway. Theirs has been employed in Wall
> Street ... He has obtained half a dozen watches. They have pock-
> eted millions of dollars.[1]

Bennett questioned the country's moral compass. Thompson, he
wrote,

> is a swindler. They are exemplars of honesty. He is a rogue. They
> are financiers. He is collared by the police. They are cherished by
> society. He is a mean, beggarly, timid, narrow-minded wretch ...
> They are respectable people, princely, bold, high-soaring

---

1   Johannes Bergmann, "The Original Confidence Man," *American
Quarterly*, Fall, 1969, vol. 21, no. 3.

"operators," who are satisfied only with the plunder of the whole community.

Thompson ended up in jail and not some "fashionable faubourg" because he aimed too low, Bennett argued. He should have gone to Albany instead and secured himself a railroad charter or issued a "flaming prospectus of another grand scheme ... He should have brought the stockholders into bankruptcy" and then "returned to a life of ease, the possessor of a clear conscience, and one million dollars." But the hapless Thompson wasn't up to it, so:

> Let him rot, then, in "the Tombs" ... while the genuine "Confidence Man" stands one of the Corinthian Columns of society ... Success, then, to the real "Confidence Man." Long life to the real "Confidence Man" ... the "Confidence Man" of Wall Street—the "Confidence Man" of the Palace uptown.[2]

James Gordon Bennett traded in demagoguery. Herman Melville did not. But they shared a mordant fascination with an emergent commercial civilization which seemed fraudulent at its core. Melville's was a remorseless gaze. That vision achieved a certain black density in what is certainly his most allusive and recondite of novels, *The Confidence-Man: His Masquerade*. It has been alleged that the novel was inspired by William Thompson's notorious arrest. True or not, the book is a veritable black mass of confidence men: religious confidence men and philosophical confidence men, literary and political confidence men, crooked businessmen and crooked philanthropists, peddlers of nostrums and miracle cures for the ailments of body and soul, all masquerading together on the steamboat *Fidéle* as it floats down the arterial heart of the country, the Mississippi River.

2　Ibid.

Predictably, among them is a speculator, experienced in the ways of the stock market. He encounters a younger man, to whom he seeks to sell stock in the Black Rapids Coal Company. Negotiations proceed, shrouded in mystery; tempting allusions are made to the stock's unavailability, suggesting its preciousness. The young man turns out to be less callow than he seemed and skeptically inquires about why the stock's price has of late been depressed. Our speculator/confidence man blames it on the "growling, the hypocritical growling, of the bears." Why "hypocritical," the young man asks. Now the modality of the negotiation shifts; it becomes a metaphysical jeremiad against speculation delivered in the interests of speculation. It is a sendup of Emerson's optimism, of a pervasive cultural optimism:

> Why the most monstrous of all hypocrites are these bears: hypocrites by inversion; hypocrites by all the simulation of dark instead of bright; souls that thrive, less upon depression, than the fiction of depression; professors of the wicked art of manufactured depressions, spurious Jeremiahs ... who, the lugubrious day done, return, like sham Lazaruses among the beggars, to make merry over the gains got by their pretended sore heads—scoundrel bears!

Bears, like gloomy philosophers, are destroyers of confidence, avers our speculator: "fellows who, whether in stocks, politics, breadstuffs, morals, metaphysics, religion—be it what it may—trump up their black panics in the naturally quiet-brightness solely with a view to some sort of covert advantage."

With this reasoning our young man is in perfect emotional sympathy, as are, presumably, most of his countrymen in their quest, undertaken in guilty innocence, for the main chance. His confidence won—he naturally gravitates to "fellows that talk comfortably and prosperously, like you"—the young man saunters off to conclude the transaction—not, however, in the "bright sunlight" but in a "private little haven" hidden from view. And there the game continues as the speculator/confidence man, his thirst for mercenary deceit unquenchable, entices his young convert with talk of stock in a "New Jerusalem, a new and thriving city, so called, in northern Minnesota."

The Conquistador

The names of Cornelius "Commodore" Vanderbilt, James "Jubilee Jim" (also known as "the Admiral") Fisk, Daniel "Unc'l Dan'l" Drew, and Jay "Mephistopheles of Wall Street" Gould are legendary. They are associated with the primordial age of the Robber Baron, the country's true baptism into the Industrial Revolution, and in particular with Wall Street's formative role in that upheaval. As their monikers may suggest—grandiloquent, folksy, and cartoonish, with a touch of evil—they still had about them the aura of the Confidence Man. As a matter of fact, they began their careers in ways not far removed from the sort of shady dealings Dickens's General or Melville's riverboat speculator trafficked in. As young men, Fisk and Drew both spent time earning a living in traveling circuses, learning the con games so common there. The Mephistophelean Gould is alleged to have made his initial stake cheating a partner in the tannery business, driving that poor fellow to suicide. The "Commodore" started off as a ferry-boat captain, a legitimate enough business, but he was well known as a sharp bargainer of minimal scruple.

Soon enough, however, they shed these less savory associations. Many of their countrymen began to think of them as Napoleonic conquerors. Of course, as Gould's moniker so strikingly indicates, many other people never saw them that way. Broad stretches of the urban and rural middle and working classes (and, for that matter, Knickerbocker patricians and New England Brahmins) continued to think of them as Confidence Men writ large, as a moral stench in the nostrils of society. This is one form of the deep ambivalence Wall Street has always provoked in American culture. Indeed, there were plenty of people who were simultaneously awestruck and repelled by what they saw in these men. Moreover, it is not incidental but rather absolutely central to their Napoleonic aura that they began life as they did—as men from nowhere. They underwent a transmutation—with some poetic license one might describe an arc from confidence man to colossus—that captured something essential, if not exactly unique, about the country's democratic faith.

Napoleon gripped the popular imagination all through the nineteenth century. The mythos had, of course, a lot to do with his imperial omnipotence. But what also counted heavily in the way people reacted to our "four horsemen" was their unprepossessing backgrounds, their earthy irreverence when it came to established ways of doing things or established social authority, their sheer audacity in taking the law into their own hands, their frontier fearlessness. Napoleon was, after all, a hero of the democratic revolution, once an obscure officer in the French army, and it was in that spirit that these new conquerors were received.

What did they conquer? Mother Nature, for one, as all four were involved in the single greatest undertaking of this phase of the Industrial Revolution; namely, the crisscrossing of the country's vastness with the world's most formidable railroad network. Other men, for another, as they all came equipped with a merciless instinct to dominate that brooked no interference, whether from rival speculators or duly constituted public authorities. And there was the marketplace, of course, whose dog-eat-dog imperatives they took with a deadly seriousness that welcomed its amorality. Finally, they conquered themselves. By that I mean everything they did—or so it seemed to their legions of admirers—entailed the greatest risk. They lived their lives as ongoing encounters with chance, with the hot breath of disaster at their backs. And they never blinked. They remained cool under fire when many lesser men—Wall Street was full of them—panicked. Risk was the arena in which they proved their manhood, in which they created themselves anew, in which they worked their will and exercised their mastery over men, machines, and the fickleness of fortune.

The market, and especially Wall Street, thus became a theater, a distinctly American theater, for enacting a heroic romance with risk. Why Wall Street? To be sure, there were robber barons aplenty, industrialists who never came anywhere near Wall Street or even intensely disliked it, like Andrew Carnegie. They too were lionized for their audacity and sangfroid and lived under the sign of the conquistador. But Wall Street's "titans of finance" occupied pride of place. First of all, there was the basic fact of life that the era's signature enterprise, the railroad, was so large it could only get off the ground with huge infusions of outside capital, which Wall Street mobilized. That alone left the Street's luminaries in a conspicuously commanding position. But more than that, Wall Street seemed to distill in the very mysteries of its machinations, the exoticism of its specialized language, the intangibility of just what it was trucking and bartering, its unpredictability, its penchant for masquerade and intrigue and dissimulation, in its sheer inscrutability and its awesome capacity to derange the whole economy, the very quintessence of risk. If you could master all that you were a hero indeed. The speculative looting and relooting of the Erie Railroad—the "scarlet woman of Wall Street"—or the bravura attempt by Gould and Fisk to corner the whole market in gold in 1869 (which came to ruin on infamous "black Friday") mesmerized the nation because they were outsized spectacles that combined the mastery of an arcane expertise with dauntless dash and were staged at the edge of a cliff. Just as the Western frontier was receding into the past and with it the proving ground of the frontier hero, that same character seemed to migrate back east to stake out his territory in the financial badlands of Wall Street.

So it was that popular media filled up with stories of financial titans whose traits mirrored the technologies they had mastered: men of iron with wills of steel, blessed with magnetic personalities and what might be called "titans' eyes"—the kind that can stare right through you. (The most celebrated example of this is Edward Steichen's photograph of J. P. Morgan, which hangs in the Metropolitan Museum of Art in New York. Steichen was so struck by Morgan's eyes that he compared looking at them to staring into the headlights of an onrushing locomotive). These men—and it goes without saying they were all men—were likened to those various historic "Napoleons," those incomparable warriors, who had appeared and reappeared down through the ages: Alexander and Caesar and Cromwell and so on. Their pronounced masculinity was of a different order than the sexuality associated with the Confidence Man. If the latter was seductive, he was so in a womanish sort of way, wily and flirtatious, an avatar of the "girlie-man." These Gilded Age buccaneers, on the contrary, were Terminators. Moreover, their triumphs were the nation's. Vanderbilt's daring as well as his more material legacy mirrored the country's urge to plunge into the unknown and emerge its master, to contend with the great powers of the earth for global supremacy.

When a monument to be known as the *Vanderbilt Memorial Bronze* was unveiled in 1869, editorial writers pulled out all the stops. It was situated at the depot of the Hudson River Railroad, which had been the object of wild speculations, commercial fraud, and rampant corruption in the governments of both New York City and the state of New York—but all that was beside the point. Everything from the lushness of the memorial's panorama and ornamentation to the immensity of its construction struck these observers as appropriate to the formidable nature of its subject. James Gordon Bennett's son, who now ran the *New York Herald*, treated it as "a monument of the greatest material inventions and enterprise of the nineteenth century"—a granite memorial to the "genius and progress of the age." The Commodore's "luminous sagacity" was on display. This was standard fare. A distinctive vocabulary inscribed these men in urban industrial legend. They were "bold," "magnificent of view," "full of verve," capable of absorbing hard blows (whether from other men or from fate) without flinching; they were "audacious," "keen," and on and on, amounting to a portrait of American primitives endowed with extraordinary virility, plebian brashness, and blunt force of personality. Drew and Vanderbilt were different in dozens of ways, yet according to one insider both had "the mind of crystal, the heart of adamant, the hand of steel, and the will of iron."

A river of second-rate novels and magazine short stories mirrored this popular preoccupation with the great capitalist as conqueror: Theodore Dreiser. Dreiser is especially illuminating not only because he was far better than second-rate, but because his reputation as a left-wing writer (which he deserved) belies the awestruck vantage point from which he viewed the financial titan. His trilogy (*The Financier*, *The Titan*, *The Stoic*) functions as a kind of hostile witness for the prosecution: evidence of how compelling the visage of the conquistador could be.

Dreiser was a social Darwinian, although of an aberrant sort. Orthodox social Darwinism, as espoused by William Graham Sumner (the Yale professor who was Herbert Spencer's chief exponent in America) held that

> the millionaires are a product of natural selection ... It is because they are thus selected that wealth ... aggregates under their hands ... They may be fairly regarded as naturally selected agents for society for certain work. They get high wages and live in luxury, but the bargain is good for society.[1]

---

1   William Graham Sumner quoted in Richard Hofstadter, *Social Darwinism in American Thought* (Boston: Beacon Press, 1992), p. 58.

Dreiser, however, wasn't having anything to do with Sumner's social meliorism or moral teleology. He was, rather, a Darwinian fundamentalist. Fitness implied nothing one way or the other about social progress or moral order. It was a cold fact of nature, barren of higher meaning, without any redeeming solicitude for the human condition.

The first volume of Dreiser's trilogy opens with a Darwinian epiphany. As a young boy, Frank Algernon Cowperwood, the story's protagonist, makes a life-defining observation. Watching a heavily armored lobster devour a vulnerable squid, young Frank discovers the answer to the question of how life is organized. "Things live on each other—that was it," is his spare and unblinking conclusion. That ethos is the red thread running through Cowperwood's whole career as a financier, a neither benign nor demonic occupation, in Dreiser's view. It is predatory, to be sure, but so is all of nature. It can bring calamity, but the universe is not, as with the social Darwinists, an orderly place, but inherently unstable and out of anyone's control. In the narrator's view it is a world of "jungle-like complexity ... a dark, rank growth of horrific but avid life—life at the full, life knife in hand, life blazing with courage and dripping at the jaws with hunger."

Over the course of the first two volumes, Cowperwood abandons every vestige of sanctified convention. He becomes a living impiety, an irreverence, a defiler of Christian ethics and bourgeois decorum, true only to the parable of the lobster and the squid. He gives up his belief in the priority and enduring worth of material production. He becomes not only a speculator but that particularly obnoxious breed, the bear that ghoulishly lives off the misery of others. He's averse to thrift, preferring to spend liberally and "get along." He jettisons even a purely rhetorical deference to the ossified maxims of competitive free-market capitalism. He mocks the culture's pious faith in the democratic way, coolly suborning loads of public officials. And his faithlessness is more encompassing than that. He cheats shamelessly on his wife, Lillian, a priggish, passionless creature of great social rectitude. Unlike his peers, whose adulteries and shady business practices are fogged over by pious pretense and feigned shock, Frank won't work to conceal his transgressions. Nor is his adultery a petty fling but rather a grand sexual passion for an indecently young girl, Aileen Butler, herself a creature of fecund beauty, impulsive, sexually ravenous, and highly dangerous to Frank's fragile social reputation. Indeed, Cowperwood's eroticism is not only as potent as his magnetic attraction to financial empire building; it is fundamentally the same unquenchable craving for conquest and control. It brooks no interference.

Dreiser is not squeamish about any of this. The trilogy avoids moralizing and harbors no second thoughts. This kind of distanced view, free of irony, is at the core of what Dreiser understands to be happening in a world reconstructed by the great forces gathering around Wall Street. Cowperwood is a kind of mighty player of the game; ruthless yet impressively powerful, an exploiter to be sure, but one whose power to exploit expresses a fundamental law of life; an exploiter who is also a creator of wealth and builder of cities. Cowperwood is a blunt, granite-like figure of considerable density, not easily reducible to the moral polarities of an earlier age. He stands at the heart of an awesome, amoral, brute matter of fact of things and exudes an aura of Olympian dirigisme.

All of this—Dreiser, along with a whole literary universe of precursors and imitators, journalists and storytellers—made up this language of Napoleonic mythmaking. It began in the Gilded Age and has been with us ever since, an integral part of the culture of Wall Street. It has always rested, first of all, on a belief that an elect group of men are innately endowed with a certain genius for triumphing over risk. While it first climaxed around the turn of the century during the age of Morgan, everyone is familiar with its more recent resurfacing. One need only recall the Reagan era and its inauguration of the second Gilded Age (which lasted well beyond his presidency). Think of names like "Chainsaw" Al Dunlap (the asset-stripper from Sunbeam), "Neutron" Jack Welch from GE, and other practitioners of the "lean and mean," crusaders on behalf of "shareholder value." Or think of books like *The Predators' Ball* recounting the high-risk financial acrobatics of the Michael Milken junk-bond gang; above all, perhaps, recall their cinematic apotheosis, Gordon Gekko (a.k.a. Ivan Boesky). The media filled up with portraits of Wall Street "gunslingers," "white and black knights," "killer bees," and "hired guns," warlike appellations borrowed helter-skelter from antiquity, the Middle Ages, and our own mythologized West. The kinship with the heroic traits of the first Gilded Age is self-evident. Indeed, for the first time in nearly a century, scholars began revising the sordid history of Fisk's own founding generation of robber barons. New studies of Jay Gould, J. P. Morgan, and Edward Harriman reconceived them as master builders. This historical revisionism did more than simply mimic the Gilded Age hagiographies of Vanderbilt and Jay Cooke or the fawning magazine literature at the turn of the century. Instead, the well-publicized faults of the old tycoonery were duly noted; more than noted, they were reconceived as the natural, necessary, inevitable, and even admirable traits of a bumptious country feeling its oats, preparing to burst onto the world stage as a new colossus.

There are differences as well, of course, and two seem worth mentioning. Our most recent cult of the titan, the maestro of risk, emerged amid a mood and even reality of national decline. It followed on from the defeat in Vietnam, the scuttling of the postwar financial system, the rise of the Organization of the Petroleum Exporting Countries (OPEC), stagflation, the wholesale deindustrialization of the country's midsection, an inferiority complex regarding the Japanese economy, the humiliation of the Iran hostage crisis, and so on. How unlike the environment of late nineteenth-century

America when, whatever else one might say about those times, the country was clearly on the rise, an awakening giant flexing its muscles. Perhaps this can in part account for what might be characterized as the declension of the masculine mystique long identified with the titan of finance. What we got in the Reagan era (not to put too fine a point on it) was the "big swinging dick" phenomenon (*Liar's Poker*), the Gordon Gekko or Larry the Liquidator (*Other People's Money*) "rip-their-eyes-out" raw bravado and violence that probably would have struck their titanic ancestors as demeaning. One senses here a certain instinct for revenge at work.

Another meaningful difference brings me to my final sketch—the one where risk wears the face of the victimized. Even during the heyday of that first generation of financial titans, there was a robust cultural (not to mention political and economic) resistance to their domination. Nothing measurably like it occurred during the Reagan era, nor until the near-implosion of the global financial system in 2008 opened up a new era of resistance (Occupy Wall Street, Bernie Sanders, and so on). There is Gordon Gekko, of course, and riotous novels like *Bonfire of the Vanities* and *The Bombardiers* and plays like *Other People's Money*, and there is the Sarbanes-Oxley Act, passed after the dot-com crash of 2001 and designed to rein in the worst skullduggery on the Street. But compared to a living religious persuasion in the nineteenth century that often consigned Wall Street to its own moral gulag; compared to a vast secular literature of ethical chastisement; compared to the Populist, Progressive, and New Deal counterreactions to the power of the titans, dissent in our own era has been meager indeed.

The Victim

A good argument can be made that the "culture of risk" suffered through a long period of disrepute lasting from 1890 through 1945.

Indeed, the "culture of risk" was not fully rehabilitated until 1980. Some caveats are in order. First, this flight from risk afflicted more than Wall Street and arose as a response to the dangerously erratic perturbations of the capitalist marketplace more generally. But again and again, Wall Street found itself in the eye of the storm—most emphatically and memorably during the crash of '29 and the Great Depression that followed. Secondly, to characterize a whole epoch this way (which at its furthest reaches measures close to a century) is obviously exaggerated. One thinks immediately, of course, about the "Roaring Twenties." And certainly before that there were champions of high-stakes speculative risk—Bernard Baruch, for one—who kept the romance alive. More remarkable, even after the crash, characters like Joe Kennedy continued to take Melville-like bearish advantage of the country's misery (until Kennedy became the first head of the Securities and Exchange Commission, that is). It is noteworthy that the board game Monopoly, whose purpose after all is not so much to get filthy rich as it is to mercilessly drive everyone else into bankruptcy, was invented and embraced by millions right in the middle of the Great Depression. The dream lived on, even under the most inauspicious circumstances.

Still, beginning with the Populist upheavals of the 1890s and continuing at least through the long era of the New Deal, more and more people became convinced that American society was much too vulnerable to the vagaries of chance—economic chance, at any rate. The problem was that the fatalities were piling up. To begin with, the economy itself seemed subject to maddeningly frequent nervous breakdowns. Look at the record: there were severe panics—some originating in Wall Street, all making an impact there—in 1837, 1857, 1873, 1882, 1893, 1901, 1907, and of course 1929, trailing social disaster in their wake. Many people looked at these episodes of unrestrained risk-taking, saw in them a virulent social pathology, and said, *Enough already!* The victims could be measured statistically but, after all, wore human faces: dispossessed farmers across the South and Great Plains, small and medium-sized business owners driven to and over the edge of bankruptcy, and workers on railroads, in factories, down in the mines—all of whom couldn't feed themselves, much less their families, when the economy rocketed downward during one of these all too frequent financial distempers. American society had seemingly overindulged the culture of risk and now found itself staring into the abyss, from which the eyes of the dispossessed and the oppressed and the extremely angry stared back.

Populism, progressivism, and the New Deal (not to mention socialism and the labor movement) are overdetermined phenomena originating in multiple grievances, articulating a variegated array of desires and objectives. But I think it is arguable that, to one degree or another, they were all preoccupied with the question of security in a capitalist economy that seemed inherently insecure. Because it seemed to be reproducing victims at an alarming rate as the nineteenth century drew to a close, an extraordinarily broad spectrum of people sought ways to control or eliminate the damage, to domesticate risk, to replace it with a culture of political or managerial control that might cure the pathology. If I say that, in this regard, J. P. Morgan and Eugene Victor Debs were on the same page, you get an idea of how widespread this persuasion became.

We expect to see the names of Debs or William Jennings Bryan or even Theodore Roosevelt among this group, but why Morgan? Because by the 1890s the country's elite circle of investment bankers (and some other corporate businessmen as well) had come to fear the chronic arrhythmia of the free market. There were severe economic costs associated with these periodic derangements, but it was just as much the social and political upheaval that followed in their wake that alarmed people like Morgan. The great banker we think of as synonymous with the free market actually hated it—hated speculation (not that he didn't indulge; he did), hated the high-risk instability of the competitive marketplace. He also feared what he thought of as "mobocracy": populism and other social insurgencies that sought to make economic life, and social life generally, less risky by subjecting them to democratic oversight.

Their sense of elite entitlement was a presumption born of their wealth as well as their social background and breeding (although the latter was often concocted in impromptu fashion, borrowed from Europe or fabricated at home on the fly; this was America, after all). They sought to master two kinds of anarchism: one that flourished in the internecine every-man-for-himself world of the marketplace, the other that flourished inside their perfervid imaginations when they remembered the Haymarket bombing, the bloody Monongahela River at the strike-bound Homestead Steel Works, the federal troops massed alongside the railroad tracks during the Pullman strike, the legions of Coxey's army of the unemployed marching cross-country demanding relief, the searing image of Bryan's "cross of gold." With some extraordinary success, Morgan and his colleagues established a modicum of order, of control from above, over the riotously self-destructive railroad industry and soon enough over broad stretches of the nation's economy by trustifying central sectors of American industry—most famously with the creation of US Steel in 1901. The other "anarchist" specter seemed to flame out with the defeat of Bryan in 1896.

Clearly, socialists like Debs, syndicalists like Big Bill Haywood of "Wobbly" fame, antitrust progressives like Louis Brandeis, and "Tory socialists" like Teddy Roosevelt had very different ideas about how to impose order on a society grown dangerously unstable, wracked by a tormenting uncertainty, who should be in charge, and what a secure society should look like. But for our purposes what is important is that the phenomenon of risk, whether viewed from Wall Street or from the other shore, no longer seemed quite so romantic, so seductive, no longer an apt proving ground for manhood, a royal road to self-creation and national glory. This disaffection came to a head, as we know, in the Great Depression.

The crash and the Depression ushered in Wall Street's age of ignominy. Its disgrace was profound, long-lasting, and multidetermined. While condemned as selfish, felonious, and conspiratorial, the Street's most grievous fault—the one that deprived it of its gravitas and left it open to demeaning ridicule—was found to be its omni-incompetence. Its sagaciously enunciated promise to deliver the good life, a "new era" of universal abundance, had turned out to be a toxic bad joke. Its faith, its speculative euphoria about the Jazz Age bull market, had morphed into a national calamity eclipsed only by the tragedy of the Civil War. This colossal failure was greeted with fear, anger, mockery, and above all a determination to once and for all domesticate risk, to erect an institutional bulwark against the fatal chanciness of unregulated capitalism. One consequence was, of course, all the regulatory legislation we associate with the New Deal. The Banking Act, the Glass-Steagall Act, the Securities and Exchange Commission, the Public Utility Holding Company Act, and so on addressed Wall Street particularly. Social Security, unemployment insurance, wage and hour legislation, the Wealth Tax Act, various forms of credit and mortgage insurance, Works Progress Administration (WPA) and other public works projects, and Keynesian fiscal policy were supposed to immunize American society more generally against the contagion of reckless risk-taking and insecurity.

I use the word *contagion* because, while Wall Street was far and away the chief culprit people blamed for the disaster, ordinary people blamed themselves as well. They had succumbed to the allure of risk, they shared in the guilt; it was almost as if the whole nation had indulged in that malignant innocence which marked the young man on the riverboat *Fidéle* as he became infatuated with the

Confidence Man. I do not want to exaggerate this; self-reproach was hardly the dominant emotion of the time. But its presence signals that the rejection of risk, the quest for security, the horror of mass victimization sank deep into the pores of American culture. This is evident in the era's popular as well as political culture. It pervades Franklin Delano Roosevelt's speeches, which were unsparing in their denunciations of Wall Street's criminal negligence. It surfaced again and again in all the public hearings into Wall Street's maledictions. It showed up in newspaper cartoons, in the movies of Frank Capra and *Dinner at Eight*, in plays like Archibald MacLeish's *Panic: A Play in Verse*, in Edmund Wilson's excoriating portraits of Wall Street felons, in the grim renderings of social suicide in *The Big Money*, the third volume of John Dos Passos's *U.S.A.* trilogy (published in 1936), in the frenzied applause for Walt Disney's cartoon short "The Three Little Pigs." Wall Street was everyone's favorite candidate for the Big Bad Wolf, and everyone had by then internalized forevermore the caution and foresight of that prudential third little pig.

Perhaps the best indication of how traumatic this encounter with risk was is how long its cultural as well as political aftershocks lingered. The fact that the infrastructure of the New Deal, as well as the cultural atmosphere that supported it, stayed relatively intact until 1980 (and of course still lives, if only on life support) is pretty good evidence that risk, wearing the face of the victim, left deep scars.

In this regard, John Marquand's 1949 novel *Point of No Return* sought to capture, in the life of one veteran of the Street, that landmark turning point in the country's long love affair with risk. That it was published during the high noon of postwar triumphalism, when the sunny vista of an American century seemed to confirm a limitless confidence about the future, is again a telling sign that, even in the United States of Amnesia, some things were not so easy to forget.

The postwar era was marked by a quixotic quest for security, and Marquand's protagonist is a clinical case study of that mordant state of mind hiding out on Wall Street. Charles Gray burrows inside the cloistered confines of an ancient firm, monkishly devoted to husbanding the blue-chip investments of its blue-blooded clientele. A sacerdotal atmosphere pervades this old-line family bank, where the very notion of risk is verboten, where rumors and hot tips are considered unseemly, where ambition must conform to the measured pace and prehistoric protocols of ascension. After hours, Charles hides out in the utterly predictable routines of an upscale Westchester suburb with meticulous attention to the subtlest nuances of social prestige, whose fixities may sometimes abrade but are at bottom reassuring.

Charles is hiding, or rather fleeing, from the past. His whole life and character were irreparably disfigured by his father's unconscionable Wall Street speculations at the height of the Jazz Age. Patriarch of a financially strapped but socially distinguished Boston family, hapless and ineffectual but yearning to recapture its fading distinction, John Gray loathes the sanctimonious, antiseptic, self-assured world of the Boston investment house. He is determined to break loose of those constraints and hypocrisies and recover the family patrimony. Instead, he loses everything. One inebriated and reckless plunge after another ends in his suicide. His son Charles is left to pick up the pieces. Romance, social elevation, career are all sacrificed on the altar of his father's malignant Wall Street fantasies. This, then, is Charles's point of no return. His life will forever after be marked by the stigma of his father's shame and by a revulsion for everything he attempted, even that daring urge to spring loose that a more callow Charles once admired.

For Marquand, Charles's point of no return is also the country's, that time to which there is no going back, when one could indulge childish dreams of erotic thrill and perpetual ease. Those Jazz Age fantasies that turned out so cheap and shabby and full of family and psychological ruin would be America's last flirtation with its indigenous optimism, its taste for the chanciness of the unknown. Life since that point of no return is filled with regret, with a chilling premonition of disaster and stultifying caution, with a poignant sense of loss and of the unforgiven. Or so it seemed.

2. Another Day Older and Deeper in Debt

Shakespeare's Polonius offered this classic advice to his son: "Neither a borrower nor a lender be." Many of our nation's Founding Fathers emphatically saw it otherwise: Always a borrower, never a lender be. As tobacco and rice planters, slave traders, and merchants, as well as land and currency speculators, they depended upon long lines of credit to finance their livelihoods and splendid ways of life. So, too, in those days did shopkeepers, tradesmen, artisans, farmers, casual laborers, and sailors. Without debt, the seedlings of a commercial economy could never have grown to maturity.

Ben Franklin, however, approached the subject warily: "Rather go to bed supperless than rise in debt" was his warning, and even now his cautionary words carry great moral weight. We worry about debt, yet we can't live without it.

Debt remains the Jekyll and Hyde of capitalism. For some the moral burden of carrying debt is a heavy one, and no one lets them

An earlier version of this chapter appeared in *Raritan*, vol. 33, no. 2, Fall 2013.

forget it. For privileged others, debt bears no moral baggage at all; it presents itself as an opportunity to prosper and, if things go wrong, can be cast off without a qualm.

Those who view debt favorably as the royal road to wealth accumulation—those who tend to be forgiven if their default is large enough—almost invariable come from the top rungs of the economic hierarchy. Then there are the rest of us, who get scolded for our impecunious ways, foreclosed upon, and dispossessed, leaving behind scars that never fade away and wounds that disable our futures. Think of this upstairs–downstairs class calculus as the politics of debt. British economist John Maynard Keynes put it like this: "If you owe your bank a hundred pounds, you have a problem. But if you owe a million, it has."

After months of journalistic chatter about an impending "debtpocalypse," debate (or lack of it) over the dreaded "debt ceiling," and the prospect of everyone careening over a "fiscal cliff," Americans remain preoccupied with debt, public and private. Austerity is what we're promised for our sins. Millions are drowning, or have already drowned, in a sea of mortgages gone bad, student loans that may never be paid off, spiraling credit-card bills, car loans, payday loans, and bizarrely complicated financial mechanisms designed by the country's "financial engineers" to dissolve what's left of the American standard of living.

The world economy almost came apart in 2007 and 2008 and still may do so under the whale-sized carcass of debt left behind by financial plunderers, who leveraged it to get ever richer. Most of them will remain in their mansions and McMansions while other debtors live outdoors, in cars or shelters, or doubled up with relatives and friends—or even in debtors' prison. Believe it or not, a version of debtors' prison, that relic of Anglo-American commercial barbarism, is back. In 2013, you can't actually be jailed for not paying your bills, but ingenious corporations, collection agencies, cops, courts, and lawyers have devised ways to ensure that debt "delinquents" will end up in jail anyway. With one-third of the states now allowing the jailing of debtors (without necessarily calling it that), it looks ever more like a trend in the making. Will Americans tolerate this or might there emerge a politics of resistance to debt? After all, it's happened before.

The World of Debtors' Prisons

Imprisonment for debt was common in colonial America and the early republic. It wasn't abolished in most states until the 1830s or 1840s, and in some cases not until after the Civil War. Today, we think of it as a peculiar and heartless way of punishing the poor—and it was. But it was more than that. Some of the richest, most esteemed members of society also ended up imprisoned for debt, like Robert Morris, who helped finance the American Revolution and ran the Treasury under the Articles of Confederation; John Pintard, a stockbroker, state legislator, and founder of the New York Historical Society; William Duer, graduate of Eton, powerful merchant and speculator, assistant secretary of the Treasury, and master of a Hudson River manse; a Pennsylvania Supreme Court judge; army generals; and other notables. Rich or poor, you were there for a long stretch, even for life, unless you could figure out some way of discharging your debts. That, however, is where the similarity between wealthy and impoverished debtors ended.

Whether in the famous Marshalsea in London, where Charles Dickens had Little Dorrit's father incarcerated (and where Dickens's father languished when the author was twelve), or in the New Gaol in New York City, where men like Duer and Morris did their time, debtors' prisons were segregated by class. If your debts were large enough and your social connections weighty enough (the two tended to go together), you lived comfortably. You were supplied with good food and well-appointed living quarters as well as books and other amusements, including, on occasion, manicurists and prostitutes. Robert Morris entertained George Washington for dinner in his "cell." Once released, he resumed his career as the new nation's richest man. Before John Pintard moved to New Gaol, he redecorated his cell, had it repainted and upholstered, and shipped in two mahogany writing desks.

Yet even for the well off and well positioned, it stung to be locked up. You were, after all, confined and unable to conduct the business that had got you there in the first place. Your political ambitions, if you had them, had to be put on hold, at the least. You would have to spend down the patrimony in order to maintain the life to which you were accustomed. Although you might live day to day in much better circumstances than your lower-call fellow inmates, you were still exposed to common and potentially fatal dangers in prison: for example, the epidemics of plague and cholera that spread amid the filth and fetid air of the jail, while outside the civilian population was fleeing town.

And then there was the shame of it. Debtors' prison was not really a form of commercial jurisprudence as much as it was an institution within the broader framework of a moral economy that had been around for centuries. Being a defaulted debtor was less a crime than a moral failure, like excessive drinking or gambling—it was a crime of dishonor. This traditional moral economy clashed with modern commercial practice: creditors often received nothing at all while the indebted languished in jail.

Broken promises punished by doing time could weigh heavily even on the consciences of those who resumed their esteemed stations in life. Pintard noted in his commonplace book that he'd spent "one year, three weeks, twenty hours" in prison—an experience, he believed, that scarred him for life. He described a Fourth of July celebration, while still locked up, with a banner that displayed "a tatter'd pair of breeches ... displayed on a constable's staff with inverted pockets" and on top, instead of a Liberty cap, an empty purse, "for Liberty alas has nothing to do within these walls."[1] Thomas Rodney, an officer in the Revolutionary Army and justice of the Supreme Court of Delaware, spent fourteen months in jail and ended up bitter and humiliated.

Meanwhile, the mass of petty debtors housed in the same institution survived, if at all, amid squalor, filth, and disease. They were often shackled and lacked heat, clean water, and adequate food—or food of any kind, since they usually had to have the money to buy their own food, clothing, and fuel. Debtors in these prisons frequently found themselves literally dying of debt. And you could end up in such circumstances for trivial sums. Of the 1,162 jailed debtors in New York City in 1787, 716 owed less than one pound. A third of Philadelphia's inmates in 1817 owed less than five dollars, and debtors outnumbered violent criminals in the city's prisons by five to one. In Boston, 15 percent of jailed debtors were women.

Scenes of public pathos were commonplace. Inmates on the upper floors of the New Gaol would lower shoes out the window on strings to collect alms for their release. Other prisons installed "beggar gates," through which those jailed in cellar dungeons could stretch out their palms for the odd coins from passersby.

Poor and rich alike wanted out. Pamphleteering against the institution of debtors' prison began in the 1750s. An Anglican minister in South Carolina denounced the jails, noting that "a person would be in a better situation in the French King's Gallies, or the Prisons of Turkey or Barbary than in this dismal place." Discontent grew. A mass escape from New Gaol of forty prisoners, armed with pistols and clubs, was prompted by extreme hunger.

In the 1820s and 1830s, as artisans, journeymen, sailors, longshoremen, and other workers organized the early trade-union movement as well as workers' political parties, one principal

---

1 Pintard quoted by Bruce H. Mann, *Republic of Debtors: Bankruptcy in the Age of American Independence* (Cambridge, MA: Harvard University Press, 2009) p.110.

demand was the abolition of imprisonment for debt. Inheritors of a radical political culture, their complaints echoed that biblical tradition of Jubilee mentioned in Leviticus, which called for the cancellation of debts, the restoration of lost house and land, and the freeing of slaves and bond servants every fifty years.

Falling into debt was a particularly ruinous affliction for those who aspired to modest independence as shopkeepers, handicrafters, or farmers. As markets for their goods expanded but became ever less predictable, they found themselves taking out credit to survive and sometimes going into arrears, often followed by a stint in debtors' prison that ended their dreams forever.

However much the poor organized and protested, it was the rich who got debt relief first. Today, we assume that debts can be discharged through bankruptcy (although that option is now either severely restricted or denied to certain classes of less-favored debt delinquents—college students, for example). Although the newly adopted US Constitution opened the door to a national bankruptcy law for which many, including the well-off, had been lobbying for years, Congress didn't walk through it until 1800.

Enough of the old moral faith that frowned on debt as sinful lingered. The United States has always been an uncharitable place when it comes to debt, a curious attitude for a society settled in large part by absconding debtors and indentured servants (a form of time-bound debt peonage). Indeed, the state of Georgia was founded as a debtors' haven at a time when England's jails were overflowing with debtors.

When Congress finally passed the Bankruptcy Act, those in the privileged quarters at New Gaol threw a party. Down below, however, life continued in its squalid way. The law, it turned out, only applied to people who had sizable debts. If you owed too little, you stayed in jail. And that was exactly the point. It made no sense for those interested in nurturing the growth of commercial civilization to stop up the arteries of commerce, which after all couldn't function without instruments of credit and debt, by taking its most successful debtors out of circulation. Not unlike today's "too big to fail" financial institutions, the larger the scale of your business operations, the more reason to keep them going and get you out of the calaboose.

Debt and the Birth of a Nation

Nowadays, the conservative media inundates us with warnings about debt from the Founding Fathers, and it's true that some of them, like Thomas Jefferson—himself an inveterate, often near-bankrupt debtor—did moralize on the subject. Yet Alexander Hamilton, an idol of the conservative movement, was the architect of the country's first national debt, insisting that "if it is not excessive, [it] will be to us a national blessing."

As the first secretary of the Treasury, Hamilton aimed to transform the former thirteen colonies, which today we would call an underdeveloped land, into a country that someday would rival Great Britain. This, he knew, required liquid capital (resources not tied up in land or other less mobile forms of wealth), which could then be invested in sometimes highly speculative and risky enterprises. Floating a national debt, he felt sure, would attract capital from well-positioned merchants at home and abroad, especially in England.

But for most ordinary people living under the new government, debt aroused anger. To begin with, there were all those veterans of the Revolutionary War and all the farmers who had supplied the revolutionary army with food; they had been paid in notoriously worthless "continentals"—the currency issued by the Continental Congress—or equally valueless state currencies. As rumors of the formation of a new national government spread, speculators roamed the countryside buying up this paper money at a penny on the dollar, on the assumption that the debts they represented would be redeemed at face value. In fact, that is just what Hamilton's national debt would do, making these "sunshine patriots" quite rich while leaving the yeomanry impoverished.

Outrage echoed across the country even before Hamilton's plan got adopted. Jefferson denounced the currency speculators as loathsome creatures and had this to say about debt in general: "The modern theory of the perpetuation of debt has drenched the earth with blood and crushed its inhabitants under burdens ever accumulating." He and others criticized the speculators as squadrons of counterrevolutionary "moneycrats" who would use their power and wealth to undo the democratic accomplishments of the revolution. In contrast, Hamilton saw them as a disinterested monied elite upon whom the country's economic well-being depended, while dismissing the criticisms of the Jeffersonians as the ravings of Jacobin Levellers. Soon enough, political warfare over the debt turned Founding Fathers into fratricidal brothers.[1]

As things turned out, Hamilton's plan worked—sometimes too well. Wealthy speculators in land, like Robert Morris, or in the building of docks, wharves, and other projects tied to trade or in the national debt itself—something William Duer and grandees like him specialized in—seized the moment. Often enough, though, they overreached and found themselves, like the yeomen farmers and soldiers, in default to their creditors.

Duer's attempts to corner the market in the bonds issued by the new federal government and in the stock of the country's first national bank represented one of the earliest instances of insider trading, as well as a lurid example of how speculation can go disastrously wrong. When the scheme collapsed, it caused the country's

---

1 *Every Man a Speculator*, Steve Fraser (New York: Harper Collins, 2005), pp. 8, 19–25.

first Wall Street panic and a local depression that spread through New England, ruining "shopkeepers, widows, orphans, butchers ... gardeners, market women, and even the noted Bawd Mrs. McCarty," as Stanley Elkins and Eric McKitrick put it in *The Age of Federalism.* A mob chased Duer through the streets of New York and might have hanged or disemboweled him had he not been rescued by the city sheriff, who sent him to the safety of debtors' prison. John Pintard, part of the same scheme, fled to Newark, New Jersey, before being caught and jailed as well.[2]

Sending the Duers and Pintards of the new republic off to debtors' prison was not, however, quite what Hamilton had in mind. And leaving them rotting there was hardly going to foster the "enterprising spirit" that would, in the Treasury secretary's estimation, turn the country into the Great Britain of the next century. Bankruptcy, on the other hand, ensured that the overextended could start again and keep the machinery of commercial transactions lubricated. Hence the Bankruptcy Act of 1800. If, however, you were not a major player, debt functioned differently. Shouldered by the hoi polloi, it functioned as a mechanism for funneling wealth into the mercantile-financial hothouses where American capitalism was being incubated.

No wonder debt excited such violent political emotions. Even before the Constitution was adopted, farmers in western Massachusetts, who were indebted to Boston bankers and merchants and in danger of losing their ancestral homes in the economic hard times of the 1780s, rose in armed rebellion. In those years, the number of lawsuits for unpaid debt doubled and tripled; farms were seized and their owners sent off to jail. Incensed, farmers led by a former revolutionary soldier, Daniel Shays, closed local courts by force and liberated debtors from prisons. Similar but smaller uprisings erupted in Maine, Connecticut, New York, and Pennsylvania, while in New Hampshire and Vermont irate farmers surrounded government offices.

---

2   Ibid., pp. 7–8.

Shays's Rebellion of 1786 particularly alarmed the country's elites. They depicted the unruly yeomen as "brutes" and their houses as "sties." They were frightened as well by state governments like Rhode Island's, which were more open to popular influence, declaring debt moratoriums and issuing paper currencies to help farmers and others pay off their debts. These developments signaled the need for a stronger central government that would be fully capable of suppressing future debtor insurgencies.

The federal authority established at the Constitutional Convention allowed for that, but the unrest continued. Shays's Rebellion was but part one of a trilogy of uprisings that continued into the 1790s. The Whiskey Rebellion of 1794 was the most serious. An excise tax ("whiskey tax") meant to generate revenue to back up the national debt threatened the livelihoods of farmers in western Pennsylvania. They used whiskey as a "currency" in a local economy where barter transactions remained common. President Washington sent in troops, many of them Revolutionary War veterans, with Hamilton at their head to put down the rebels.

Debt Servitude and Primitive Accumulation

Debt would continue to play a vital role in national political affairs throughout the nineteenth century, functioning as a form of capital accumulation in the financial sector and often choking precapitalist forms of life in the process. Soon enough, manufacturers and other capitalists would invest directly in the production process, employing wage labor and selling into the marketplace. But before that, and long after, banks and other financial institutions accumulated from outside the spheres of production by extending credit to productive enterprises and subscribing to loans by public authorities, supported by tax revenues. The mechanisms of public and private debt made the lives of farmers, craftsmen, shopkeepers, and other increasingly insupportable.

This parasitic economic metabolism helped account for the riotous nature of Gilded Age politics. Much of the high drama of late nineteenth-century political life circled around "greenbacks," "free silver," and the "gold standard." These issues may strike us as arcane today, but they were incendiary then, threatening what some called a second Civil War. In one way or another they were centrally about debt, especially a system of indebtedness that was driving independent farmers to extinction.

All the highways of global capitalism found their way into the trackless vastness of rural America. Farmers there were not in dire straits because of their backwoods isolation. On the contrary, it was because they turned out to be living at ground zero of the capitalist economy, where the explosive energies of financial and commercial modernity detonated. A toxic combination of railroads, grain-elevator operators, farm-machinery manufacturers, commodity-exchange speculators, local merchants, and, above all, the banking establishment had farmers at their mercy. Their helplessness was only aggravated when the nineteenth-century version of globalization left their crops in desperate competition with those from the steppes of Canada and Russia as well as the outbacks of Australia and South America.

To survive this mercantile onslaught, farmers hooked themselves up to the long lines of credit that stretched back to the financial centers of the East. These lifelines allowed them to buy the seed, fertilizer, and machines they needed to farm; pay the storage and freight charges that went with selling their crops; and keep house and home together while the plants ripened and the hogs fattened. When market day finally arrived, the farmers found out just what all that backbreaking work was really worth. If the news was bad, then those credit lines were shut off and they found themselves dispossessed. The family farm and the network of small-town life that went with it were being swept into the rivers of capital that were heading for metropolitan America. On the "sod house" frontier, poverty was a "badge of honor which decorated all," as Lawrence Goodwyn put it in his study of the Populist movement. In his *Devil's Dictionary*, the acid-tongued humorist Ambrose Bierce defined the dilemma this way: "Debt is an ingenious substitute for the chain and whip of the slave driver."

Across the Great Plains and the cotton-growing South, discontented farmers spread the blame for their predicament far and wide. Anger tended to pool around the strangulating system of currency and credit run out of the banking centers of the Northeast. Beginning in the 1870s with the emergence of the Greenback Party and Greenback Labor Party, and culminating in the 1890s with the People's Party, or Populist Party, independent farmers, tenant farmers, sharecroppers, small business owners, and skilled workers directed ever more intense hostility at "the money power."

That "power" might appear locally in the homeliest of disguises: in coal mines and other industrial sites, among "coolies" working to build the railroads or imported immigrant gang laborers and convicts leased to private concerns, workers were typically compelled to buy what they needed in company scrip at company stores, at prices that left them perpetually in debt. They were so precariously positioned that going into debt—whether to pawnshops or employers, landlords or loan sharks—was unavoidable. Often they were paid in kind: wood chips, thread, hemp, scarps of canvas, cordage—nothing, that is, that was of any use in paying off accumulated debts. In effect they were, as they called themselves, "debt slaves."

In the South, hard-pressed growers found themselves embroiled in a crop-lien system, dependent on the local "furnishing agent" to supply everything needed, from seed to clothing to machinery, to get through the growing season. In such situations, no money changed hands; a note was scribbled in the merchant's ledger, with payment due at "settling up" time. This granted the lender a lien, or title, to the crop—a lien that never went away.

In this fashion, the South became (to use Goodwyn's phrase) "a great pawnshop," with farmers perpetually in debt at interest rates exceeding 100 percent per year. In Alabama, Georgia, and Mississippi, 90 percent of farmers lived on credit. The first lien you signed was essentially a life sentence. Either that or you became a tenant farmer—or you simply left your land, something so commonplace that everyone knew what the letters "G.T.T." on an abandoned farmhouse meant: "Gone to Texas." (One hundred thousand people a year were doing that in the 1870s.) The merchant's exaction was so steep that African Americans and immigrants, in particular, were regularly reduced to peonage—forced, that is, to work to pay off their debt, an illegal but not uncommon practice. And that neighborhood furnishing agent was often tied to the banks up north for his own lines of credit. In this way, the sucking sound of money leaving for the great metropolises reverberated from region to region.

Facing dispossession, farmers formed alliances and set up cooperatives to extend credit to one another and market crops themselves. As one Populist editorialist remarked, this was the way "mortgage-burdened farmers can assert their freedom from the tyranny of organized capital." But when they found that these groupings couldn't survive the competitive pressure of the banking establishment, politics beckoned.

From one presidential election to the next, and in state contests throughout the South and West, irate grain and cotton growers demanded that the government either expand the paper currency supply ("greenbacks," also known as "the people's money") or monetize silver (again, to enlarge the money supply), or that it set up public institutions to finance farmers during the growing season. With a passion hard for us to imagine, they railed against the "gold standard," which, Democratic Party presidential candidate William Jennings Bryan famously cried, should no longer be allowed to "crucify mankind on a cross of gold." Should that cross stay fixed in place, one Alabama physician prophesied, it would "reduce the American yeomanry to menials and paupers, to be driven by monopolies like cattle and swine." As Election Day approached, Populist editors and speakers warned of an approaching war with the money power, and they meant it: "The fight will come and let it come!"[1]

The idea was to deliberately force the government to inflate the currency and so raise farm prices. This, Populists thought, would allow farmers to get out of the sea of debt in which they were submerged. Inflation, accomplished by expanding the supply of money, would make it easier for debtors to pay off loans with the additional proceeds they received from those rising farm prices. It would, on the other hand, infuriate creditors, who would then have to accept a cheapened currency in payment for debts originally denominated in more precious gold. For the dependent mass of sorely afflicted debtors, this was a cry from the heart. It echoed across the heartland, coming nearer to upsetting the established order than any American political upheaval before or since.

Yet the passion of those Populist farmers and laborers was matched by that of their enemies, men at the top of the economy and government for whom debt had long been a road to riches rather than destitution. They dismissed their foes as "cranks" and "calamity howlers." And in the election of 1896, they won. Bryan went down in defeat, gold continued its pitiless process of crucifixion, and a whole human ecology was set on a path to extinction.

The Return of Debt Servitude

When populism died, debt as a spark for national political confrontation died, too. The great reform eras that followed—Progressivism, the New Deal, and the Great Society—were preoccupied instead with inequality, economic collapse, exploitation in the workplace, and the outsized nature of corporate power in a consolidated industrial-capitalist system.

---

1 Ibid., pp. 205–11.

Rumblings about debt servitude could certainly still be heard. Foreclosed farmers during the Great Depression mobilized, held "penny auctions" to restore farms to families, hanged judges in effigy, and forced the Prudential Insurance Company, the largest land creditor in Iowa, to suspend foreclosures on 37,000 farms (which persuaded the Metropolitan Life Insurance Company to do likewise). A Kansas City realtor was shot in the act of foreclosing on a family farm; a country sheriff was kidnapped while trying to evict a farm widow and dumped ten miles out of town. Urban renters and homeowners facing eviction formed neighborhood groups to stop local sheriffs or police from throwing families out of their houses or apartments. Furniture tossed into the street in eviction proceedings would be restored by neighbors, who would also turn the gas and electricity back on. New Deal farm and housing-finance legislation bailed out banks and homeowners alike. Right-wing populists, like the Catholic priest Father Charles Coughlin, carried on the war against the gold standard in tirades tinged with anti-Semitism. Signs like one in Nebraska that said "The Jew System of Banking," illustrated with a giant rattlesnake, showed up too often. But the age of primitive accumulation, in which debt and the financial sector had played such a strategic role, was drawing to a close.

Today we have entered a new phase. In what might be called capitalist underdevelopment, once again debt has emerged as both a central mode of capital accumulation and a principal mechanism of servitude. Warren Buffett (of all people) has predicted that in the coming decades, the United States is more likely to turn into a "sharecropper society" than an "ownership society."

In our time, the financial sector has enriched itself by devouring the productive wherewithal of industrial America, starving the public sector of resources, and saddling ordinary working people with every conceivable form of consumer debt. The deindustrialization of America, which began in the 1970s and has continued ever since at an accelerating rate, was set in motion by the country's leading financial institutions. All those mergers and acquisitions, leveraged buyouts, junk-bond acquisitions, and the "lean and mean" asset-stripping that followed saddled the productive sectors of the economy with insupportable debts. These were, on the one hand, lucrative securities for the banks and private-equity and venture-capital firms that issued them. But for ordinary working people, they delivered plant shutdowns, massive layoffs, declining real wages, diminished pensions, and reduced or nonexistent health care. And then came the unconscionably profitable securitizing of the homes where people lived—and in due time could no longer live. Taking on ever greater loads of debt has become, for many, the only way to tread water. Household debt, which in 1952 was at 36 percent of total personal income, had by 2006 hit 127 percent. Even financing poverty became a lucrative enterprise. Taking advantage of the low credit ratings of poor people and their need for cash to pay monthly bills or simply feed themselves, some check-cashing outlets, payday lenders, tax preparers, and others levy interest rates of 200 percent, 300 percent, and more. As recently as the 1970s, a good part of this would have been illegal under usury laws that no longer exist. These poverty creditors are often tied to the largest financiers, including Citibank, Bank of America, and American Express.

Credit has come to function as a plastic safety net in a world of job insecurity, declining state support, and slow-motion economic growth, especially among the elderly, young adults, and low-income families. More than half the pretax income of those three groups goes to servicing debt. Nowadays, however, the company store is headquartered on Wall Street. Debt is driving this system of autocannibalism that, by every measure of social well-being, is relentlessly turning a developed country into an underdeveloped one. Jekyll and Hyde are back. Is a political resistance to debt servitude once again imaginable?

Some argue that it is wiser to confront the underlying reason debt has become such an onerous burden for so many: namely, that the core of the economy has been hollowed out—the core which once generated decently paying, often unionized jobs that came with the wherewithal to vacation, stay healthy, educate the kids, and retire. A political movement, they argue, ought to concentrate its energies in that direction (rather than detouring into debt resistance), mobilizing for the collective redevelopment of the commonwealth.

This is a strong argument. But taking on the financial sector on its home turn has a certain compelling logic, especially in a new era based on capital disaccumulation—that is, the cannibalization of the life-supporting economy by a fictitious one deploying arcane forms of securitized debt. Not to mention that millions of people face day to day and in every way what their ancestors once did: thralldom to the banks. Breaking that dependency on institutions too big to fail won't bring on the end of the world, as official opinion warns us. That is one domestic version of a more general politics of fear that elites now manufacture with greater and greater frequency.

How to "break their haughty power" is not a simple matter. But there are plenty of proposals afloat, ranging from the modest to the more radical, about how to take them on. Why not, for example, pass some version of the Tobin tax that penalizes financial transactions of a purely speculative nature? Aren't banks that are too big to fail also banks that shouldn't exist? How about empowering the Federal Reserve with the authority to adjust interest rates to reward banks borrowing for productive investments, while charging them more when they access government credit for less justifiable purposes? That would be a first step toward altering our whole perspective about the people banks need to serve. Since several billion people depend on the resources they privately control, why not treat them as we sometimes do public utilities and own them outright, or at least include on their governing boards representatives of the public to help determine how their enormous capital resources are deployed? In some towns and cities, public and community organizations are buying up foreclosed houses and returning them to their owners at affordable rates. Perhaps it's time for another Jubilee Day.

3. Locking Down an American Workforce: Prison Labor as the Past—and Future—of American "Free-Market" Capitalism

Steve Fraser and Joshua B. Freeman

Sweatshop labor is back with a vengeance. It can be found across broad stretches of the American economy and around the world. Penitentiaries have become a niche market for such work. The privatization of prisons in recent years has meant the creation of a small army of workers too coerced and rightless to complain.

Prisoners, whose ranks increasingly consist of those for whom the legitimate economy has found no use, now make up a virtual brigade within the reserve army of the unemployed whose ranks have ballooned along with the US incarceration rate. CoreCivic (formerly Corrections Corporation of America) and G4S (formerly Wackenhut), two prison privatizers, sell inmate labor

An earlier version of this chapter was co-written with Joshua Freeman and published in *TomDispatch* on April 19, 2012.

at subminimum wages to Fortune 500 corporations like Chevron, Bank of America, AT&T, and IBM.

These companies can, in most states, lease factories in prisons or prisoners to work on the outside. Prisoners are now making office furniture, working in call centers, fabricating body armor, taking hotel reservations, working in slaughterhouses, or manufacturing textiles, shoes, and clothing, while getting paid somewhere between 93 cents and $4.73 per day.

Rarely can you find workers so pliable, easy to control, stripped of political rights, and subject to martial discipline at the first sign of recalcitrance—unless, that is, you traveled back to the nineteenth century when convict labor was commonplace nationwide. Indeed, a sentence of "confinement at hard labor" was then the essence of the American penal system. More than that, it was one vital way the United States became a modern industrial capitalist economy—at a moment, eerily like our own, when the mechanisms of capital accumulation were in crisis.

A Yankee Invention

What some historians call "the long Depression" of the nineteenth century, which lasted from the mid-1870s through the mid-1890s, was marked by frequent panics and slumps, mass bankruptcies, deflation, and self-destructive competition among businesses designed to depress costs, especially labor costs. So, too, we are living through a twenty-first-century age of panics and austerity with similar pressures to shrink the social wage.

Convict labor has been and once again is an appealing way for business to address these dilemmas. Penal servitude now strikes us as a barbaric throwback to some long-lost moment that preceded the Industrial Revolution, but in that we're wrong. From its first appearance in this country, it has been associated with modern capitalist industry and large-scale agriculture.

And that is only the first of many misconceptions about this peculiar institution. Infamous for the brutality with which prison laborers were once treated, indelibly linked in popular memory (and popular culture) with images of the black chain gang in the American South, it is usually assumed to be a Southern invention. So apparently atavistic, it seems to fit naturally with the retrograde nature of Southern life and labor, its economic and cultural underdevelopment, its racial caste system, and its desperate attachment to the "lost cause."

As it happens, penal servitude—the leasing out of prisoners to private enterprise, either within prison walls or in outside workshops, factories, and fields—was originally known as a "Yankee invention."

First used at Auburn prison in New York State in the 1820s, the system spread widely and quickly throughout the North, the Midwest, and later the West. It developed alongside state-run prison workshops that produced goods for the public sector and sometimes the open market.

A few Southern states also used it. Prisoners there, as elsewhere, however, were mainly white men, since slave masters, with a free hand to deal with the "infractions" of their chattel, had little need for prison. The Thirteenth Amendment abolishing slavery would, in fact, make an exception for penal servitude precisely because it had become the dominant form of punishment throughout the free states.

Nor were those sentenced to "confinement at hard labor" restricted to digging ditches or other unskilled work; nor were they only men. Prisoners were employed at an enormous range of tasks from rope- and wagon-making to carpet, hat, and clothing manufacturing (where women prisoners were sometimes put to work), as well as coal mining, carpentry, barrel-making, shoe production, house-building, and even the manufacture of rifles. The range of petty and larger workshops into which the felons were integrated made up the heart of the new American economy.

Observing a free-labor textile mill and a convict-labor one on a visit to the United States, novelist Charles Dickens couldn't tell the difference. State governments used the rental revenue garnered from their prisoners to meet budget needs, while entrepreneurs made outsized profits by either working the prisoners themselves or subleasing them to other businessmen.

Convict Labor in the "New South"

After the Civil War, the convict-lease system metamorphosed. In the South, it became ubiquitous, one of several grim methods—including the black codes, debt peonage, the crop-lien system, life-time labor contracts, and vigilante terror—used to control and fix in place the newly emancipated slave. Those "freedmen" were eager to pursue their new liberty either by setting up as small farmers or by exercising the right to move out of the region at will or from job to job as "free wage labor" was supposed to be able to do.

If you assumed, however, that the convict-lease system was solely the brainchild of the apartheid all-white "Redeemer" governments that overthrew the Radical Republican regimes (which first ran the defeated Confederacy during Reconstruction) and used their power to introduce Jim Crow to Dixie, you would be wrong again. In Georgia, for instance, the Radical Republican state government took the initiative soon after the war ended. And this was because the convict-lease system was tied to the modernizing sectors of the postwar economy, no matter where in Dixie it was introduced or by whom.

So convicts were leased to coal-mining, iron-forging, steel-making, and railroad companies, including Tennessee Coal and Iron (TC&I), a major producer across the South, especially in the booming region around Birmingham, Alabama. More than a quarter of the coal coming out of Birmingham's pits was then mined by prisoners. By the turn of the century, TC&I had been folded into J. P. Morgan's United States Steel complex, which also relied heavily on prison laborers.

All the main extractive industries of the South were, in fact, wedded to the system. Turpentine and lumber camps deep in the fetid swamps and forest vastnesses of Georgia, Florida, and Louisiana commonly worked their convicts until they dropped dead from overwork or disease. The region's plantation monocultures in cotton and sugar made regular use of imprisoned former slaves, including women. Among the leading families of Atlanta, Birmingham, and other "New South" metropolises were businessmen whose fortunes originated in the dank coal pits, malarial marshes, isolated forests, and squalid barracks in which their unfree peons worked, lived, and died.

Because it tended to grant absolute authority to private commercial interests and because its racial makeup in the post-slavery era was overwhelmingly African-American, the South's convict-lease system was distinctive. Its caste nature is not only impossible to forget, but should remind us of the unbalanced racial profile of America's bloated prison population today.

Moreover, this totalitarian-style control invited appalling brutalities in response to any sign of resistance: whippings, water torture, isolation in "dark cells," dehydration, starvation, ice-baths, shackling with metal spurs riveted to the feet, and "tricing" (an excruciatingly painful process in which recalcitrant prisoners were strung up by the thumbs with fishing line attached to overhead pulleys). Even women in a hosiery mill in Tennessee were flogged, hung by the wrists, and placed in solitary confinement.

Living quarters for prisoner-workers were usually rat-infested and disease-ridden. Work lasted at least from sunup to sundown and well past the point of exhaustion. Death came often enough and bodies were cast off in unmarked graves by the side of the road or by incineration in coke ovens. Injury rates averaged one per worker per month, including respiratory failure, burnings, disfigurement, and the loss of limbs. Prison mines were called "nurseries of death." Among Southern convict laborers, the mortality rate (not even including high levels of suicides) was eight times that among similar workers in the North—and it was extraordinarily high there.

The Southern system also stood out for the intimate collusion among industrial, commercial, and agricultural enterprises and every level of Southern law enforcement as well as the judicial system. Sheriffs, local justices of the peace, state police, judges, and state governments conspired to keep the convict-lease business humming. Indeed, local law officers depended on the leasing system for a substantial part of their income. (They pocketed the fines and fees associated with the "convictions," a repayable sum that would be added on to the amount of time at "hard labor" demanded of the prisoner.)

The arrest cycle was synchronized with the business cycle, timed to the rise and fall of the demand for fresh labor. County and state treasuries similarly counted on such revenues, since the postwar South was so capital-starved that only renting out convicts assured that prisons could be built and maintained.

There was, then, every incentive to concoct charges or send people to jail for the most trivial offenses: vagrancy, gambling, drinking, partying, hopping a freight car, tarrying too long in town. A "pig law" in Mississippi assured you of five years as a prison laborer if you stole a farm animal worth more than $10. Theft of a fence rail could result in the same.

Penal Servitude in the Gilded Age North

All of this was only different in degree from prevailing practices everywhere else: the sale of prison labor power to private interests, corporal punishment, and the absence of all rights including civil liberties, the vote, and the right to protest or organize against terrible conditions.

In the North, where 80 percent of all US prison labor was employed after the Civil War and which accounted for over $35 billion in output (in current dollars), the system was reconfigured to meet the needs of modern industry and the pressures of "the long Depression." Convict labor was increasingly leased out only to a handful of major manufacturers in each state. These textile mills, oven makers, mining operations, hat and shoe factories—one in Wisconsin leased that state's entire population of convicted felons—were then installing the kind of mass production methods becoming standard in much of American industry. As organized markets for prison labor grew increasingly oligopolistic (like the rest of the economy), the Depression of 1873 and subsequent depressions in the following decades wiped out many smaller businesses that had once gone trawling for convicts.

Today, we talk about a newly "flexible economy," often a euphemism for the geometric growth of a precariously positioned, insecure workforce. The convict-labor system of the nineteenth century offered an original specimen of perfect flexibility.

Companies leasing convicts enjoyed authority to dispose of their rented labor power as they saw fit. Workers were compelled to labor in total silence. Even hand gestures and eye contact were prohibited for the purpose of creating "silent and insulated working machines."

Supervision of prison labor was ostensibly shared by employers and the prison authorities. In fact, many businesses did continue to conduct their operations within prison walls where they supplied the materials, power, and machinery, while the state provided guards, workshops, food, clothing, and what passed for medical care. As a matter of practice though, the foremen of the businesses called the shots. And there were certain states, including Nebraska, Washington, and New Mexico, that, like their Southern counterparts, ceded complete control to the lessee. As one observer put it, "Felons are mere machines held to labor by the dark cell and the scourge."

Free-market industrial capitalism, then and now, invariably draws on the aid of the state. In that system's formative phases, the state has regularly used its coercive powers of taxation, expropriation, and in this case incarceration to free up natural and human resources lying outside the orbit of capitalism proper.

In both the North and the South, the contracting out of convict labor was one way in which that state-assisted mechanism of capital accumulation arose. Contracts with the government assured employers that their labor force would be replenished anytime a worker got sick, was disabled, died, or simply became too worn out to continue.

The Kansas Wagon Company, for example, signed a five-year contract in 1877 that prevented the state from raising the rental price of labor or renting to other employers. The company also got an option to renew the lease for ten more years, while the government was obliged to pay for new machinery, larger workshops, a power supply, and even the building of a switching track that connected to the trunk line of the Pacific Railway and so ensured that the product could be moved effectively to market.

Penal institutions all over the country became auxiliary arms of capitalist industry and commerce. Two-thirds of all prisoners worked for private enterprise.

Today, strikingly enough, government is again providing subsidies and tax incentives as well as facilities, utilities, and free space for corporations making use of this same category of abjectly dependent labor.

The New Abolitionism

Dependency and flexibility naturally assumed no resistance, but there was plenty of that all through the nineteenth century from workers, farmers, and even prisoners. Indeed, a principal objective in using prison labor was to undermine efforts to unionize, but from the standpoint of mobilized working people far more was at stake.

Opposition to convict labor arose from workingmen's associations, labor-oriented political parties, journeymen unions, and other groups which considered the system an insult to the moral codes of egalitarian republicanism nurtured by the American Revolution. The specter of proletarian dependency haunted the lives of the country's self-reliant handicraft workers who watched apprehensively as shops employing wage labor began popping up across the country. Much of the earliest of this agitation was aimed at the use of prisoners to replace skilled workers (while unskilled prison labor was initially largely ignored).

It was bad enough for craftsmen to see their own livelihoods and standards of living put in jeopardy by "free" wage labor. Worse still was to watch unfree labor do the same thing. At the time, employers were turning to that captive prison population to combat attempts by aggrieved workers to organize and defend themselves. On the eve of the Civil War, for example, an iron-molding contractor in Spuyten Duyvil, north of Manhattan in the Bronx, locked out his unionized workers and then moved his operation to Sing Sing penitentiary, where a laborer cost forty cents, $2.60 less than the going day rate. It worked, and Local 11 of the Union of Iron Workers quickly died away.

Worst of all was to imagine this debased form of work as a model for the proletarian future to come. The workingman's movement of the Jacksonian era was deeply alarmed by the prospect of "wage slavery," a condition inimical to their sense of themselves as citizens of a republic of independent producers. Prison labor was a sub-species of that dreaded "slavery," a caricature of it perhaps, and intolerable to a movement often as much about emancipation as unionization.

All the way through the Gilded Age of the 1890s, convict labor continued to serve as a magnet for emancipatory desires. In addition, prisoners' rebellions became ever more common—in the North particularly, where many prisoners turned out to be Civil War veterans and dispossessed working people who already knew something about fighting for freedom and fighting back. Major penitentiaries like Sing Sing became sites of repeated strikes and riots; a strike in 1877 even took on the transplanted Spuyten Duyvil iron-molding company.

Above and below the Mason Dixon line, political platforms, protest rallies, petition campaigns, legislative investigations, union strikes, and boycotts by farm organizations like the Farmers Alliance and the Grange cried out for the abolition of the convict-lease system, or at least for its rigorous regulation. Over the century's last two decades, more than twenty coal-mine strikes broke out because of the use of convict miners.

The Knights of Labor, that era's most audacious labor movement, was particularly exercised. During the Coal Creek Wars in eastern Tennessee in the early 1890s, for instance, TC&I tried to use prisoners to break a miners' strike. The company's vice president noted that it was "an effective club to hold over the heads of free laborers."

Strikers and their allies affiliated with the Knights, the United Mine Workers, and the Farmers Alliance launched guerilla attacks on the prisoner stockade, sending the convicts they freed to Knoxville. When the governor insisted on shipping them back, the workers released them into the surrounding hills and countryside. Gun battles followed.

The Death of Convict Leasing

In the North, the prison abolition movement went viral, embracing not only workers' organizations, sympathetic rural insurgents, and prisoners, but also widening circles of middle-class reformers. The newly created American Federation of Labor denounced the system as "contract slavery." It also demanded the banning of any imports from abroad made with convict labor and the exclusion from the open market of goods produced domestically by prisoners, whether in state-run or private workshops. In Chicago, the construction unions refused to work with materials made by prisoners.

By the latter part of the century, in state after state penal servitude was on its way to extinction. New York, where the "industry" was born and was largest, killed it by the late 1880s. The tariff of 1890 prohibited the sale of convict-made wares from abroad. Private leasing continued in the North, but under increasingly restrictive conditions, including federal legislation passed during the New Deal. By World War II, it was virtually extinct (although government-run prison workshops continued as they always had).

At least officially, even in the South it was at an end by the turn of the century in Tennessee, Louisiana, Georgia, and Mississippi. Higher political calculations were at work in these states. Established elites were eager to break the inter-racial alliances that had formed over abolishing convict leasing by abolishing the hated system itself. Often enough, however, it ended in name only.

What replaced it was the state-run chain gang (although some Southern states like Alabama and Florida continued private leasing well into the 1920s). Inmates were set to work building roads and other infrastructure projects vital to the flourishing of a mature market economy and so to the continuing process of capital accumulation. In the North, the system of "hard labor" was replaced by a system of "hard time," that numbing, brutalizing idleness where masses of people extruded from the mainstream economy are pooled into mass penal colonies. The historic link between labor, punishment, and economic development was severed, and remained so ... until now.

Convict Leasing Rises Again

"Now" means our second Gilded Age and its aftermath. In these years, the system of leasing out convicts to private enterprise was reborn. This was a perverse triumph for the law of supply and demand in an era infatuated with the charms of the free market. On the supply side, the United States holds captive 25 percent of all the prisoners on the planet: 2.3 million people. It has the highest incarceration rate in the world as well, a figure that began skyrocketing in 1980 as Ronald Reagan became president. As for the demand for labor, since the 1970s American industrial corporations have found it increasingly unprofitable to invest in domestic production. Instead, they have sought out the hundreds of millions of people abroad who are willing to, or can be pressed into, working for far less than American workers.

As a consequence, those back home—disproportionately African-American workers—who found themselves living in economic exile, scrabbling to get by, began showing up in similarly disproportionate numbers in the country's rapidly expanding prison archipelago. It didn't take long for corporate America to come to view this as another potential foreign country, full of cheap and subservient labor—and better yet, close by.

What began in the 1970s as an end run around the laws prohibiting convict leasing by private interests has now become an industrial sector in its own right, employing more people than any Fortune 500 corporation and operating in thirty-seven states. And here's the ultimate irony: our ancestors found convict labor obnoxious in part because it seemed to prefigure a new and more universal form of enslavement. Could its rebirth foreshadow a future ever more unnervingly like those past nightmares?

Today, we are being reassured by the president, the mainstream media, and economic experts that the Great Recession is over, that we are in "recovery" even though most of the recovering patients haven't actually noticed significant improvement in their condition. For those announcing its arrival, "recovery" means that the mega-banks are no longer on the brink of bankruptcy, the stock market has made up lost ground, corporate profits are improving, and notoriously unreliable employment numbers have improved by several tenths of a percent.

What accounts for that peculiarly narrow view of recovery, however, is that the general costs of doing business are falling off a cliff as the economy eats itself alive. The recovery being celebrated owes thanks to local, state, and federal austerity budgets, the starving of the social welfare system and public services, rampant anti-union campaigns in the public and private sector, the spread of sweatshop labor, the coercion of desperate unemployed or under-employed workers to accept lower wages, part-time work, and temporary work, as well as the relinquishing of health-care benefits and a financially secure retirement—in short, the surrender of the hope that is supposed to come with the American franchise.

Such a recovery, resting on the stripping away of the hard-won material and cultural achievements of the past century, suggests a new world in which the prison-labor archipelago could indeed become a vast gulag of the downwardly mobile.

4. Uncle Sam Doesn't Want You: America's Reserve Army of Labor Marches Through Time

Steve Fraser and Joshua B. Freeman

Not long ago, the city council of Ventura, California, passed an ordinance making it legal for the unemployed and homeless to sleep in their cars. At the height of the Great Recession of 2008, one-third of the capital equipment of the American economy lay idle. Of the women and men idled along with that equipment, only 37 percent got a government unemployment check and that check, on average, represented only 35 percent of their weekly wages.

Meanwhile, there are now two million "99ers"—those who have maxed out their supplemental unemployment benefits because they have been out of work for more than 99 weeks. Think of them as a full division in the "reserve army of labor." That "army," in turn, accounts for 17 percent of the American labor force, if one includes part-time workers who need and want full-time work and the

An earlier version of this chapter was co-written with Joshua Freeman and was published in *TomDispatch* on September 11, 2011.

millions of unemployed Americans who have grown so discouraged that they've given up looking for jobs and so aren't counted in the official unemployment figures. As is its historic duty, that force of idle workers is once again driving down wages, lengthening working hours, eroding on-the-job conditions, and adding an element of raw fear to the lives of anyone still lucky enough to have a job.

No one volunteers to serve in this army. But anyone, from Silicon Valley engineers to Florida tomato pickers, is eligible to join what, in our time, might be thought of as the all-involuntary force. Its mission is to make the world safe for capitalism. Today, with the world spiraling into a second "Great Recession" (even if few, besides the banks, ever noticed that the first one had ended), its ranks are bound to grow.

The All-Involuntary Army (of Labor)

As has always been true, the coexistence of idling workplaces and cast-off workers remains the single most severe indictment of capitalism as a system for the reproduction of human society. The arrival of a new social category—"the 99ers"—punctuates that grim observation today.

After all, what made the Great Depression "great" was not only the staggering level of unemployment (no less true in various earlier periods of economic collapse), but its duration. Years went by, numbingly, totally demoralizingly, without work or hope. When it all refused to end, people began to question the fundamentals, to wonder if, as a system, capitalism hadn't outlived its usefulness.

Nowadays, the 99ers notwithstanding, we don't readily jump to such a conclusion. Along with the "business cycle," including stock market bubbles and busts and other economic perturbations, unemployment has been normalized. No one thinks it's a good thing, of course, but it's certainly not something that should cause us to question the way the economy is organized.

Long gone are the times when unemployment was so shocking and traumatic that it took people back to the basics. We don't, for instance, even use that phrase "the reserve army of labor" anymore. It strikes many, along with "class struggle" and "working class," as embarrassing. It's too "Marxist" or anachronistic in an age of postindustrial flexible capitalism, when we've grown accustomed to the casualness and transience of work, or even anointed it as a form of "free agency."

However, long before leftists began referring to the unemployed as a reserve army, that redolent metaphor was regularly wielded by anxious or angry nineteenth-century journalists, government officials, town fathers, governors, churchmen, and other concerned citizens. Something new was happening, they were sure, even if they weren't entirely clear on what to make of it.

Unemployment as a recurring feature of the social landscape only caught American attention with the rise of capitalism in the pre–Civil War era. Before that, even if the rhythms of agricultural and village life included seasonal oscillations between periods of intense labor and downtime, farmers and handicraft workers generally retained the ability to sustain their families.

Hard times were common enough, but except *in extremis* most people retained land and tools, not to speak of common rights to woodlands, grazing areas, and the ability to hunt and fish. They were—we would say today—"self-employed." Only when such means of subsistence and production became concentrated in the hands of merchant capitalists, manufacturers, and large landowners did the situation change fundamentally. A proletariat—those without property of any kind except their own labor power—made its appearance, dependent on the propertied to employ them. If, for whatever reason, the market for their labor power dried up, they were set adrift.

This process of dispossession lasted more than a century. In the early decades of the nineteenth century, its impact remained limited.

The farmers, handicraftsmen, fishermen, and various tradespeople swept into the new textile or shoe factories, or the farm women set to work out in the countryside spinning and weaving for merchant capitalists still held on to some semblance of their old ways of life. They maintained vegetable gardens, continued to hunt and fish, and perhaps kept a few domestic animals.

When the first commercial panics erupted in the 1830s and 1850s and business came to a standstill, many could fall back on precapitalist ways of making a living, even if a bare one. Still, the first regiments of the reserve army of the unemployed had made their appearance. Jobless men were already roaming the roads, an alarming new sight for townspeople not used to such things.

Demobilizing the Workforce Becomes the New Norm

When industrial capitalism exploded after the Civil War, unemployment suddenly became a chronic and frightening aspect of modern life affecting millions. Panics and depressions now occurred with distressing frequency. Their randomness, severity, and duration (some lasted half a decade or more) only swelled the ranks of the reserve army. Crushing helplessness in the face of unemployment would be a devastating new experience for the great waves of immigrants just landing on American shores, many of them peasants from southern and eastern Europe accustomed to falling back on their own meager resources in fields and forests when times were bad.

The very presence of this "army" of able-bodied but destitute workers seemed to catch the essential savagery of the new economy and it stunned onlookers. The "tramp" became a ubiquitous figure, traveling the roads and rails, sometimes carrying his tools with him, desperate for work. He proved a threatening specter for villagers and city people alike.

Just as shocking was a growing realization—made undeniable by each dismal repetition of the business cycle—that the new industrial economy wasn't just producing that reserve army, but depended on its regular mobilization and demobilization to carry on the process of capital accumulation. It was no passing phenomenon, no natural disaster that would run its course. It was the new normal.

Initial reactions were varied and dramatic. Local governments rushed to pass punitive laws against tramping and vagrancy, mandating terms of six months to two years of hard labor in work-houses. Meanwhile, the orthodox thinking of that moment raised steep barriers to government aid for those in need. During the devastating depression of the 1870s, for instance, President Ulysses Grant's secretary of the Treasury put things succinctly: "It is not part of the business of government to find employment for people."

Punishment and studied indifference were, however, by no means the only responses as emergency relief efforts—some private, some public—became common. The ravaging effects of unemployment, the way it spread like a plague, and its chronic reappearance also put more radical measures on the agenda, proposals that questioned the viability and morality of what was then termed the "wages system."

Calls went out to colonize vacant land and establish state-run factories and farms to productively re-employ the idled. Infuriated throngs occupied state houses demanding public works. Elements of the labor and Populist movements advocated manufacturing and agricultural cooperatives as a way around the ruthlessness of the Darwinian free market. Business "trusts" or monopolies were often decried for driving other businesses under and so exacerbating the unemployment dilemma. In some cases, their nationalization was called for. Militants of the moment began to demand work not as a sop to the indigent, but as a right of citizenship, as precious and inviolable as anything in the Bill of Rights.

The greatest and most prolonged mass mobilization of the mid-1880s was the national movement for the eight-hour work day. It was animated partly by a desire for more leisure time, but also by a vain hope that its passage by Congress might effectively raise wages. (Industrialists, however, had no intention of paying the same amount for eight hours of work as they had for 12.) Its main impetus, though, was a belief that mandating a national reduction in the hours of work would spread jobs around and so diminish the ranks of the reserve army.

Some were convinced that capitalism's appetite for human labor was too voracious for business ever to agree to such limits. So long as the business cycle was on its upward arc, the compulsion to exploit labor power was insatiable. When the market went south, all that surplus humanity could be left to fend for itself. Its partisans nonetheless believed that the movement for an eight-hour day would expose the barbarism of the economic system for all to see, opening the door to something more humane.

In other words, a wide spectrum of responses to unemployment was enfolded within a broad and growing anticapitalist culture. Within the organized labor movement, that proto-union, the Knights of Labor, was part of an anticapitalist insurgency. Most trade unions of the time, however, accepted that the "wages system" was here to stay and focused instead on the issues of job security, fighting for unemployment benefit funds for members, seniority, prohibitions against overtime, and the shortening of working hours.

Even agitation to ban child labor and limit female employment was motivated in part by a desire to temper the pervasiveness of unemployment by curtailing the pool of available labor. Other trade union procedures and proposals were more mean-spirited, including attempts to ban immigration or exclude African Americans and other minorities or the unskilled from membership in the movement.

As part of this tumultuous season of upheaval, which lasted from the 1870s through the Great Depression, the unemployed themselves organized demonstrations. A gathering in Tompkins Square Park of thousands of New Yorkers left destitute by the panic and depression of 1873 was dispersed with infamous brutality by the police. Local newspapers labeled the protestors "communards."

(The recently defeated Paris Commune had ignited a hysterical fear of "un-American" radicalism, a toxin that has never left the American bloodstream.)

Although the Tompkins Square rally was mainly a plea for relief and public works, there was some talk of marching on Wall Street. Such radical rhetoric, not to speak of actual violence, was hardly unusual in such confrontations then, a measure of how raw class relations were and how profoundly disturbed people had become by the haunting presence of mass unemployment.

Just as telling, the unemployed and those still at work but at loggerheads with their bosses frequently displayed their solidarity in public. During the "Great Insurrection" of 1877, when railroad strikers from coast to coast faced off against state militias, federal troops, and the private armies of the railroad barons, they were joined by regiments of the "reserve army." Often these were their neighbors and family members, but also strangers who, feeling an affinity for their beleaguered brethren, preferred setting fire to railroad engine houses over going to work in them as scabs. Amid the awful depression of the 1890s, a cigar maker caught the temper of the times simply: "I believe the working men themselves will have to take action. I believe those men that are employed will have look out for the unemployed that work at the same business they do."

Marching Armies (of the Unemployed)

Demonstrations of the unemployed resurfaced with each major economic downturn. In the depression winter of 1893–1894, for example, ragged "armies" of the desperate gathered in various parts of the country, forty of them in all. (Eighteen-year-old future novelist Jack London joined one in California.) The largest commandeered a train in an effort to get to Washington, D.C., and was chased for 300 miles across Montana by federal troops.

The most famous of them was led by Jacob Coxey, a self-made Ohio businessman. "Coxey's Army" (more formally known as "the Commonwealers" or the "Commonwealth of Christ Army") made it all the way to the capital, a "living petition" to Congress. It was led by his seventeen-year-old daughter as "the Goddess of Peace" riding a white horse.

In the nation's capital, the "Army" lodged its plea for relief, work, and an increase in the money supply. (Jacob's son was called "Legal Tender Cox.") President Grover Cleveland wasn't hearing any of it, having already made his views known in 1889 during his first term in office: "The lessons of paternalism ought to be unlearned and the better lesson taught that while the people should patriotically and cheerfully support their government, its functions do not include support of the people."

Christian charity was not Cleveland's long suit. Others of the faith, however, believers in the social gospel and Christian socialism especially, staged spectacular public dramas on behalf of the "shorn lambs of the unemployed"—even a mock "slave auction" in Boston in 1921 during a severe post–World War I slump, in which the jobless were offered to the highest bidders as evidence of what "wage slavery" really meant.

The Great Depression brought this protracted period of labor turmoil to a climax and to an end. In its early years, the ethos of "mutualism" and solidarity between the employed and unemployed was strengthened. In those years, railroads began to report startling jumps in the numbers of Americans engaged in "train hopping"—the rail equivalent of hitchhiking. On one line, the "hoppers" went from 14,000 in 1929 to 186,000 in 1931.

In 1930, when the unemployment rate was at about today's level, in cities across the country the first rallies of the unemployed began with demands for work and relief. Later, there were food riots and raids on delivery trucks and packinghouses, as well as the occupations of shuttered coal mines and bankrupt utility companies by the desperate who began to work them.

"Leagues" and "councils" of the unemployed, sometimes organized by the Communist Party, sometimes by the Socialist Party, and sometimes by a group run by radical pacifist A. J. Muste, marshaled their forces to stop home evictions, support strikes, and make far-reaching proposals for a permanent system of public works and unemployment insurance. Muste's groups, strong in the Midwest, set up bartering arrangements and labor exchanges among the jobless.

In support of striking workers, unemployed protestors shut down the Briggs plant in Highland Park, Michigan—it manufactured auto bodies for Ford—pledging that they would not scab on the striking workers. A march of former and current employees of the Ford facilities in Dearborn, Michigan, made the unusual demand that the company (not the government) provide work for the jobless. For their trouble, they were bloodied by Ford's hired thugs and five of them were killed.

President Herbert Hoover took similar action. In a move that shocked much of the nation, he ordered Army Chief of Staff General Douglas MacArthur to use troops to disperse the Bonus Expeditionary Army, World War I jobless veterans gathered in tents on Anacostia Flats in Washington asking for accelerated payments of their wartime pensions. They were routed at bayonet point and MacArthur's troops burned down their tent city.

How the New Deal Dealt

The Great Depression was, however, so profoundly unsettling that the unemployed finally became a political constituency of national proportions. The pressure on mainstream politicians to do something grew ever more intense. The Conference of Mayors that meets to this day was founded then to lobby Washington for federal relief for the jobless. Even segments of the business community had begun to complain about the "costs" of unemployment when it came to workplace efficiency.

Unemployment insurance, work relief, welfare, and public works—all of which had surfaced in public debate since the turn of the twentieth century—made up the basic package of responses offered by President Franklin Roosevelt's New Deal to the inherent insecurity of proletarian life. None were exactly expansive either in what they provided or in their execution, and yet all of them found themselves under chronic assault from birth (as they are today).

The most daring legislation under consideration, the Lundeen bill (authored by a Minnesota congressman), would have provided unemployment insurance equal to prevailing wages for anyone over eighteen working part or full time. Though it never became law, it was to be financed by a tax on incomes exceeding $5,000, and administered by elected worker representatives. It was not atypical in its most basic assumption which once would have been thought intolerable—that unemployment at significant levels would continue into the indefinite future.

Unemployment was now to be ameliorated, but also accepted. Harry Hopkins, who ran the New Deal's relief efforts, was typical in predicting that "a probable minimum of four to five million" Americans would remain out of work "even in future 'prosperity' periods." Consequently, the new relief reforms were to be considered defense mechanisms designed to recharge the batteries of a stalled economy and to minimize the political fallout from outsized joblessness. This menu of "solutions" has constituted the core of the labor and progressive movement's approach to unemployment ever since.

"The Natural Rate of Unemployment"

After World War II, unemployment became, for the most part, a numerical and policy issue rather than a social phenomenon. By the 1960s, what once struck most Americans as unnatural and ghastly had been fully transformed by economists and political elites into "the natural rate of unemployment"—a level of joblessness that should never be tampered with because it was futile to do so and to try would induce inflation.

More recently matters have turned truly perverse. Neoliberals, who during the Reagan era of the 1980s eclipsed Keynesians as the dominant thinkers when it came to economic policy, were worried that unemployment might not be high enough. It was increasingly feared that, if the ranks of the jobless were not large indeed, both labor costs and inflation would rise, threatening the future value of capital investments. The world, in other words, had turned upside down.

As official society adapted to the permanence of unemployment, the unemployed themselves subsided into political quiescence. There were exceptions, however.

Perhaps the most massive unemployment demonstration in the nation's history took place in 1963 when 100,000 Americans marched on Washington for "Jobs and Freedom." It is a telling commentary on the political sensibilities of the last half-century that the March on Washington, recalled mainly for Martin Luther King's famed "I Have a Dream" speech, is rarely if ever remembered as an outpouring of righteous anger about a system that consigned much of a whole race to the outcast status first experienced by the young women of New England textile mills in antebellum America.

Today, the question is: As the new unemployment "norm" rises, will the "99ers" remain just a number, or will anger and systemic dysfunction lead to the rebirth of movements of the unemployed, perhaps allied, as in the past, with others suffering from the economy's relentless downward arc? Keep in mind that the extent of organized protest by the unemployed in the past should not be exaggerated. Not even the Great Depression evoked their sustained mass mobilization. That's hardly surprising. By its nature, unemployment demoralizes and isolates people. It makes of them a transient and chronically fluctuating population with no readily discernable common enemy and no obvious place to coalesce.

Another question might be: In the coming years, might we see the return of a basic American horror at the phenomenon of joblessness? And might it drive Americans to begin to ask deeper questions about the system that lives and feeds on it?

After all, we now exist in an underdeveloping economy. What new jobs it is creating are poor paying, low skill, and often temporary, nor are there enough of them to significantly reduce the numbers of those out of work. The 99ers are stark evidence that we may be witnessing the birth of a new permanent class of the marginalized. (The percentage of the unemployed who have been out of work for more than six months has grown from 8.6 percent in 1979 to 19.6 percent today.) Moreover, our mode of "flexible capitalism" has made work itself increasingly transient and precarious.

Until now, ideologues of the new order have had remarkable success in dressing this up as a new form of freedom. But our ancestors, who experienced frequent and distressing interruptions in their work lives, who migrated thousands of miles to find jobs which they kept or lost at the whim of employers, and who, in solitary search for work, tramped the roads and hopped the freight cars, were not so delusional.

We have a choice: Americans can continue to accept large-scale unemployment as "natural" and permanent, even—a truly grotesque development—as a basic feature of a bipartisan road to "recovery" via austerity. Or we can follow the lead of the jobless young in the Arab Spring and of protestors beginning to demonstrate en masse in Europe. Even the newly minted proletarians of Ventura, California, sleeping in their cars, may decide that they have had enough of a political and economic order of things so bankrupt it can find no use for them at any price.

5. Making Disaster Pay: From the San Francisco Earthquake to Superstorm Sandy, How Capitalism Stacks the Deck on Disaster

In 2007, a financial firestorm ravaged Wall Street and the rest of the country. In 2012, Superstorm Sandy obliterated a substantial chunk of the Atlantic seaboard. We think of the first as a human-made calamity, the second as the malignant innocence of nature. But neither notion quite captures how the power of a few and the vulnerability of the many determine what goes on at ground level. Causes and consequences, who gets blamed and who leaves the scene permanently scarred, who goes down and who emerges better positioned than before: these are matters often predetermined by the structures of power and wealth, racial and ethnic hierarchies, and despised and favored forms of work, as well as the moral and social prejudices in place before disaster strikes.

An earlier version of this chapter first appeared in *TomDispatch* on April 4, 2013.

When it comes to our recent financial implosion, this is easy enough to see, although great efforts have been expended trying to deny the self-evident. "Human beings" did not bring the system to its knees; the country's dominant financial institutions and a complicit government did that. They've recovered; the rest of us haven't.

Sandy seems a more ambiguous case. On the one hand, it's obvious enough that an economy resting on fossil fuels played a catalytic role in intensifying the storm. Those corporate interests profiting from that form of energy production and doing all they can to defend it are certainly culpable—not the rest of humanity, which has no choice but to depend on the energy system we're given.

On the other hand, rich and poor, big businesses and neighborhood shops suffered; some, however, more than others. Among them were working-class communities; public-housing residents; outer-borough New York City homeowners; communities in Long Island, along the New Jersey shore, and inland; workers denied unemployment compensation; and the old, the sick, and the injured abandoned for days or weeks in dark and dangerous high-rises without medical help or access to fresh food or water. Help, when it came to these "disadvantaged" worlds, often arrived late, or last, or not at all.

Cleaning up and rebuilding New York City and other places hit by the storm will provide a further road map of who gets served and whose ox gets gored. It's ominous, if hardly shocking, that New York mayor Michael Bloomberg has already appointed Mark Ricks of Goldman Sachs to the business-dominated team planning the city's future. Where would this billionaire mayor turn other than to his fraternity brothers, especially in this era when, against all the odds, we still worship at the altar of the dealmakers, no matter their malfeasances and fatal ineptitudes?

Still, it is early days and the verdict is not in on the post-Sandy future. However, *Crisis Cities*, an incisive analysis by sociologists

Kevin Fox Gotham and Miriam Greenberg of what happened after the 9/11 attacks in New York and in New Orleans after Hurricane Katrina, offers some concrete forebodings. Everyone knows that, as soon as Katrina made landfall, the racial divisions of New Orleans determined which communities were drowned and which got help, who got arrested (and shot), and who left town forever. To be poor in New Orleans during and after Katrina was a curse. To be poor and black amounted to excommunication.

Gotham and Greenberg prove that, after 9/11 and after Katrina, reconstruction and rehabilitation were also skewed heavily in favor of the business community and the wealthy. In both cities, big business controlled the redevelopment process—where the money landed and where it didn't.

Tax breaks and private-sector subsidies became channels for federal aid. "Public benefit" standards, which once accompanied federal grants and tax exemptions to ensure that projects served some public purpose, especially to "benefit persons of low and moderate income," were eliminated, leaving poorer people out in the cold while exacerbating existing inequalities. Governments scurried around inventing ways to auction off reconstruction projects to private interests by issuing tax-exempt "private activity bonds." These were soon gloriously renamed "Liberty Bonds," though the unasked question was: Whose liberty?

The lion's share of grants and exemptions went, of course, to the biggest corporations. In New York, more than 40 percent of all bonds, or $2.4 billion, went to a single developer, Larry Silverstein. Second to Silverstein was Goldman Sachs. Yet these institutions and their inhabitants represented at best a mere 15 percent of those affected, most of them low-wage workers who, in some cases, ended up getting evicted from their homes thanks to those business-oriented tax breaks. Federal aid, hypothetically tied to building affordable housing and the creation of living-wage jobs, ended up as just that: hypothetical.

Naturally, these mechanisms proved lucrative. More than that, they are the means by which elites use disasters as opportunities to turn wrecked cities or regions into money-making centers and playlands for what in the nineteenth century was called the "uppertendom" and what we now call the "1 percent."

Indeed, the original "uppertendom" faced its own "natural" disasters during the Gilded Age. Then, too, such catastrophes exposed the class and racial anatomy of America to public view. Then, too, one person's disaster was another's main chance. Whether you focus on the cause of the calamity, the way people reacted to it, or the means and purposes that drove the reclamation afterward, disasters and capitalism metabolized together long before "disaster capitalism" became the *nom du jour*.

Fire

Mrs. O'Leary's infamously rambunctious cow did not kick a lantern into a batch of hay and start the Chicago fire of 1871. To this day, however, many probably still believe the story, even though the journalist who first reported it admitted a mere twenty years later that he'd made it up.

It was a story that stuck because it meshed with the ethnic and social fears and prejudices of bourgeois Chicago. Irish and German immigrants then filled up the congested warrens of that Midwestern center of industry and commerce. Their customs, religions, languages, political beliefs, and proletarian status were alien and alarming—especially because that was the year of the Paris Commune, when proletarians took over the French national capital for two months. It scared the daylights out of the "uppertendom," and broad stretches of the middle classes as well, in cities and towns throughout the United States.

Chicago's papers were full of stories about "petroleuses,"

"Amazon-like women" with "long flaming hair" coursing through the streets of Paris hurling the equivalent of Molotov cocktails at the French National Guard. Could it happen here? That was the question. Impoverished immigrant workers were already raising a ruckus in mines and on railroads. Perhaps as in France, so in Chicago, they would become conspirators and incendiaries. Perhaps the great fire that gutted the city was no accident. Even if it was, weren't there those prepared to make malevolent use of it?

Rumors of secret societies, revolutionary arsonists, and mass assaults on property circulated widely by word of mouth and through the Chicago media. So Mrs. O'Leary proved an especially apt scapegoat for the conflagration, fitting perfectly the temper of the time. She was, after all, "low-class" Irish at a moment when her immigrant countrymen were still despised as rustic potato-eaters, bestial and good for nothing but backbreaking labor. It was also known that they were all too Catholic, notoriously fond of alcohol, and quite capable of terrorizing British landlords back home.

Less talked about was the likelier cause of the fire: the unimaginably congested neighborhoods of the poor were made entirely out of wood—houses, signs, and sidewalks, too. These had for years been the sites of frequent fires (two a day in 1870). Such frail structures became kindling for the flames that would in 1871 end up leveling downtown banks, businesses, and the homes of the rich.

These fears leaped with the flames that were burning up the city, killing 3,000 and leaving 100,000 homeless, and in the days and weeks that followed they hardly subsided. Immigrant, poor, and proletarian, Chicago's working class was held in deep moral suspicion. Believing is often seeing, so when one upper-class eyewitness looked, here's what he saw: "Vice and crime had got the first scorching. The district where the fire got firm foothold was the Alsatia of Chicago. Fleeing before it was a crowd of blear-eyed, drunken and diseased wretches, male and female, half naked, ghastly with painted cheeks cursing, uttering ribald jests."

Relief agencies, mainly privately run, were charged with aiding only the "worthy," who were deemed "deserving" of help only after close inspection of their work habits, family arrangements, home economics, drinking customs, and so on. Civil War general Philip Sheridan established martial law and was quick to fire on suspected looters, while enforcing a curfew to keep the "twilight population" in check.

At the same time, Chicago's business elite, its civic leaders, and a remarkable roster of first-rate architects went about reshaping downtown Chicago into a modern hub of commerce and culture that they hoped would rival New York. Real-estate speculators made a fortune, although none were known to have been shot for looting. For some, in other words, the fire functioned as a fortuitous slum-clearance/urban-renewal program on speed.

Angry working people marched against new restrictions on cheaper building materials, seeing them as discriminatory against labor and immigrants and as attempts to force them out of their city. They paraded to the Common Council, where they threw bricks through the windows while the Council dutifully passed the ordinances. For their efforts, the protestors were denounced as the "scum of the community" and "mongrel firebugs" and likened to the Parisian communards, intent on establishing a "reign of terror."

The fire was out, but only for the time being. The fires of social insurrection were still smoldering and would flame up again and again in the streets of Chicago throughout the rest of the century.

Flood

An unnatural disaster! With a "roar like thunder," a wall of water sixty feet high from Lake Conemaugh, believed to be the largest artificial body of water in the world in 1889, came racing down a canyon near Johnstown, Pennsylvania, at forty miles an hour.

Everything in its path was swept away, starting with Woodvale, a company town run by the Cambria Iron Works. Johnstown itself was next as the tidal wave rushed on, relentlessly drowning and destroying bridges, oil tankers, and factories. It tossed locomotives, railroad cars, and even houses into the air. It ended the lives of more than 2,200 people. Seven hundred and seventy-seven were never identified and are buried in the "Plot of the Unknown." Johnstown has been memorialized ever since in song and story.

Was it fate, as well as an especially rainy spring, that did the trick in 1889? At the top of the canyon, members of the South Fork Fishing and Hunting Club, men like iron and steel magnates Andrew Carnegie, Henry Clay Frick, and Andrew Mellon, as well as the *crème de la crème* of Pittsburgh high society (the city was only sixty miles away), had long enjoyed the pleasures of that artificial lake. They had gone fishing, paddle boating, and sailing there for years. And for years, engineers had kept informing them that the earthen dam holding back its waters was defective. The spillway was too small and clogged with fencing materials, meant to keep the expensive sports fish stocked in the lake from escaping into a nearby river. Auxiliary discharge pipes had decayed and leaks had been routinely noticed at the base of the dam, even when the weather was especially dry.

The club's sportsmen did nothing. In fact, they ordered several feet shaved off the top of the dam to make way for a road so members could get to their "cottages" faster from the nearby railroad station. After the horror, there were lawsuits aplenty, but no one was ever held responsible for what quickly became a legendary tragedy. In 1989, the centennial of the disaster, an article in the *Journal of Civil Engineering* confirmed that the actions of the South Fork Club were the proximate cause of this "natural disaster."

All was not lost, however. Some years after Johnstown was rebuilt, Andrew Carnegie donated one of the libraries for which he would become so widely celebrated.

Earthquake

Bubonic plague ravaged San Francisco when the earthquake of 1906 sent hordes of rats racing through the rubble, chasing through the raw sewage spilling into the streets as the city's sewer pipes crumpled. Anyone was susceptible. In one way, the earthquake had been an equal-opportunity destroyer: Chinatown, with its masses of poor living in squalid wooden shacks, was razed to the ground by the quake and subsequent fire. Other working-class precincts were similarly leveled and burned. But so too was Nob Hill, where the city's gilded elite lived.

A mythic memory of communal suffering, self-sacrifice, and mutual aid emerged in the immediate aftermath of the San Francisco disaster, as it still does in the wake of many similar collective traumas. After 9/11, as after Superstorm Sandy, stories of how people from all walks of life banded together to help one another were commonplace. This was even true in Chicago after the fire, notwithstanding the white-hot hostilities between the classes and the masses. These are not fables but moving accounts drawn from real life. They offer a kind of hope in disaster and, consoling as they are meant to be, linger on, sometimes forever. Meanwhile, the disaster's darker doings are often interred and resting in peace.

Looking back on earthquake-ravaged San Francisco, a well-off refugee remembered that the calamity "did not discriminate between tavern and tabernacle, bank and brothel." Yet the wife of the president of Levi Strauss and Co. drove up to one of the relief centers in her limousine (in those early days, cars were still mainly luxury machines; she owned one of the handful of limos in the city). She was, of course, ushered right to the head of its endless line.

Even in these immediate post-quake reports, one can detect other motivations at work. So, for example, while San Francisco was ravaged, the death toll was calculated at only about 375 people. Given the savage firestorm coursing through the most densely packed of neighborhoods, that low figure surprised people and left some wondering. The answer turned out to be this: the city fathers were determined to cite a low number so as not to discourage San Francisco's rebuilding and the outside investments it would require. For many years, the figure was nonetheless accepted as accurate. Recently, however, through the diligent efforts of researchers, we know that the numbers of dead were probably ten times higher. News of the bubonic plague was suppressed for similar reasons.

Calculations of that kind informed many aspects of the tragedy. While sitting atop the San Andreas Fault is not ideal, should the underlying tectonic plates move a bit, not much was said about other contributory causes. Minor earthquakes had for decades been set off, at least in part, by the hydraulic mining that accompanied the California gold rush in its later years.

The operation to relieve the distress of hundreds of thousands of homeless people after the quake was tainted by class and ethnic biases not unlike those in Chicago. Relief camps segregated refugees by class as well as race and gender. Firefighters pooled water and equipment to save the homes of the wealthy first. In working-class districts, firefighting focused on commercial properties like a Folgers Coffee warehouse and freight sheds, not on saving homes. Seventeen hundred troops under General Frederick Funston guarded richer precincts because, as he explained, "San Francisco had its class of people no doubt who would take advantage of any opportunity to plunder the banks and rich jewelry and other stores of the city." Chinatown did not die an entirely natural death, either. It was dynamited to create firebreaks that would prevent the fires already raging there from spreading to tonier neighborhoods.

Two years after the event, poor people were still living in "relief cottages," tents, and other makeshift accommodations which, at rental rates of six dollars a month, many couldn't afford. To get relief required a letter from a clergyman testifying to one's moral worth. Working-class women took to the streets to protest.

Meanwhile, former residents of Nob Hill had moved into equally luxurious digs elsewhere in the city. However, they did have a problem in those early months: there was a crying lack of domestic help. As the *San Francisco Chronicle* reported, "Everyone had wondered where the cooks had gone. They had been lost since the fire." So working women, who were bending all their efforts to restoring their devastated families by making use of what relief was available, were chastised for not returning to the kitchens of the elect. One paper claimed that the women "were loafing ... when families needed help"; a Red Cross matron observed, "Women [domestics] prefer to live ... in relief camps."

Help was, however, on the way. Special rehabilitation funds were reserved for helping single women resume their lives of domestic service.

Being solicitous about the needs of the rich could reach heights of absurdity. It was recommended, for instance, that special philanthropic pawn shops be established for the upper classes, where "people who saved their jewels could be rehabilitated by having such a place to go where they would not have to pay too much interest."

If rehabilitation and recovery were on the civic mind, certain minds counted more than others. Everybody knew that the city's wood-frame buildings could not stand up to the pressures of another earthquake, which—they also knew—was a reasonable future possibility. So the city adopted new building codes calling for the use of reinforced concrete and steel in structures over six stories high. Those codes lasted a year. Pressure from the business community and builders caused the city to relax those rules, except in the new downtown, which was urgently readying itself for the Panama-Pacific International Exposition of 1915, where the city's boosters hoped to eradicate the last pungent odors of the calamity.

A $500 "bonus plan" to help rebuild homes favored the native-born and two-parent households. Housing rehabilitation began with the wealthy and worked its way very slowly to the poor. There were lots of jobs for "earthquake mechanics," but at wages that could never keep up with escalating rents driven by real-estate speculators.

Insurance companies had by then rewritten their homeowner policies to exempt earthquakes from coverage. Fire was covered, however, and it's clear that people deliberately set fire to their own homes, already ruined by the tremors, since without insurance money there was no way they could recover and rebuild. Not surprisingly, payoffs were highest for the wealthy. The insurance companies worked at delaying payments to the hardest hit, the poor. This fit with the mood of the moment—that those working-class shacks were "no loss to the city."

Neither was Chinatown. San Francisco's upper crust, as well as large portions of its white middle and working classes, had never been fond of the Chinese in their midst, even though they depended on their labor. The quake struck the city's burghers as an opportunity to funnel them out of the center of the city—the old Chinatown had largely been destroyed—to some enclave on its outskirts. (One resident remarked that "fire has reclaimed civilization and cleanliness from the Chinese ghetto.") Their plans were, however, successfully thwarted by the concerted resistance of the Chinese community.

Resistance notwithstanding, Chicago and San Francisco emerged from their trials by fire as bustling centers of capitalist enterprise. Disaster capitalism has a long history. One of the last remaining "relief cottages" built by Funston's army at the cost of one hundred dollars and rented for two dollars was sold in 2013 for $600,000.

Recently, when the Republican majority in Congress temporarily blocked funds for Sandy relief and rehabilitation efforts, it was a chilling reminder that no matter how universal a calamity is, the commonwealth regularly takes a backseat to wealth. Appeals to fellowship, to mutual assistance and shared sacrifice, seem to give way with scandalous speed to the commanding imperatives of a warped economy and political plutocracy.

More Sandys are surely headed our way, more climate-driven disasters of all sorts than we can now fully imagine. Rest assured, they will be no more "natural" than the Chicago fire, the Johnstown flood, or the San Francisco earthquake. More than fire itself, what we need to deal with now is the power of the finance, insurance, and real estate—or FIRE—sector, whose leading corporations now effectively run our economy. Without doing that, the "nature" these interests have helped create will punish us all while providing a ghoulish boondoggle for a few.

Part 2

The Ages of Capitalism

6. Two Gilded Ages

Red-baiting has once again become a weapon of choice on the American political battlefield. John McCain called Barack Obama a socialist, when after all the new president is really a liberal, and more a neoliberal than a New Deal one at that. Not so long ago it would have been enough to declare him anathema on those grounds alone. McCain's resort to the "s-word" signals that, thanks to the recent collapse of our "second Gilded Age," matters of economic justice, inequality, class conflict, the relationship between democracy and concentrated wealth, and the efficacy and credibility of the free-enterprise system are rising to the surface of public life after a long submergence. Even that system's patron saint, former Federal Reserve chair Alan Greenspan, has abandoned the faith. Hallelujah!

Omens appeared before the crash of 2008, even before the first intimations of the subprime mortgage meltdown nearly two years before. References to our "second Gilded Age" were already in the air well before the turn of the new century and became commonplace

An earlier version of this chapter appeared in *Raritan*, vol. 29, no. 1, Summer 2009.

thereafter. At first they carried with them a certain Marie Antoinette–like playful insouciance about the exhibitionism of the superrich. After the dot-com bust of 2000–2001 and the avalanche of Wall Street and corporate scandals that followed, the mood grew more somber. If talk about our second Gilded Age at first evoked comparisons to the masked balls of the "gay nineties," in time the emphasis shifted to recovered memories of stark inequality, to Jacob Riis's late nineteenth-century world, inhabited by have-nots as well as haves.

One small but telling sign that the zeitgeist is changing is the reissuing of *The Politicos* by Matthew Josephson.[1] Written in the 1930s and once considered a classic history of the political economy of the first Gilded Age (at the time, many thought it a more important book than *The Robber Barons*, which made Josephson famous), it has been out of print and out of mind for decades. Moreover, its class-inflected analysis of that period was revisited quite recently by Jack Beatty in *Age of Betrayal*.[2] As the inverse of McCain's red-baiting of Obama, these publications are welcome signs that the intellectual universe is opening up. Beatty's book in particular is an explicitly present-minded history that finds striking likenesses between what his subtitle calls "The Triumph of Money in America, 1865–1900" and the last quarter-century of American public and private life. Just how much these two Gilded Ages resemble each other is a pregnant question, and the works by Josephson and Beatty, among others, illuminate three dimensions of this conundrum: the role of primitive accumulation; the transformation and decline of the "labor question"; and the interplay of wealth, democracy, and the politics of consent.

No country in history industrialized itself as rapidly as the United

---

1   *The Politicos, 1865–1896*, Matthew Josephson (New York: Commons, 2007 [1938]).

2   *Age of Betrayal: The Triumph of Money in America, 1865–1900*, Jack Beatty (New York: Knopf, 2007).

States (with the possible exception of China). It qualifies as a "miracle" and has been treated that way for a long time by historians, economists, and social commentators. Over the course of a single generation, during the last third of the nineteenth century, the face of the country changed utterly. The elements of the story are familiar: giant industries; a historic shift to fossil-fuel-based energy; stunning new means of transportation and communication (the railroad above all); revolutionary scientific and technological wonders like the telegraph, telephone, electric light, elevator, and phonograph; the settlement and cultivation of a vast, largely unexplored hinterland; the systematic discovery, conversion, and exploitation of naturally occurring "raw materials"; the rise of the city as the dominant mode of human habitation, social mixing, and commercial invention. At the same time, numerous innovative corporate and bureaucratic organizations emerged to manage it all, organizations that dwarfed, in their reach and complexity, the puny undertakings of the government or its army. By the end of the nineteenth century, this extraordinary leap into the future left the United States in possession of an industrial machine grander in size and scope than the combined powers of the most developed countries of Western Europe.

A drama of epic proportions, this tale has been told and retold for generations, but not always in the same way. Once upon a time and again lately, it's been recounted as essentially a story of Progress, in the Whiggish sense. Walter Rostow's *Stages of Economic Growth*, and especially its emphasis on the "takeoff" stage of industrial modernization, was a famous and influential popularization of this view back in the 1950s, part of a Cold War intellectual celebration of the West and the American way. Maury Klein's *The Genesis of Industrial America, 1870–1920,* is emblematic of that viewpoint today.[3] This well-crafted book conveys a nuts-and-bolts depiction

---

3 *The Genesis of Industrial America, 1870–1920*, Maury Klein (New York: Cambridge University Press, 2007).

of all the particular miracles of production, transportation, communication, invention, and distribution that together made up the big miracle. It is an Olympian and naturalized view of the whole process. Klein emphasizes technology, science, and the country's natural resource endowment. A perfect combination of the factors of production—land, labor, and capital—together gave us the skeletal structure of the modern world. A sense of the inexorable pervades the text—but with one crucial exception.

Above all, what Klein considers the ghost in the machine, the spirit that gave life to all its inanimate components, was the unique entrepreneurial genius of the American businessman. Alexis de Tocqueville had discovered this quality in antebellum America (as would Calvin Coolidge in his America a century later), and Klein never tires of quoting the French aristocrat-*cum*-savant. Klein himself puts it bluntly: "Since the founding of the Republic in 1789 the business of Americans has always been business." As a historian he has made it his own business to capture that special talent in biographical portraits of men once thought of as robber barons, in particular the railroad empire builder Edward Harriman as well as Jay Gould, known far and wide by his contemporaries and for generations afterward as "the Mephistopheles of Wall Street." Klein's purpose has been to rescue these men from what he considers history's unfair verdict, which Klein argues singled out their moral transgressions but turned a blind eye to their inventive organizational and financial genius and their appetite for risk, which transformed the country's blessed endowment of natural resources into undreamed-of progress. This kind of triumphalist retelling of American business and economic history during the first Gilded Age marked the late 1980s and 1990s especially. It is reasonable to detect here an echo of the Reagan-era zeitgeist. Klein's book generalizes that view.

Klein (and others who take this approach) would acknowledge that progress was not cost-free. Abuses occurred. The endowment was drawn down without regard to the future, and the natural environment bore the scars. Farmers lost their homesteads. Handicraft workers lost their trades. Industrial workers lost some of their humanity. Cities developed slums and sweatshops staffed by children. Businesses went belly-up in the competitive maelstrom. Social unrest boiled over now and then. All of this is lamentable in the same way that our political overlords today wring their hands over the collateral damage that sometimes accompanies the crusade for democracy. But acknowledging the dark side of progress does not change the underlying assumption: Gilded Age industrialism was the irresistible and empyrean story of the forces of production in the hands of great men. Joseph Schumpeter would later call the period one of "creative destruction."

Dispossession, however, need not be treated as an ancillary story, a kind of subplot to the principal drama. Instead, the whole industrializing enterprise may be seen to rest on the systematic cannibalizing of various forms of precapitalist social economies. To one degree or another, this is the approach taken by Josephson, Beatty, and Rebecca Edwards in her recent treatment of the Gilded Age, *New Spirits*. Although Edwards's book lacks an overarching narrative and structural logic, it is full of brilliantly rendered depictions of this process of capital accumulation at the expense of the "other." For example, her treatment of what happened to undermine the capacity of Native American societies to reproduce themselves is superb. Even the Dawes Act of 1887, Edwards notes, ostensibly designed to convert Native American communalists into private family farmers, ended up finishing the bloodier process of mass Indian removal. Under the act's allotment system, most tribes suffered catastrophic losses of land and resources that reduced their members to a state of woeful dependency.

Slaves, artisans, homesteaders, European peasants, small-town storekeepers, Southern hillbillies, and prairie sodbusters weren't consigned to reservations. But they were the raw material, as were Native American buffalo hunters and subsistence agrarians, of a process of primitive accumulation which drove them to extinction and without which Klein's miracle is inconceivable. If Native Americans ended up on reservations, all these other refugees from preindustrial ways of life and of making a living ended up as the proletarians of factory and field or as their near relations, toiling away as convict laborers, indebted tenants and sharecroppers, and contract laborers, comprising a whole menagerie of semifree peonage. The miracle of capital accumulation in the Gilded Age depended on a second miracle of disaccumulation happening outside the boundaries of capitalism proper. It proceeded relentlessly, appropriating land and resources both human and natural that had once been off limits because they were enmeshed in alternative forms of slave, petty, and subsistence economies: plantation monocultures, smallholder agriculture both in America and across southeastern and central Europe, handicraft production on both sides of the Atlantic, mercantile activities serving local markets, and an enormous variety of family businesses filling up the arteries of production and distribution. Liberated from these premodern systems of social reproduction, some of their denizens were free (or, rather, were compelled) to take on their fateful role as wage labor or its close facsimile; that is, they became the bone and sinew of the industrial capital accumulation celebrated by Rostow, Klein, and others.

How that liberation or dispossession took place is one way of telling the story of the first Gilded Age that sheds light on our own second Gilded Age. Josephson and Beatty are both sensitive to the fundamental rupture with the past as the first Gilded Age got under way. They grapple with the political mechanisms and social consequences of what Josephson calls a counterrevolution and Beatty indicts as a betrayal. *The Politicos* describes the intricate machinations that transformed a Republican Party of economic emancipation and democracy into the creature of a new corporate plutocracy. *Age of Betrayal* decries the forsaking of Lincoln's vision of a nation of roughly equal, independent smallholders in town and country, and with it the foundations of the republic. Both books pay special attention to the politics of capital accumulation in a way that Klein's does not.

War, the ultimate pursuit of politics by other means, ended the slave system. In the course of a single generation, ex-slaves were reduced to various forms of agricultural peonage thanks to the failure of the Republican Party to provide them the landed where-withal to become freeholders. If slaves were abandoned, so too were those millions who took Horace Greeley seriously and thought they'd reinvent themselves out West. The Homestead Act, passed during the Civil War, was supposed to make a reality out of Lincoln's version of the free-labor and free-soil dream. It ended up a cruel hoax. Less than a half-million people actually set up viable farms. Most public land was overtaken by the railroads thanks to the government's beneficent land-grant policy (another form of primitive accumulation), or by land speculators backed by Eastern bankers (who sometimes hired pretend "homesteaders" in acts of outright fraud), or by giant cattle ranches and timber companies and the like, who worked hand in glove with government land agents. Beatty observes that as early as 1862, two-thirds of Iowa (or 10 million acres) was owned by speculators. Railroads closed off one-third of Kansas to homesteading, and that was the best land available. Mushrooming cities back east became, in a kind of historical inversion, the safety valve for overpopulated rural areas to the west. Beatty has some rich material on this. He quotes Henry Demarest Lloyd's remark that by the mid-1880s "our young men can no longer go West; they must go up or down." And, as Beatty points out, few city workers had the capital to migrate west anyway; when one Pennsylvania state legislator suggested that the state subsidize such moves, he was denounced as "the Pennsylvania Communist" for his trouble.

Moreover, the South in particular became a colonial dependency of the industrializing North, partly a function of its defeat and political subordination. The tariff on imported goods, which moved irresistibly upward all through the era, protected industry while worsening the terms of trade for rural America in the South and West. Those regions were compelled to absorb the high-priced output of America's "infant industries," relegating the South especially to a condition of permanent underdevelopment. Not only former slaves but much of the white yeomanry of the South and homesteaders on the Great Plains fell into penury. They were whipsawed by the crushing competition generated by the vastly expanded world market in agricultural goods (including Russian wheat, Argentine meat, and staples from Canada and Australia) and by railroad, grain-elevator, and agricultural-machinery monopolies whose rates and prices made staying alive as an independent farmer yeoman labor indeed. You could do it only by leveraging everything in sight. The crop-lien system in the South and the mortgaging of the Western prairies to Eastern bankers made smallholders into captives of finance capitalism, one drought or flood or blizzard or locust invasion away from the auction block. In the South especially, impoverished sharecroppers and tenants had to borrow money to pay for essential supplies. They turned to large planters or local "furnishing" merchants and pledged a portion of their next year's crop as collateral. They paid such usurious interest rates that, often enough, their debts exceeded the value of the crops just harvested; an endless recycling of debt dependency was the result.

Debt-based capital formation, which may or may not be reinvested in industry, has been a classic mode of primitive accumulation around the world. Here in the United States, it was enforced by bipartisan adherence to the gold standard, which offered debtors no relief, safeguarded creditors, and kept foreign investment capital, particularly British funds, flowing into what was, after all, still a developing country and a risky one.[1]

Globalized capitalist agriculture also wiped out or imperiled peasant proprietors and other small producers in Sicily and southern Italy and all across the Balkans, Austro-Hungary, Poland, and Scandinavia. As miraculous as the rapidity and scope of American industrialization (and as enmeshed in its triumph) was the overnight uprooting of millions of people from their ancestral villages and from traditional ways of life that could no longer be sustained. If local populations managed to hang on, they could do so only by a process of social amputation, sending off their young and not-so-young men and eventually whole kin networks to work in the New World, there to remit back what they could to those left behind. Once in the United States, they joined their efforts with homegrown superannuated farmers and handicrafters displaced by the machine and the factory's finely reticulated division of labor to mine the coal, lay the tracks, and staff the megaworkshops of the New World's Industrial Revolution. These legions of the displaced became charter members of an American proletariat. Their new existence was both a promise and a reproach.

Little wonder that this wrenching upheaval in the lives and identities of so many incited extraordinary conflict, great fears, and great expectations. This is the age of the Haymarket bombing, an explosion that killed seven Chicago police and led to the judicial murder of four anarchist suspects. This is the age of protracted strikes at the Carnegie Steel Works in Homestead, Pennsylvania, and the Pullman Palace Car Company in Pullman, Illinois, strikes that exposed the paternalist pretensions of Andrew Carnegie and George Pullman as little more than shams. This is the age of violent confrontations pitting private corporate armies and state and

---

1 Richard Bensel provides an intricate and probing analysis of this whole dynamic in *The Political Economy of American Industrialization, 1877–1900* (Cambridge: Cambridge University Press, 2000).

federal militias against striking workers and their families, friends, and neighbors. This is the age of the mass strike and the general strike, events that escaped the confines of any particular employer-employee relationship and became instead the *cri de coeur* of a whole new world, as for example in the national crusade for the eight-hour day. Armed worker militias, dressed up in their own homespun regalia, paraded in the streets of America's major cities, making bluntly clear that if shot at, they would shoot back. During the 1880s especially, the Knights of Labor, for a brief and electrifying moment, leapt the forbidden barriers of ethnicity, race, gender, and skill to embrace all those engaged in productive labor. Farmer alliances in the South and West took on the railroads and bankers and their political enablers in both parties, created the People's (or Populist) Party, and even threatened to breach the racial divide that ensured the South's colonial subservience.

Literature, high and low, filled up with utopian longings and dystopian premonitions. People were infatuated with didactic novels like *Looking Backward* and *A Traveler from Altruria*, which imagined a future cooperative commonwealth infused by Christian good fellowship. *Caesar's Column*, by Populist tribune Ignatius Donnelly, and, from the other side, *The Bread Winners*, by Republican Party sachem John Hay, prophesied the bloody end of civilization in a conspiratorial mayhem. These books too were devoured by thousands. A politics of fear and of apocalyptic promise was born out of the experience of dispossession. Rebecca Edwards echoes the views of many at the time that the country was descending into a "second Civil War," scarcely more than a decade after the first one ended.

How to interpret this rising of the dispossessed? And why did it fail? The two questions are linked. As Richard Bensel notes, perhaps the greatest miracle of all is that the country underwent a brutal and often tyrannical process of industrialization while preserving the protocols of political democracy, however warped and decayed. The latter registered and ensured a real measure of consent to a wrenching experience that might otherwise have fomented open and protracted rebellion.

One can exaggerate this degree of consent, however. Voter fraud and disenfranchisement occurred not only in the South but everywhere, and Beatty documents it meticulously. Terror—including vigilante justice, lynchings, village massacres, and racial cleansings, along with more pedestrian forms of intimidation—was the order of the day in the South, leaving the Republican Party a cadaver and preserving the power of the white Democrats' oligarchy. Nor was terror confined to the old Confederacy. In the aftermath of Haymarket, state and local officials, as well as civic-minded business in cities around the country, rounded up anarchists and labor radicals of all stripes, built massive urban fortresses equipped with Gatling guns, and made known their readiness to use them. The Knights of Labor never recovered from this reign of terror.

So too the power of the judiciary was deployed over and over again to enjoin strikes, most notoriously to crush the Pullman strike at the point of a federal bayonet in 1894. The Supreme Court nullified the efforts, victorious in state legislatures, of farmer and antimonopoly activists to regulate railroads and other giant businesses. Beatty provides an exhaustive (and exhausting) analysis of the role of the Court, in particular its use of the Fourteenth Amendment, originally designed to safeguard the civil rights of the freedmen, to immunize corporations against democratic interference. For Josephson, writing in the 1930s, and Beatty, writing in the early 2000s, all of this contributes to a prima facie case that the Gilded Age's new business elite betrayed the country's democratic birthright.

Still, the two parties functioned and competed. Millions voted for one or the other of them instead of third parties, of which there were many, beginning with the Greenback-Labor party of the 1870s and culminating with the Populists. One must reckon with an element of consent—not enthusiastic consent, perhaps, but consent nonetheless.

Fissures separated might-have-been allies, undermining the prospects of the resistance. This was self-evident in the South, where the racial divide, breached here and there, could never be overcome. These animosities were deliberately provoked and aggravated by the region's master class of planters and merchants to undermine every act of incipient solidarity between black and white tenants and sharecroppers. Their sense of mutual dispossession was suffocated by shrill cries for regional and racial loyalty, preventing the emergence of a durable political alternative—either Republican or Populist—to the apartheid rule of the white *Herrenvolk* democracy. Beatty recounts harrowing instances of this plotting. He notes a record number of lynchings in 1892 and 1893 as Populist fervor heated up the Southland, many of them what Beatty calls sadistic "spectacle" lynchings, deliberately designed to send a political message.

Outside the South, the experience of primitive accumulation and dispossession led its victims to remedies that had little or no appeal to people—industrial workers particularly—whose lives were increasingly defined not by their exclusion from but by their assimilation into the mechanisms of modern capital accumulation. On the one hand, the Knights of Labor, the Populists, and the profusion of antimonopoly movements in cities and states together anticipated, in their programmatic thinking, many of the essential economic reforms or attempted reforms of the next century: the graduated income tax, public ownership of public utilities, government-subsidized agriculture, trust-busting, public works, and rigorous regulation of the railroads. Yet even as they pursued these objectives, they did so in order to hold on to ways of life and of making a living that could, under the right set of altered conditions, preserve their self-respect, propertied independence, and cherished identities. The historic pathos of these efforts is undeniable. But they hardly spoke to the multitudes for whom wage labor had become a permanent fate.

Thus, the cooperative commonwealth was to be a prophylactic against proletarian dependency, an alternative to the degradation of wage slavery. Cooperative ventures sponsored by farm organizations (jointly owned marketing, distribution, purchasing, and other enterprises) and cooperative industrial undertakings set up by the Knights of Labor in towns and cities all over the country were practical expressions of that more profound desire. But they succumbed to the merciless pressures of the marketplace.

Intervention in the political arena seemed a more promising alternative, itself a symptom of how relatively open to popular influence the electoral system still was in late nineteenth-century America. Inflating the currency—whether through issuing greenbacks, monetizing silver, or both—became the general panacea for a vast class of debtors trying desperately to stay afloat as independent proprietors. All this political resistance and visionary longing came to a head in the election of 1896 and received its most eloquent articulation in William Jennings Bryan's unforgettable "cross of gold" speech. Attacking the gold standard for tightening bankers' grip on debtors, Bryan warned the plutocracy: "You shall not crucify mankind upon this cross of gold." His Christian idiom captured the conflation of moral and economic belief that had inspired generations.

Bryan's speech is also noteworthy because, in it, the "Great Commoner" jettisoned almost the entire Populist program—public ownership of railroads and utilities, government price supports for farmers, a graduated income tax, the eight-hour day, and so on—focusing instead on the call for coining silver. That's why the anti-monopolist Henry Demarest Lloyd called the silver issue the "cowbird of the Populist Party." Josephson uses his scalpel of class analysis to observe that the Nebraskan's electrifying remarks echoed a version of the "labor question" as it was once understood by Lincoln and later by the Knights of Labor and others. Bryan struggled mightily to include the new world of proletarian dependency within the capacious universe of autonomous productive labor:

> We say to you that you have made the definition of a business man too limited ... The man who is employed for wages is as much a business man as his employer ... the miners who go down a thousand feet into the earth or climb two thousand feet upon the cliffs, and bring forth from hiding places the precious metals to be poured into channels of trade are as much business men as the few financial magnates who, in a backroom, corner the money of the world. We come to speak for the broader class of businessmen.

Somehow, by opening up the sluice gates of commercial credit, by curbing the appetite of a voracious class of moneyed overlords, by restoring popular rule to the temples of civilization, the country might yet escape a proletarian future, or so he hoped.

But the cry for free silver, for inflating the currency, struck a discordant note among millions of urban industrial workers who dreamed less of setting themselves up as petty entrepreneurs than of keeping the cost of living as low as possible. If the gold standard helped them do that, if the tariff kept American industry humming and safe from foreign competition, if restricting immigration could buoy up wages, the wisdom of making common cause with indebted agrarians was not self-evident. Moreover, thanks to the steady price deflation characteristic of the period, and notwithstanding the most brutal and exhausting varieties of exploitation, the economy's extraordinary growth generated a slow but perceptible rise in the material standard of living for many industrial workers, particularly those uprooted from abroad. Werner Sombart's famous remark about socialist hopes in America running aground on "shoals of roast beef and apple pie" carries a blunt truth, one Rebecca Edwards emphasizes by describing the formidable growth of mass consumption and consumer culture. Private debt, for example, was roughly estimated at $11 trillion in 1890, 300 times what even the boldest guesses had previously predicted.

Voting Republican under this set of circumstances, even if the party was run by big businessmen and their lawyers, as everyone acknowledged, was not as outlandish an idea as it might seem. Workers all across the country's industrial midsection did so in considerable numbers, and only in part because they were scared into it by Republican Party propagandists and by their own employers, who threatened to close up shop should Bryan win.

For a long generation, then, the national political arena was dominated by the experience of dispossession and primitive accumulation. All fundamental issues, including gold and silver, the tariff, antitrust, Reconstruction and redemption, and eventually immigration, were in one way or another tethered to that tragic historic transformation. Meanwhile, as Richard Bensel has argued, the modern labor question, the one about the industrial class struggle and its denouement, remained confined to the shop floor and the hurly-burly of the streets. There it was contested with extreme violence. Indubitably its energies added to the social incandescence of the era. Its distinctive perspective about exploitation and the darker logic of Progress flowed into and overlapped with those shut out of capitalism's mainstream and headed for extinction. That is why it was possible for all to agree that the "labor question" was preeminent without agreeing on precisely what question was being asked. But the proletarian purgatories of Homestead and Pullman, of Coeur d'Alene and Haymarket, never managed to define the contours of national political debate during the first Gilded Age.

Two labor questions existed side by side: one concerned itself with the vanishing of the independent producer of town and country, the other with the fate of the newly born propertyless wage slave. Some dreamed of a grand coalition that would unite the ranks of both imperiled worlds, a movement restorationist and revolutionary all at the same time. Perhaps that coming together was fated not to be, or inherently impossible given their divergent outlooks and objectives; Josephson would take that view. But just to make sure, American politicians worked away at the tactics of political distraction and stagecraft long before Karl Rove perfected the art. Serious attempts to join forces among blacks and whites, between farmers and workers, caused anxiety at the upper reaches of the two national parties and among the business elite. Echoes of the new labor question could be heard in mainstream party planks censuring the convict and contract labor systems. The Populists included a demand for the eight-hour day and inveighed against the courts' use of injunctions to outlaw strikes. The craving for some form of regulatory legislation led to the passage of the Interstate Commerce Act and the Sherman Antitrust Act. Both laws turned out to be toothless—and that was not by accident.

Ex-president Rutherford B. Hayes confided to his diary in 1886, "This is a government of the people, by the people, and for the people no longer. It is a government by the corporations, of the corporations, and for the corporations." But neither Hayes nor anyone else belonging to the country's emergent political business class was about to confess this in public. Rather, the corporate elite and the political machines increasingly subject to its will deliberately diverted public attention away from this brute reality and onto matters more likely to divide and distract their gathering enemies. Josephson and Beatty both dwell on this effort. The Republicans tirelessly "waved the bloody shirt" to keep wartime sectional and racial enmities aflame. Pamphlets and political broadsides filled the air with talk of "rum, Romanism, and rebellion" to incite ethnic and religious passions dividing Protestants from Catholics, wets from dries. When the deadly depression of the 1890s took hold, President Grover Cleveland whipped up jingoist emotions over a trivial Venezuelan boundary dispute with the British.

A certain degree of cynical manipulation was at work. Nelson Aldrich, senator from Rhode Island and (more important) John D. Rockefeller's factotum in that body, called the Interstate Commerce Act, passed in 1887, "a delusion and a sham ... An empty menace to the great, made to answer the clamor of the ignorant and unreasoning." Onetime corporate lawyer and President Cleveland's attorney general, Richard Olney, concurred. The Interstate Commerce Commission, he noted,

> satisfies the popular clamor for a government supervision of railroads, at the same time that the supervision is almost entirely nominal ... It thus becomes a sort of barrier between the railroad companies and the people and a sort of protection against hasty and crude legislation hostile to railroad interests.

Following the bloody debacle at Homestead, which helped reelect the Democrat Cleveland in 1892, Andrew Carnegie, a nominal Republican, confided his true feelings about the outcome to Henry Clay Frick: "Cleveland! Landslide! Well, we have nothing to fear and perhaps it is best. People will now think the Protected Manufacturers are attended to and quit agitating. Cleveland is a pretty good fellow. Off for Venice tomorrow." As Henry Adams noted, "The amazing thing is that no one talks about real interests. By common consent they agree to let these alone. We are afraid to discuss them." After all, as William McKinley, campaigning in 1896 from his front porch in Ohio, explained, "In America we spurn all class distinctions. We are all equal citizens and equal in privilege and opportunity."

In our own time, that refrain still reverberates. Indeed, for the past quarter-century, it might be taken as an understatement. Our political vocabulary has been wiped clean of all references to the class struggle, except insofar as they may be used to stigmatize any such allusions as heinously alien to the American way. On the one hand, the age of Reagan was marked by inequalities in income and wealth that exceeded those of the first Gilded Age. Crony capitalism and subordination of the state to private interests have been at least as naked and, if anything, more systematically organized than what was decried as the "Great Barbecue" of post–Civil War politics. The piggish display of wealth characteristic of the "gay nineties" has nothing on the hedge-fund hog heaven of our own day. Yet if America during the first Gilded Age might be thought of as society living on the edge, its ruling class and ruling beliefs subject to chronic resistance and Jehovian denunciation, the country passed through its second Gilded Age in a state of acquiescent torpor. The more things stay the same, the more they change.

Even as the curtain descends on the second Gilded Age, even as we enter a new era that seems bound to open up political possibilities not dreamed of for a long generation, the mystery remains: How is it that such similar moments in the national saga could elicit such starkly different reactions? Solving this mystery may even have some bearing on what lies ahead. Two books that examine, in turn, the underlying economic transformations and the politics of consent that defined the second Gilded Age illuminate this subject.

Bad Money, by Kevin Phillips, takes up the subject of the financialization of the US economy during what he calls the "age of Reagan" (the period from 1980 to the collapse of Lehman Brothers and the rest of the American and global financial system in the fall of 2008).[1] Phillips and others have been sounding alarm bells about this development for well over a decade. Financialization, or what he sometimes aptly characterizes as financial mercantilism, is one way of describing a reordering of our economic life that is, in certain essential ways, the opposite of what happened during the first Gilded Age.

Industrial capital accumulation at home has been supplanted by

---

1 *Bad Money: Reckless Finance, Failed Politics, and the Global Crisis of American Capitalism*, Kevin Phillips (New York: Viking, 2008).

disaccumulation. Primitive accumulation at the expense of noncapitalist economies has been replaced by the autocannibalism of domestic industry by the financial sector. Upward mobility and a general, if slow, rise in the standard of living has been overtaken by stagnation and regression, by a general lowering of the social wage. Primitive accumulation has shifted from the American heartland to the global South and has become the engine house of prosperity for the postindustrial world.

Bad money is bad, in Phillips's view, because it derives from the hollowing out of the real productive capacity of the country. He notes that the FIRE sector represents roughly 20 percent of the economy while manufacturing's share has declined precipitously from about a third to 12 percent. Investment in research and development and in new plant and equipment petered out in the 1980s, even sinking below the miserly levels of the previous desultory decade. Once the world's greatest exporter of manufactured goods, now its chief importer; once the world's creditor, now its leading debtor nation; the US economy today is the mirror image of what it once was.

Moreover, financialization and deindustrialization are not parallel developments but organically connected ones. While the process was already under way in the 1970s, it took off, so to speak, with the merger-and-acquisition, junk-bond, leveraged-buyout mania of the 1980s. It was then that the systematic stripping of the assets of American industry made billionaires overnight out of financial speculators like Michael Milken, Carl Icahn, Ivan Boesky, and a host of others. Once undertaken, this industrial triage never stopped and was abetted by the massive outsourcing and offshoring of industrial production to the global South.

As the primary mode of capital accumulation in the financial sector, autocannibalism inflicted a second fatal wound. Deindustriali-zation and the shriveling up of the labor movement that followed inevitably in its wake actually depressed the general material and cultural standard of living of ordinary working people. The gears of Progress, that demiurge of the first Gilded Age, were set in reverse. The public investment in the infrastructure that makes life in a complex industrial society possible dwindled, even as bridges and tunnels and dams and roads and railroads and public utilities rotted away in plain sight. Poverty levels rose. Wage levels fell or stood still. The "family wage" once supplied by one wage-earner now required two. Smokestack jobs, along with their security and menu of benefits, were eviscerated and replaced by contingent, part-time, low-wage employment in the retail and service sectors. Surgical strikes directed against the armature of public programs designed to soften the free fall of the free market (education, welfare, and urban rehabilitation, among others) further undermined the social wage. Autocannibalism was the dark secret of second-Gilded-Age prosperity.

None of this happened naturally, or by some inexorable logic of technological progress, or by accident. If deindustrialization alone wasn't enough to defang the labor movement, Reagan's firing of striking air traffic controllers in 1981 announced open season on unions everywhere. Soon enough, the National Labor Relations Board, originally conceived as a mechanism of industrial democracy, was converted—by presidential appointments, deliberate understaffing, relaxed enforcement, and judicial ingenuity—into a tool of industrial autocracy. Moreover, from the moment Reagan took office, part of the strategic purpose behind the widely acknowledged silliness of supply-side economics was to starve social services of tax revenues. The insatiable appetite of the military-industrial sector, which every second Gilded Age regime was always ready to feed, provided an evergreen excuse for putting human welfare on short rations. Indeed, the continuing investment in Eisenhower's military-industrial complex was itself a major form of economic parasitism, concealing its wasting disaccumulation under a mountain of high-tech munitions.

Electoral contests notwithstanding, rule by the blunt instrument typified the first Gilded Age. In our time, the state has been no less aggressive—indeed, arguably even more so—but not in the same way. The striking decline in political violence (at home, that is) as compared to those days testifies to this fact. It is true, of course, that the counterrevolution against the New Deal order did much to undermine the social provisions and regulatory apparatus that defined the mid-twentieth-century American administrative welfare state. Certainly, the financial quagmire of high-risk, arcane, parasitic debt that has sucked the life out of the real economy might never have existed without the deregulatory mania of the last decade and more. In spirit if not in concrete policy, this hands-off attitude mimics the first Gilded Age.

What is distinctly new, however, is the opposite: the proactive intervention of the state on behalf of our new finance-driven, highly leveraged economic order whenever that order is under serious duress. This is the bailout state, what Phillips characterizes as financial mercantilism. And it wasn't born on Saint Patrick's Day 2008, when Bear Stearns nearly went under. It goes back, as Phillips notes, at least to the rescue of Chrysler in the late 1970s, and more pointedly to the savings-and-loan debacle and government bailout engineered by the Resolution Trust Corporation in the early 1990s. It has continued ever since.

However many favors to the business community wended their way down the chain of command from Josephson's spoilsmen and two-party hierarchs of the first Gilded Age, they never dreamed of this kind of spectacular offloading of the risks of industrial and financial accumulation onto the backs of ordinary taxpayers. Instead, the whole system was allowed to collapse periodically into panic and depression. Such a turn of events is no longer considered economically, politically, or socially tolerable. A counterrevolution headed back to the future could not escape history entirely. The Great Crash, the Great Depression, and the Great Upheaval of the

New Deal happened and they were not to be allowed to happen again. (The train may have already left the station, however, and it is doubtful that even heroic acts of salvationist finance can alter the course of events.)

Financial mercantilism and autocannibalism have, until now, elicited little political opposition, a silence strikingly at odds with the big noise of a century ago. One reason may be that the bailout state managed to keep the economy aloft and generate a kind of prosperity—half-real, half-illusory. But it could never have done so without initiating a process of primitive accumulation abroad across much of Asia and Latin America. Hundreds of millions of peasants in China, India, and elsewhere were either swept into the orbit of sweated industry, expelled from their smallholdings, or left hanging on for dear life. Others enlisted in the armies of the immigrant working poor in the service sectors of the West or (as in the case of thousands of Indian farmers) were driven to suicide: primitive accumulation with a vengeance.

Capital accumulation in the Third World's industrial zones in turn allowed for the financing of the West's heavily leveraged economy and the absorption of tidal waves of debt generated by the FIRE sector and US government borrowing. While the United States managed to export very little democracy, it did very successfully export its toxic mortgages and its vast supply of collateralized debt obligations and financial derivatives. This has been so for a long time and amounts to bipartisan policy, pursued with vigor, for example, during the "Washington Consensus" years of Bill Clinton and his Treasury secretary Robert Rubin. Now, however, the implosion of developing economies is a direct outcome of their massive ingestion of that "bad money" originating in the United States and the shriveling up of their export markets in Europe and America.

To the degree that domestic prosperity, such as it was, depended on that peculiar form of financial export, we can thank the dispossessed peasantry and the new industrial working classes of the global South. This might be thought of as a kind of social imperialism, one whose life cycle is nearing an end. What may turn out to be even more fatally characteristic of our leveraged economy than the recklessness of its financial oligarchs is the degree to which ordinary people are deeply implicated and dependent on what these "masters of the universe" have invented. Consumer spending, in all its wondrous variety, is still the country's real engine, accounting for two-thirds of the economy. But the engine has been running on fumes for some time. The subprime-mortgage collapse alerted everyone to just how deeply in debt the average American consumer has become, and not just when it comes to buying a home. The FIRE sector overextended itself and, thanks to that sector's diligence and ingenuity, the whole mass-consumption economy now finds itself underwater in debt.

Moreover, it would be hard to exaggerate the extent to which the consumer economy and culture of the late twentieth century exceeded the first Gilded Age in depth and scope. Today it penetrates into the lowest depths of proletarian life; its seductions inveigle even the working poor.

And why not? In a world overrun with quests for psychic identity, this is the arena that matters most, that promises so much by way of personal liberation and reinvention. It may rest on primitive accumulation abroad and financial mercantilism at home, but it can ease the pain of autocannibalism. If dispossession excited the political and social imagination of the first Gilded Age, consumer culture, leveraged by debt, has helped make the state of permanent wage labor, even a declining, downwardly mobile one, tolerable. So too, along with deindustrialization and the evisceration of the labor movement, it has disarmed most of those collective instincts and institutions that once offered resistance.

Consent, however, is as much a matter of mobilization, manipulation, and management as of the fallout of late twentieth-century consumer economics. Larry Bartels tries to come to grips with this in *Unequal Democracy*.[1] The book has two missions. The first is to extend his demolition (begun in an earlier journal article) of Thomas Frank's *What's the Matter with Kansas?* Frank argued that the conservative triumph of the past quarter-century depended on working-class voters voting against their own material interests and for a party run by their enemies. They did so, Frank argued, in defense of cultural conservatism, even though their hardcore "family values" were hardly shared or rewarded by the Republican business elite that really ran things. *Unequal Democracy* presents a statistical refutation of Frank. Bartels's numbers seem to show that working-class voters have not deserted the Democratic Party in anything close to Frank's estimates; that they continue to treat economic issues as critical and more important than cultural ones; and that on abortion, LGBTQ rights, and other cultural matters their views have been, most of the time, less rightward-leaning than those of middle- and upper-income voters. The singular exception to all this is the white section of the Southern working class, which can account for almost the entire shift in working-class voting and whose behavior can be explained on the basis of race. Bartels and Frank have debated the numbers, and the categories of class analysis that give rise to them. (Frank's working class is defined by those lacking a college education; Bartels's by those who fall into the bottom one-third of the income distribution.) Bartels gets the better of this argument, if only because of Frank's breezy way of generalizing from anecdotes, as if two or more of them rise to the level of data.

Bartels's second mission is to explain why the gross inequality of the second Gilded Age moved ahead with little opposition. Here he is not much more useful than Frank. Frank's book does not attempt a full explanation of what it describes and decries. Bartels points to

---

1   *Unequal Democracy: The Political Economy of the New Gilded Age*, Larry M. Bartels (Princeton, NJ: Princeton University Press, 2008).

a series of contingencies to account for Republican success: that voters are myopic, focused on short-term economic results, and that Republicans have managed to turn in good economic performances in election years; that all voters, rich and poor, react well, especially in election years, to high rates of income growth at the top of the pyramid, taking it as a sign of general economic good health, and so Republicans have reaped the political benefit of their own affluence; that the GOP has been better at fundraising, giving them a propaganda advantage; and that while Democrats have been consistently better at responding to the material needs of everyday people, their record of doing so peaks in off years and so doesn't deliver electorally. None of this seems robust enough to describe the skewed political economy of the new Gilded Age, which is Bartels's purpose. It all seems too much of a matter of good luck and good timing to account for the transvaluation of political values over a whole political era. Something more basic must have occurred to account for the sea change in the political culture.

For all his superficiality, Frank is describing something real. Nelson Aldrich and Andrew Carnegie might have learned a thing or two from Karl Rove about the arts and crafts of political diversion. Rove and company developed a whole inventory of "bloody shirts" and waved them with considerable success. Why not allow for the real appeal that the assault on "limousine liberalism" had, and still has, for working people caught up in the trials of their own economic and social decline? It is congruent, after all, with Bartels's own view of this population's sense of itself as underrepresented. Indeed, perhaps Bartels means to include this without expressly saying so when he talks of the GOP's fundraising and propaganda advantage. Why begrudge the brilliance of a conservative business offensive against the New Deal that got away with depicting itself as antielitist, as a revolution against capitalism in the interests of capitalism? The triumph here was thoroughgoing and, in order fully to account for it, one has to acknowledge the complicity of the

Democratic Party in its conversion to neoliberalism, something Bartels won't do.

Anecdotes and datasets may overlook something, however. Both writers depend on a naturalized profile of the working class, as if that category were a function of income, educational level, or some other "objective" measure of the social structure. But the category may come alive only when it acts consciously in history, animated by a coherent view of the world around it. Many have noted that the voting behavior of the unionized sector of whatever one chooses to define as the working class is starkly different—"more progressive" will do as shorthand—from the unorganized mass, of which it is a distinctly small minority on virtually all issues. This may be to some degree a function of union education and propaganda. Arguably, however, it is a more profound outcome of the sociology of knowledge; that is, the way people perceive, understand, and then act in the world has everything to do with their social relationships, with the organizational filters that make sense out of chaos. Autocannibalism stripped away the flesh and bone of a movement and its institutions that, in however limited a way, provided the medium for the working class to exist as a social fact. Its absence has been sorely missed.

The politics of dispossession lit up the first Gilded Age. The politics of proletarian demoralization, autocannibalism, and consumer anomie help account for the drear gloom of the second.

7. American Labor and the Great Depression

"We are in a new era to which I do not belong." So confided ex-president Calvin Coolidge to a close friend on a cold December day in 1932. He punctuated that melancholic thought a few weeks later by dying.[1]

Coolidge's premonition proved to be uncannily accurate. The Great Depression was, except for the Civil War, the most traumatic moment in the history of the United States. Nothing was quite the same after it. In an American culture that normally lives in the windowless room of the current event, the economic devastation of the 1930s and the New Deal which tried to repair it remain to this day deeply imprinted on the national psyche. Indeed, the current global financial meltdown and "Great Recession" are constantly and inevitably compared to what befell the country and the rest of the world seventy-five years ago.

An earlier version of this chapter first appeared in the *International Journal of Labour Research*, vol. 2, no. 1, 2010.

1 Arthur M. Schlesinger, Jr., *The Crisis of the Old Order* (New York: Houghton Mifflin, 1956), p. 457.

A watershed event, the Great Depression lives on in memory. The national income was halved in three years, beginning with the stock-market crash in 1929. One-quarter of the workforce (about 15 million people) was unemployed by 1933.[1] Joblessness had tripled in those same three years. In fact, if we leave out of account people employed in one way or another in agriculture, unemployment amounted to an astounding 37 percent. In industrial cities like Toledo, the number was a surreal 80 percent. Of the 75 percent of the national workforce actually employed, one-third could only get part-time work, so in reality only one-half of the active laboring population did so on a full-time basis.[2]

The payroll of full-time workers at United States Steel went from 225,000 in 1929 to zero in early 1933. Industrial construction practically evaporated, plunging from $949 million to $74 million in 1932. Manufacturing output dropped 29 percent between 1929 and 1933. Thirteen million bales of cotton went unsold in 1932, while food crops rotted in the fields and cattle were slaughtered by the millions.[3] Five thousand banks had failed by the time Franklin Roosevelt took office in March of 1933. Exports had bottomed out at a level not seen since 1904. The money supply, thanks in part to mass hoarding by ordinary people terrified by the banking crisis, had fallen by one-third between 1929 and 1933, aggravating what was already a crushing price deflation that affected everything from home prices to wages. So, for example, 80 percent of the stock market's value in 1929 had vanished into thin air by 1933. Six hundred thousand properties, including not only farms but also urban and rural residences, were in foreclosure. In early 1933,

---

1   William Leuchtenburg, *Franklin Roosevelt and the New Deal, 1934–40* (New York: Harper and Row, 1963).

2   Jonathan Alter, *The Defining Moment: FDR's Hundred Days and the Triumph of Hope* (New York: Simon Schuster, 2006).

3   Leuchtenburg, *Franklin Roosevelt and the New Deal*.

thirty-six of forty key economic indicators had arrived at the lowest point they were to reach during the whole eleven grim years of the Great Depression.[4]

Not until war in Europe stimulated a huge demand in America for war and war-related materials did employment and general economic well-being pick up rapidly. To many people, the depth and the length of the Great Depression suggested that capitalism itself had entered a systemic and perhaps terminal crisis.

Because the breakdown was so severe and total, many looked for underlying problems to explain why everything fell apart. Stark indeed was the presence of plenty amid poverty. And even starker was the apparent organic connection between the two: poverty not only lived alongside abundance but seemed to be caused by it. The output of capitalism's productive machinery had outgrown the capacity of the market to absorb it. Thanks to that insufficient effective demand, the dynamos of industrial and agricultural abundance shut down, only worsening the dilemma.

The Old Order Called into Question

Observation of this grotesque cycle of plenty begetting poverty led to a deeper indictment of the old order. Gross inequalities in the distribution of wealth and income (at levels not matched again until the turn of our own new century) were clearly at fault. Those inequalities were partly the consequence of a tax system favoring the wealthy. More fundamentally, they stemmed from the low-wage policy—at least when compared to the dramatic increases in worker productivity of the 1920s—that had characterized American industry since the consolidation of corporate control in the late nineteenth century. Meanwhile, farm income dropped precipitously

---

4   Alter, *The Defining Moment.*

with the revival of European agriculture after the war. Oligopolistic corporate control of major industrial sectors generated artificially high prices. Capital resources were pooled, coagulated, and idled in the hands of an investment banking elite—what, during the Progressive era, had been identified by Louis Brandeis and Woodrow Wilson as the "money trust." Determined to defend the fictitious paper values associated with its aging investments, the "trust" locked down access to capital and credit to fund newer, competitive enterprises and new technological innovations, especially in emerging mass-consumption-oriented industries. Systemic underconsumption and a dearth of new, productive investment were the twin evils (abetted by the power of a rentier class of speculative coupon clippers) identified by Keynes and others as the prime factors behind the collapse and stagnation.

Government intervention was essential, many critics agreed, and should be diverse. By 1933, who could any longer believe that the free market was self-correcting? With private and local forms of relief exhausted, who could any longer believe the federal government should stand aside? By that time, the most august financiers had been paraded before congressional investigating committees where their helplessness, ignorance, and multifarious schemes of self-enrichment had been made public and excoriated.

So by 1933, the first signs of extraparliamentary direct action signaled that it might be possible, even necessary, to break new ground. Twenty thousand veterans from World War I gathered on Anacostia Flats in the nation's capital to demand an early installment of their war service pensions. The "Bonus Army," as it came to be called, only dispersed at the point of federal bayonets, ordered into action by President Hoover and commanded by Douglas McArthur. Four thousand farmers occupied the Nebraska state house and 5,000 people crowded into a Seattle municipal building demanding government help. Political leaders were chased through the streets by crowds crying, "When do we eat?

We want action."[1] A demonstration of unemployed marching past Henry Ford's auto plant in Dearborn, Michigan, was violently driven away and some demonstrators were killed by the auto tycoon's private police. Coal miners seized food from company stores, and on some occasions even seized the closed mines to sell the ore. Some of the jobless who had been cut off by utility companies tapped into gas and electric lines with the help of unemployed workers in those industries; nor would local juries convict them of trespassing or theft when the coal companies sued. The governors of Minnesota and North Dakota declared moratoriums on mortgage foreclosure sales.[2] On city streets, neighbors gathered to forcibly prevent the evictions of their friends. For those who yearned to overthrow the past and directly confront the structural and institutional dilemmas that had run the economy into the ditch, these were promising, if also anxiety-producing, signs that it just might be possible.

The New Deal

Looking back at those times there is a popular tendency today to romanticize Roosevelt and the New Deal. Actually, he was in some ways a prisoner of the past, at least when he first entered office and continuing through the first two years of his administration. Some historians have identified that period as the "first New Deal," to distinguish it from the more audacious and social-democratic-minded reforms of the "second New Deal." For instance, the president believed in the orthodox wisdom of the balanced budget and never entirely abandoned that faith, even when he was later convinced to depart from it in Keynesian fashion by using deficit

---

1   Ibid., p.18.
2   Leuchtenburg, *Franklin Roosevelt and the New Deal*, pp. 25–6.

spending not only for relief but to prime the pump of recovery. Roosevelt shared the traditional repugnance for what was then called "the dole," or welfare. Moreover, he feared, as much as Hoover did, parting company with the country's business and financial elite. He tried instead, until it proved unworkable, to forge a partnership with that community in much the same way Hoover had. The two key pieces of recovery legislation passed during the first hundred days—the National Industrial Recovery Act (NIRA) and the Agricultural Adjustment Act—were premised on the idea of business-government collaboration. Given these conservative-minded philosophical maxims and cautious political calculations, a decisive rupture with the past might have seemed highly unlikely.

Yet that is just what happened. It had begun even during the legendary first hundred days of the new administration. The creation of the Tennessee Valley Authority (TVA) was a stunning venture into the realm of economic planning and regional development, which included the government creating and owning a major electrical power-generating facility. Regional electrification was in turn designed to sweep the whole Tennessee Valley into the orbit of a modern mass-consumption economy, inspiring satellite industrial and urban settlements and making the whole region a new market for the output of American industries. The private-sector electrical-power industry bitterly opposed the TVA, resenting its "unfair" competition. But the TVA prevailed.

Other key pieces of legislation were introduced during those formative days. The Securities Act passed during the first hundred days, and the second such act introduced a year later, created the Securities and Exchange Commission to regulate the markets. Neither act called for draconian measures. But the very idea that Wall Street's old guard would be a bit more open to public inspection—and would have to obey rules against insider trading and the like—was obnoxious to an arrogant milieu long grown accustomed to making their own rules to their own advantage. They embarked on permanent and poisonous opposition to the New Deal and its presidential architect, whom they thought of as a "traitor to his class." Even more germane when it came to dismantling the "securities bloc" of older investment banks and infrastructural heavy industry was the passage of the Glass-Steagall Act, another product of Roosevelt's first hundred days. The law separated commercial from investment banking, whose merging had been particularly extensive and rapid during the 1920s and had consolidated the power of the "money trust."

Finally, it is critical to note that these preliminary days of the New Deal included the first hesitant steps in the direction of what we would today consider Keynesian fiscal innovation, social welfare and labor reform. Legislation included a Public Works Administration whose mission was to undertake large-scale public projects to boost employment and created the Civilian Conservation Corps, a sizable if limited federal venture into work relief and precursor of more ambitious undertakings. The NIRA called for wage minimums, hour maximums, and the end of child labor. It also included a provision—one hated by the tycoons of heavy industry—that seemed to place the authority of the government behind the right of workers to form unions and appeared to oblige employers to negotiate with them. Over the next couple of years, it became clear that in fact the government was not yet ready to enforce its own laws, whether on wage and hour standards or on the right to organize. Nonetheless, it was a premonition of things to come.

Labor's Role

Looking at the lay of the land in 1932, no one could have expected much of anything from the labor movement. Like the rest of the country, it was flat on its back, leading a ghostly existence. Never commanding much of a presence, except in a restricted set of crafts and industries, it had at least represented 12.1 percent of the labor force in 1920. By 1930, that share had shrunk to 7.4 percent—even less than it is today.[1] Most of that membership belonged to the craft unions that dominated the American Federation of Labor (AFL). These institutions hung on by virtue of their leverage, however dwindling, over the markets for skilled labor. Even here, though, the Depression pushed hundreds of thousands of construction-trades craftsmen, skilled tool-and-die makers, mechanics, and others onto the breadlines. Where the AFL did enjoy a broader reach over industrial labor generally, as in coal mining, the railroads, or the garment and textile industries, mass bankruptcies placed unions like the United Mine Workers and the Amalgamated Clothing Workers on short rations. Not only did they lose numbers in droves as mines and shops closed up, they were also forced to cut back severely on the resources devoted to organizing, internal education, and other matters. Whole union locals folded. In the case of the clothing workers, much of their innovative work on negotiating unemployment insurance plans with management ended in insolvency. The United Mine Workers (UMW) had already lost 80 percent of its members during the 1920s, a sorry state that was repeated in sectors like meatpacking, textiles, and paper-making. Where unions continued to cling to life, wage and hour standards deteriorated irresistibly. When strikes did take place to organize at new sites or to hold on to existing ones or resist wage cuts, as for example in the Southern textile industry, they almost invariably failed in the years leading up to Roosevelt's victory. Not surprisingly, between 1929 and 1930, the number of strikers fell by 80 percent.

Most inauspicious of all was the brute fact that the heart of American industry—steel, auto, glass, rubber, electrical, farm

---

[1]   Barry Hirsch and David MacPherson, "Union Membership and Coverage Database from the Current Population Survey Note," *Industrial Labor Relations Review*, vol. 56, vo. 2, Jan. 2002, pp. 349–354.

machinery, meatpacking, maritime, and more—was almost completely unorganized. In 1930, 90 percent of the auto workforce was unorganized.[2] And to make matters worse, the craft elite that ran the AFL displayed a real aversion to confronting this world. After all, American heavy industry was deeply hostile to unions, and was armed and ready to use all measures—legal, extralegal, and violent—to stop their incursion. Just as problematic was that workers in heavy industry were largely first- and second-genera-tion immigrants, hailing from southeastern and eastern Europe. Their ethnic, cultural, and religious backgrounds, along with the fact that they performed unskilled and semi-skilled labor, left the native-born, skilled, and Protestant milieu in the AFL suspicious and even contemptuous of their abilities, including their ability to organize.

Politically, the labor movement's situation seemed nearly as unpromising at the outset of the New Deal. True, it had enough friends in Congress to pass the Norris–La Guardia Act in 1932 while Hoover was still in office. The law sharply restricted the use of the court-ordered labor injunction to break strikes, an enormously effec-tive weapon in the arsenal of antiunionism for at least two genera-tions. The provision in the NIRA proclaiming the right to organize was called "labor's Emancipation Proclamation." Union organizers deployed it to convince workers that "the president wants you to join a union." But soon enough, the NIRA became known in labor circles as the "national runaround." It was an apt sobriquet, as the Labor Board set up to enforce those good intentions failed to do so. Indeed, less than 10 percent of the code authorities set up to administer the act in specific industries even had labor representatives.[3]

---

2   Robert Zeiger, *The CIO: 1935–1955* (Chapel Hill: University of North Carolina Press, 1995).

3   Eric Rauchway, "Learning from the New Deal's Mistakes," *The American Prospect*, 22 Jan. 2008.

What did change was the reality in the field, beginning with the state of the economy. During Roosevelt's first two terms, the US economy grew at an annual average rate of 9 to 10 percent. Durable goods expenditures and the value of construction rose substantially. Unemployment dropped in each year, except during the calamitous recession of 1937–38, due both to publicly created jobs (about 3.6 million) and an uptick in private manufacturing. Agriculture picked up thanks in part to price supports and crop restrictions. Home foreclosures abated as well, due to the mortgage subsidies made available through the Home Owners' Loan Corporation. Stabilization and regulation of the financial system, including the creation of the Federal Deposit Insurance Corporation to guarantee bank deposits, stopped the hoarding and helped open the arteries of commercial credit. Most of all, the stimulus provided by federal spending, even haltingly applied, seems to have encouraged investment in the private sector.

Consequently, the political and social psychology of the nation shifted seemingly overnight. Common sense might suggest that popular insurgencies arise as a function of mass misery. Often enough, however, the opposite is the case. Many, although certainly not all, of the expressions of resistance and outrage that occurred in the earliest years of the Great Depression were momentary pleas for help without any sustained organizational momentum. By the end of 1934, however, the picture looked entirely different. It is reasonable to think that the economy's improvement gave people the courage, the optimism, and the material leverage with which to fight back.

Something was already stirring in 1933, when the number of strikes doubled from the previous year. Then 1.5 million workers went on strike in 1934.[1] Some of the most notable of these conflicts had the character of mass strikes; that is, they rapidly spread beyond

---

1   Zeiger, *The CIO*.

the borders of a conventional trade-union dispute with a particular employer and into whole communities. At the same time, other forms of working-class-based mobilization—rent strikes, demonstrations by leagues of the unemployed, consumer protests, tenant-farmer mobilizations—made the air electric with possibility.

Political Impact

This sort of combativeness heated the political atmosphere, which in turn further encouraged grassroots militancy and broadened social aspirations. One might call the relationship symbiotic. At the national level, the midterm elections of 1934 were a telling case. Not only did the Democratic Party substantially increase its congressional majority but, more importantly, that majority was far readier to contemplate major reform—readier than the president himself—than the one elected in 1932. The edgier and more demanding popular mood had registered. Some measure of that change in the complexion of the legislative branch was undoubtedly due to the gathering challenge to the rule of industrial autocracy in the workplace. By 1936, Roosevelt himself would be condemning "Tories of industry" for their selfishness and antidemocratic behavior. A Senate subcommittee formed that year began a systematic exposure of the lengths to which the country's leading industrial corporations were willing to go—including using spies and heavily armed private police and stockpiling lethal munitions—to crush all attempts at union organizing. Even earlier, by the end of 1934, the National Labor Relations Act—which would create a statutory right to organize and make it the legal obligation of employers to engage in collective bargaining with the freely chosen representatives of their employees—was retrieved from the bottom of the president's inbox pile and soon enough became a top priority of the administration.

State and local politics and extraparliamentary activity, much of it powered by the "labor question," accelerated this drift to the left. In California, the famous novelist and socialist Upton Sinclair won the Democratic primary in 1934 and campaigned for the governorship under the slogan "End Poverty in California." Sinclair's platform was avowedly anticapitalist and advocated replacing the older system with one based on production for use. Similar language informed Floyd Olson's Farmer-Labor Party in Minnesota and Philip La Follette's in Wisconsin and led to their electoral triumphs after earlier defeats in 1932. Down South, the firebrand senator from Louisiana, Huey Long, inspired a multimillion-member populist "Share Our Wealth" outcry. "Share Our Wealth" clubs sprang up all over the country, calling, among other things, for confiscatory taxes on the superrich, minimum wages, and government ownership of public utilities. Father Charles Coughlin, the "radio priest" from Royal Oak, Michigan, mesmerized millions of listeners on a weekly basis as he condemned Wall Street speculators and supported the right of workers, particularly his auto-worker audience in nearby Detroit, to organize unions. (Only later would Coughlin's anti-Semitism and Christo-fascism supplant his earlier Catholic corporatism and its criticisms of tooth-and-claw capitalism.)

As the country's social and political center of gravity shifted, the labor movement in turn grew bolder, both on the shop floor and in the political arena. But this new audacity came with a price. Fissures within the upper echelons of the trade-union hierarchy had been widening for some time. The labor upsurge of 1934 included hundreds of thousands of workers in heavy industry practically demanding that the old labor federation organize them. Although the AFL established new "federal locals" to accommodate this initial rush, soon enough it began parceling out members in haphazard fashion into existing craft unions, which then did nothing. The AFL was reluctant, as it always had been, to entertain a new strategy of mass industrial unionism aimed at creating universal unions that would encompass all the workers in particular industrial sectors. All of its nativist cultural prejudices, its fear of confronting the country's largest corporations, and its nose-in-the-air snobbery regarding the unskilled came into play.

Politically, the craft-dominated federation adhered to a tradition of voluntarism that also aggravated relations with rising elements of the labor movement, which looked to the state and public policy as a way out of labor's cul-de-sac. The role of the judiciary in "enjoining" (prohibiting) strikes—a practice stretching well back into the nineteenth century—along with the remarkable frequency with which state and national governments had resorted to armed force to quell labor uprisings, left the AFL wary of any government involvement in labor relations. The federation at first opposed Social Security legislation for fear that it would compete with long established trade-union welfare and pension funds and leach away the loyalty of its members. Until 1932, it even opposed government unemployment insurance. This arm's-length suspicion of the state ran headlong into the contrary strategy developing within the ranks of industrial unionism, which increasingly came to see the New Deal administration and its allies in Congress as not only useful but essential.

And then there was the question of radicalism. The strikes and organizing drives that lit up the industrial landscape beginning in 1934 were not spontaneous eruptions, popular folklore notwithstanding. In virtually every case, they were prepared for and led by a menagerie of radicals: socialists, Communists, Trotskyists, remnants of the Industrial Workers of the World (the "Wobblies"), anarcho-syndicalists, and others. Moreover, the leadership of the industrial-union faction within the AFL often included similarly minded people. John L. Lewis of the UMW, who became the public face of the new industrial union movement, did not fit this profile; in fact, he had been a Republican, never shy about purging his union of radical oppositionists back in the 1920s. But as the movement grew in the mid-1930s, he was more than willing to make use of radicals as key organizers and strategists. Others, like Sidney Hillman of the Amalgamated Clothing Workers and David Dubinsky of the International Ladies' Garment Workers' Union, were Russian-immigrant Jewish socialists. The new industrial-union movements that began to emerge in auto, rubber, and electrical goods and among West Coast longshoremen, seafarers, packing-house and tobacco workers, and teamsters were invariably led by political radicals of one variety or another. For these cadres, more was at stake than the creation of effective new institutions of collective bargaining or even than the triumph of industrial unionism as a form more appropriate to modern mass production. They sought to address the "labor question" more broadly and envisioned a social movement prepared to champion the needs of working people generally, whether members of unions or not, black or white, skilled or unskilled, male or female, immigrant or native born. Simmering divisions within the house of labor finally came to a head with the creation of the Committee for Industrial Organization in 1935, which was soon purged from the ranks of the AFL and emerged as independent labor organization, the Congress of Industrial Organizations (CIO). The CIO immediately embarked on a strategy—simultaneously political and industrial—that not only ended the reign of industrial autocracy in basic industry but provided the social energy that made possible the Keynesian social-welfare state with which the New Deal is most enduringly identified. In the industrial arena, this meant pooling resources (organizers and money, first of all) into risky joint campaigns to organize basic industries like steel, meatpacking, and textiles. But even as the CIO put together the steelworkers' organizing committee and analogous multiunion undertakings, it assiduously pursued its political options.

Senator La Follette's subcommittee exposed the intimidating and violence-prone antiunion machinations of companies like General Motors and Republic Steel. Its staff also met regularly with CIO organizers to coordinate the release of the committee's most damning revelations with the tactical maneuvers of the union's campaign. The Wagner Act passed in the spring of 1935, establishing the National Labor Relations Board (NLRB), which was empowered to enforce the right to organize and employers' obligation to engage in collective bargaining. Once the CIO got under way, the NLRB, heavily staffed by sympathizers of the new movement, again and again ruled in its favor, making the CIO-affiliated union the sole bargaining agent and effectively eroding industry's attempt to skirt around the law by setting up multiple or company unions.

Early in 1936, the CIO formed Labor's Nonpartisan League to mobilize for the upcoming presidential election. The league established local offices all over the country in working-class cities and towns. Programmatically, it did not confine itself to union issues narrowly conceived. It depicted Roosevelt and the New Deal as a bulwark against reaction, a foe of the plutocracy, and a muscular champion of wide-ranging reform. After all, 1934 to 1937 witnessed the enactment of the Wagner Act and Social Security (including government-funded pensions, unemployment insurance, and Aid to Families with Dependent Children), as well as the Wealth Tax Act, the Public Utility Holding Company Act (designed to break up the combines of holding companies that had dominated the power industry and saddled it with enormous, enervating debt), a vast expansion of public works under the auspices of the Works Progress Administration, and a low-income housing program, among other socially minded innovations. Some of these reforms looked better on paper than they did in practice; the Wealth Tax Act did very little to redistribute income, and the housing program was severely limited. But to one degree or another they represented ruptures with the self-reliant individualism, growing inequality, and laissez-faire political culture of the past.

Roosevelt, for his part, became increasingly willing to collaborate with, even instigate, this transformation in the country's political chemistry. By the middle of 1934, he had little to lose, as the old elites had deserted him. For example, the du Ponts, Morgans, and other leading business circles from the "securities bloc" established the American Liberty League, whose animus for the New Deal—and for Roosevelt personally—knew no limits. Class polarization, a rare phenomenon in American political life, increasingly colored public rhetoric. If in the eyes of the American Liberty League the president was a "Communist," he in turn was prepared to identify them as "economic royalists" and to announce proudly that if they hated him, he "welcomed their hatred." The CIO cheered and mimicked such language in the 1936 campaign and thereafter. Meanwhile, the temporary coalescence in the runup to the 1936 election of the Huey Long movement with Father Coughlin's followers and those of the Francis Townsend movement (demanding universal old-age pensions) made Roosevelt wary of losing constituencies to the populist left, a further incentive to realign his campaign against the "captains of industry."

Syncopation of political and industrial initiatives culminated in the pathbreaking Flint sit-down strike against General Motors by the fledgling United Auto Workers (UAW) that began hardly more than a month after Roosevelt's landslide re-election and ended with the company's reluctant recognition of the UAW (at least in certain plants). That smashing victory was a real tonic to the CIO and to millions of working people. An epidemic of sit-down strikes erupted all across the country that lasted into the middle of 1937.

Roosevelt's overwhelming triumph of 1936 inspired the high point of the CIO's strategic ambitions. It was the moment when the New Deal administration felt most beholden to the labor movement for its contribution to that victory. Together, they embarked on a daring attempt to reconfigure the two-party system, to make it reflect more clearly than the semicoherent coalitions that customarily defined the political order, the distinct class interests, and outlook that the Great Depression had made so transparent. By American standards it was an audacious undertaking. In the end, it turned out to be a fateful failure.

Everything depended on upending the ancien régime in the South. While the New Deal faced its natural antagonists in the Republican Party, it was hobbled internally by the considerable power of Southern Democrats in Congress. To move ahead with bolder plans of social reform, there needed to be a day of reckoning, one that would confront the political overlords who ran the South and defended its racially inflected political economy, which rested on low-wage peonage. Ever since the late nineteenth century, the South had been a one-party region. As a result, its Democratic Party representatives in Washington enjoyed disproportionate seniority in the power-wielding committees that helped determine the fate of New Deal legislative initiatives. Thanks to their inordinate influence, New Deal provisions were systematically rewired in the South to exclude African Americans, tenant farmers, and share-croppers. Moreover, so long as the South remained a bastion of low-wage labor, hardened its hostility to unionization, and maintained its segregated caste system, it would continue to undermine labor and social-welfare standards throughout the country.

Together, New Deal political operatives and the CIO embarked upon a three-pronged strategy to take on the old South and in the process transform the internal chemistry of the Democratic Party. First, beginning in 1937, the CIO launched a major drive to organize the Southern textile industry: the site of runaway textile manufacturers since the turn of the century and the region's primary industrial enterprise. The Textile Workers Organizing Committee inundated the South with organizers and money. Complementary efforts by other elements of the CIO made simultaneous forays into the tobacco sheds and steel mills of the Carolinas and Virginia. Many, although not all, were racially integrated undertakings and where unions managed to get started, they often sustained that flagrant challenge to Southern mores. Second, the Roosevelt administration, in close cooperation with the labor movement, doggedly campaigned for a minimum-wage/maximum-hour law. Although designed to cover the whole country, it was particularly targeted at the South, where bare subsistence wages were the rule even in industry, but especially among agricultural and domestic workers. The third leg of this strategic démarche made the unprecedented attempt to purge the Democratic Party of its mainly Southern conservative elements during the primary campaigns leading up to the 1938 midterm elections. This was initiated by the president, but he relied on the CIO to provide the shock troops.

All three undertakings failed to one degree or another. Concerted resistance by the whole Southern oligarchy, including a storm of red- and race-baiting, along with the frailty of what amounted to Southern liberalism, doomed the textile organizing campaign. The minimum-wage law—the Fair Labor Standards Act (FLSA)—did pass in 1938. But before it did, it was subject to a thousand amendments that exempted much of the Southern labor force—agricultural and domestic workers particularly. Finally, so too did the purge of the party go down to defeat, as most of the Democratic old guard in the South fought off the administration's primary challenges. For this reason, 1938 and the passage of the FLSA mark the endpoint of the "second New Deal." After that, as attention shifted to the war in Europe, there would be no more social and economic reform of the sort that we now think of as the heart of the New Deal.

Did the New Deal Work?

How to assess the whole experience? First, the question is often asked whether the New Deal cured the Great Depression. The answer is "yes and no." So long as the administration kept up its courage and adhered to robust deficit spending, along with other measures designed to shore up demand, there was real recovery. However, because Roosevelt himself was never entirely convinced this was right and proper and because conservative forces within both the Republican and Democratic parties mounted effective opposition to this kind of Keynesianism, the New Deal oscillated between spending and retrenchment. So, for example, the Civil Works Administration, set up in 1933, created four million public-works jobs but was dissolved less than a year later. The even more ambitious Works Progress Administration, created in 1935, suffered serious cutbacks by 1937.[1] The latter arguably led to what was called "the Roosevelt Recession" of 1937–38, a very severe one that nearly matched the declines of the earlier part of the decade.

In the realm of economic and social reform, the New Deal certainly accomplished much. Financial regulation, labor reform, Social Security, public works, relief, and regional planning together comprise no mean achievement, especially when measured against an American political tradition that had found most of this repugnant. But more was arguably possible, and the failure to extend the reach of the social-democratic welfare state had consequences that haunt America to this day. Although the CIO mounted heroic efforts to confront the racism that impoverished and degraded African Americans and divided the working class, the New Deal never really did. It was too intimidated by its conservative allies in the South and its opponents elsewhere. Moreover, fledgling efforts to extend social insurance to include health care and low-income housing were either abandoned or left on life support. The audacious foray into government ownership and social and economic planning represented by the Tennessee Valley Authority (and the "little TVAs" that sprang up in the western United States) would never again make it onto the political agenda. Efforts at major income redistribution through the tax system never proceeded very far, even during the height of the "second New Deal." Antitrust sentiments clung to life, but as bygone rhetoric that informed public policy less and less. By the end of the decade, the New Deal had run out of gas as a reform movement and had begun mending fences

---

1   Rauchway, "Learning from the New Deal's Mistakes."

with the old business establishment, a process that would accelerate enormously during World War II: the war mobilization apparatus was honeycombed with corporate personnel from what President Eisenhower would later call the "military-industrial complex."

Labor's Mixed Record

How do we assess the role of the labor movement in this story of triumph and frustration? Without its social and political muscle, it is hard to imagine the New Deal evolving in the direction of social democracy even to the extent that it did. The reign of industrial autocracy that had terrorized workers since the Gilded Age was over. Industrial democracy, however flawed in execution, took its place. Moreover, industrial unionism was an extraordinary accomplishment, and not just as a stunning piece of organizational architecture. It required overcoming, at least partially, a multitude of ethno-cultural, religious, racial, and gender divisions. In that sense, it brought into life as a self-conscious act the modern American proletariat, up until then a mere statistical artifice. At a time when racial subordination was still an unquestioned axiom of American life, the CIO defied it and sometimes succeeded, so that substantial numbers of African-American workers joined its ranks and enjoyed its victories. The labor movement left a lasting imprint on American culture. An ethos of social solidarity and a concern for and appreciation of the role and traditions of the ordinary working person remained a vibrant part of American life until a half-century later, when the Reagan era ushered in a new age of Mammon-worship.

Nonetheless, in the end, the labor movement was never strong or determined enough—either ideologically or politically—to force matters beyond the reformed capitalism that distanced America from the more thoroughgoing social-democratic innovations characteristic of postwar Western Europe. Whatever real progress the

CIO made in overthrowing the racial order could not measure up against the New Deal's failure to even try, leaving the politics of race behind like a ticking time bomb. It would detonate in the 1960s and help dismantle the New Deal order and renew deep fissures within the labor movement. The sit-down strikes of the mid-1930s, while inspirational, were also fear-inducing, setting off tremors about the threat to private property that registered with middle-class folk and made the Roosevelt administration more inhibited about hitching its fate to the new labor movement.

The outcry against the sit-down tactic also led to reservations within the CIO itself, as the leadership sensed, at least on this vital matter, its estrangement from popular opinion. This signaled a deeper problem. True, the CIO was a kind of social miracle in so far as it managed to transcend the more parochial identities that had crippled the labor movement for so long. But those fractious divisions still carried force. If the leading cadre in many of the new unions were secular radicals willing to imagine real alternatives to capitalism, that was hardly the case throughout the ranks, where old loyalties to the church, ethnic traditions, private property, and patriarchal and racial hierarchies, not to mention good old-fashioned American individualism, endured, constraining more daring social and political ambitions.

At the same time, the CIO in particular became so enamored of and dependent on its relationship with a friendly government that it was reluctant, when times changed, to shift gears and rely on itself. World War II brought matters to a head. At the outset of the war, the labor movement still exercised real influence within the economic mobilization bureaucracy. It even lobbied for tripartite councils of labor, business, and government to run the economy and particular industries. Very soon, however, big business assumed all the major levers of power. Evicted from its more influential enclaves in the war-mobilization bureaucracy but afraid to challenge the administration, the CIO found itself enforcing a regimen of patriotic sweating that would widen the distance between the leadership and the ranks. Dreams of extending the welfare state after the war were scrapped. Friends of labor became scarcer and scarcer within the inner councils of the national government, especially after Roosevelt died.

Social-democratic Keynesianism was inexorably supplanted by its commercial variant, which left the basic institutions of the free market in a commanding, if no longer omnipotent, position. In one last spasm of social and political upheaval, the whole industrial labor movement went on strike during 1945 and 1946 (although not all at one time) and made one last heroic effort to organize the South. Simultaneously, it vigorously campaigned for national health insurance, a widening of what today is called the "social safety net," a commitment by the national government to use its fiscal power to guarantee full employment, and a national income policy to prevent the kind of unequal distribution that had helped cause the Great Depression. Although Truman squeaked to victory in 1948 by mending his damaged relations with the labor movement, by the end of the decade much of the visionary momentum of the movement had dissipated. The Cold War and domestic anticommunism soon enough took their toll; an intimidated CIO purged its ranks of some of its most militant and socially conscious unions, and the country grew accustomed to thinking of things like racial justice and national health insurance as sneaky forms of Communism. After that, the labor movement reconciled itself to defending its bastions of power in the private sector through the mechanisms of collective bargaining and assumed its position as a junior member of the new power elite.

8. The Age of Acquiescence

Why, during what many have aptly called America's "second Gilded Age," has there been so little opposition to the rule of big business and finance? Why this timorousness in the teeth of a cynical crony capitalism, gross inequalities of income and wealth, the subversion of democracy by money, the nauseating conspicuous display of riches, and the exaltation of a savage selfishness? This has never happened before. No matter the outcome, Americans of all kinds—farmers, workers, urban and small-town business owners and professionals, oppressed minorities—have always contested the reign of capital. No more! At least, nothing remotely on the scale of what once was. Why? Why now? Something went missing, beginning with the age of Ronald Reagan. What became of that long and noble and often enough efficacious tradition of opposition—political, moral, religious, social—to the reign of money? This essay is a provisional attempt to probe that enigma.

Google "second Gilded Age" and you will get ferried to 7,000

An earlier version of this chapter appeared in *Salmagundi*, no. 170/171, Spring–Summer 2011.

possible sites where you can learn more about what you already instinctively know. That we have just recently lived through a Gilded Age has become a journalistic commonplace. Most would now acknowledge that for a generation, beginning with the election of Ronald Reagan, the economic throw-weight, political power, and social prestige of the country's business and financial elite went virtually unchallenged. Crony capitalism luridly lit up the political landscape. Government was charged with either getting out of the way of businesspeople on the make or supplying them with boatloads of favors (cost-plus contracts, subsidies, tax abatements, and the like) to help them pile up the booty. A "leisure class" holed up in gated communities or "housoleums" as gargantuan as the imported castles of their first Gilded Age forerunners. They supped on lion meat and made ready to decamp to their private islands aboard their private jets should the spirit move them. Reagan's splendid inaugural ball was described as a "bacchanalia of the haves." The division of wealth and income polarized. It became so extreme that, by any measure, inequality exceeded the highest levels ever before reached in American history: that is, just before the Great Crash and Depression of the 1930s.

Our gilded elites were hardly embarrassed by their Mammon-worship, nor were the rest of us. Style guru Diana Vreeland, stylishly blunt, captured the moment: "Everything is power and money and how to use them both ... we mustn't be afraid of snobbism and luxury." And the plight of those less fortunate proved no cause for alarm. Endless ideological justifications were fabricated for this stark inequality. Poverty, to the degree that it was acknowledged at all, was conveniently treated as a cultural and moral problem of the impoverished (remember Clinton's historic "welfare-to-work" termination of the New Deal's "welfare as we know it"). A reinvigorated belief in the free market as the fairest (not to mention the most efficient) way to allocate wealth worked like a tonic to soothe uneasy consciences and exculpate the workings of the merciless marketplace.

Crony capitalism, inequality, extravagance, social Darwinian self-justification, blame-the-victim callousness, free-market hypocrisy: thus it was once, back in the late nineteenth century; thus it was once again in the late twentieth. A "second Gilded Age" indeed. Yet how shockingly different than the first one! Back then the country rumbled to the thunder of mass strikes, moral outrage, and political revolution, mayhem on city streets and in the countryside. There was then a Great Noise. There is now, in our time, a Great Silence.

Even after the global meltdown of the financial system, even in the wake of the most severe economic calamity since the Great Depression, at a moment when we might reasonably expect our gilded elite to get its comeuppance, that hasn't happened; not yet, anyway. Indeed, those circles continue to exercise extraordinary political influence, within the inner sanctum of a regime that came to power promising "change we can believe in." So too, their economic preeminence has, if anything, gotten weightier thanks to the rescue efforts mobilized on their behalf by the government. While they've suffered through some queasy moments—Bernie Madoff's $50 billion Ponzi scheme; Merrill Lynch's John Thain and his $1,400 wastebasket; Richard Fuld, ex-CEO of the deceased Lehman Brothers, reaping a $22 million retirement bonus as his firm collapsed into oblivion; Goldman Sachs's gaming of its own clients—it is astonishing how well they've weathered the storm. What storm?

But hold on a second: What about the Tea Party? What about all that "Don't Tread on Me" belligerence? No spinal collapse there, certainly. Except that once it got over its initial fury about bailing out bankers, the Tea Party rising has directed the lion's share of its anger elsewhere: at the efforts of big government, tepid as they may be, to resurrect the economy; or at the "illegal immigrant plague"; or at proposals to domesticate the rogue financial establishment; or at efforts to punish the ecocide perpetrated by BP. When it comes to standing up to the power blocs that really rule, these rebels from yesteryear lapse into silence.

Perhaps this shouldn't surprise us. After all, as President Calvin Coolidge once famously observed, "The business of America is business." The puritanical president from taciturn Vermont was widely, if gently, mocked as "Silent Cal." (Dorothy Parker, when informed of his passing, waspishly remarked "How could they tell?") But in this case, he said a mouthful. Since the first colonial settlements, the New World had invited the ambitions of the high and mighty as well as the hoi polloi to enrich themselves. The freedom to do just that was the dream, the promise. If history or fate favored a fortunate few in that race to heap up wealth and power, Americans tended to be distinctly tolerant: all agreed that was part of the game.

But did they? Some of America's most esteemed historians have accepted that premise. The country has been remarkably free of the kinds of social antagonisms, class conflicts, and fundamental political assaults on capitalism that bedeviled the Old World. That good fortune (if you choose to see it that way) may be credited to a universally shared belief in acquisitive individualism and to a richly endowed continental economy that has made that belief reality for so many. Americans, in the words of one of these historians, have been "a people of plenty." Abundance, even if unevenly shared, was the New World's solution to the Old World's faceoff between landlords and peons, aristocrats and democrats, capital and labor, socialism and capitalism. In the United States, whatever other abrasive relations between racial, religious, and ethnic groups may have disturbed the country's social and political equanimity, no pitched battles or Armageddon-like confrontations between the haves and have-nots happen here. On fundamental matters about private property and its prerogatives, a rough consensus has reigned. But has it? Until now—until our own Age of Acquiescence—the answer sometimes has been yes, and sometimes emphatically no. A tradition of resistance to moneyed power stretches all the way back to the earliest days of the republic. Thomas Jefferson and his legions of democratic followers mounted the barricades in a bitter standoff against Alexander Hamilton and upper-crust Federalists, who they suspected harbored counterrevolutionary designs to install a moneyed aristocracy in place of the country's new plebian government. Andrew Jackson waged a holy war against the second Bank of the United States, run by a mainline Philadelphia aristocrat and known far and wide as "the monster bank." The president accused the "monster" of monopolizing the country's financial resources and privileging well-connected "moneycrats."

During the first Gilded Age, simmering class resentments boiled over. As a title, *Apocalypse Now* could easily have been applied to a movie made about late nineteenth-century America. Whichever side you happened to be on, there was an overwhelming dread that the nation was dividing in two and verging on a second Civil War, that a final confrontation between the "classes and the masses" was unavoidable. Irate farmers mobilized in the Populist Party. Farmer-Labor Parties in states and cities from coast to coast challenged the dominion of the two-party system. Rolling waves of strikes enveloped whole communities and paralyzed the nation's brand-new railroads, steel mills, coal mines, and factories. Legions of small business owners, trade unionists, urban consumers, and local politicians raged against monopoly and the "trusts." Armed workers' militias paraded in the streets of many American cities. Business and political elites built massive urban fortresses, public armories equipped with Gatling guns, preparing to crush the insurrections they saw headed their way.

The first Gilded Age was a moment of great fear, but also of great expectations—a period infatuated with a literature of utopias as well as dystopias. Everyone was seeking a way out, something wholly new to replace the rancor and incipient violence of Gilded Age capitalism. All the insurgencies of that era expressed a deep yearning to abolish, in one way or another, the prevailing industrial order. They were disturbed enough, naïve enough, desperate enough, inventive enough, desiring enough, deluded enough—some still drawing cultural nourishment from the fading homesteads and workshops of preindustrial America—to believe that out of all this could come a new way of life, a cooperative commonwealth.

When Rockefeller ally Senator William McKinley defeated populist tribune and "boy orator of the Platte" William Jennings Bryan for the presidency in the election of 1896, that particular dream died. But the spirit of resistance and rebellion lived on. The trust-busting movement actually grew stronger after the turn of the century, directing its ire at the mother of all trusts, "the money trust." It helped elect Woodrow Wilson president in 1912. The years before World War I were aflame with violent encounters between labor and capital, from the massacred coal miners in Ludlow, Colorado, to the mass strikes in the immigrant barrios of Paterson, New Jersey, and Lawrence, Massachusetts, back east. Socialist Party presidential candidate Eugene Debs polled a million votes, and elected Socialists sat in city councils and state legislatures. Former president Teddy Roosevelt became the standard bearer for a new, albeit short-lived, Progressive Party whose platform anticipated many of the social and economic reforms of the next great standoff between the haves and the have-nots.

I speak, of course, of the Great Depression and the New Deal. We still live in its shadow. FDR is in part famous for his excommunication of the rich and powerful. He called them out as "economic royalists," "Tories of industry," and predatory looters of "other people's money." On the eve of his 1936 re-election, he defiantly announced to the nation that those circles hated him and he "welcomed their hatred." That kind of presidential anathema would never have been delivered without the spectacular social uprisings of that era. Sit-down strikes and factory takeovers in the industrial heartland, Farmer-Labor Parties in the Midwest and out in California, prairie-fire populist movements to "share the wealth" led by demagogues like "Kingfish" Louisiana senator Huey Long and the "radio priest" Father Charles Coughlin: all challenged the power of concentrated wealth and moved the New Deal irresistibly to the left.

And then there were "the sixties." Say what you like, there is no question that the spirit of rebellion against racial oppression, against imperial war, against conventional morality and gender discrimination, against the overwhelming power of the military-industrial complex was alive and well. The establishment remained in the crosshairs of a variegated protest movement that penetrated even the inner sanctums of power.

Fast-forward to our second Gilded Age—the Age of Acquiescence—and the stage seems bare indeed. No great fears, no great expectations, no looming social apocalypse, no utopias or dystopias—just a kind of flatline sense of the end of history. Where are all the roiling insurgencies, the breakaway political parties, the waves of strikes and boycotts, the infectious communal upheavals, the chronic sense of "enough is enough"? Where are the earnest efforts to invoke a new order? What's left of mainstream populism exists on life support in some attic of the Democratic Party. In a society so saturated in Christian sanctimony, as ours is, would anyone today describe "mankind crucified on a cross of gold" as Bryan once famously did, let loose against "Mammon-worship," or condemn aristocratic "parasites" and "vampire speculators"? Where nineteenth-century evangelical preachers—some of them, at least—pronounced anathema on capitalist greed, our second Gilded Age televangelists deify it.

How mysterious! And what makes this great silence even more curious is that it can't be too easily attributed to the narcosis of abundance. Beginning in the 1970s, the income of working-class

Americans has essentially remained stagnant—and only has achieved that level of remuneration because two wage-earners now bring home what used to be earned by one. The country's infrastructure, which is after all part of the quality of life, has steadily decayed and at times collapsed. Insecurity of employment, even before the Great Recession, has become the norm. Moreover, that insecurity has crept into the nightmares of ill and aged Americans as health care and reliable pensions elude the grasp of millions. Poverty, after a long hiatus following the war on it waged by the Great Society, has made a comeback, its levels rising ominously. Welfare, once conceived as at least a partial solution to poverty, is now seen as its cause. Not only that, but poverty, which for several generations had become a function of exclusion from the workforce, now instead arises often enough out of superexploitation at work. Sweatshop labor, once thought to be a relic of industrial medievalism, pockmarks whole sectors of the economy—mass retailing, service, even construction—encompassing millions of the working poor. Many are immigrants, legal and undocumented; now many more come from the ranks of the modestly well-off middle and working classes who find themselves, in a word, dispossessed.

All of this and much more were the signposts of a long secular decline. Until very recently it was masked by bubbles of debt-based prosperity. For a not inconsiderable number of people that worked quite well, but for so many others it offered a fable of abundance in place of the real thing. And then came the global financial meltdown, record-shattering foreclosures and unemployment, and the withering of a dream. Yet still the sounds of silence reign, at least when compared to the great noise of the past.

Something vital went missing from the American collective psyche and moral makeup, from its political will to resist and its social imagination.

The End

The metabolism of capitalism has changed. From the nineteenth century through the golden age of postwar prosperity, the country's material well-being and its moral fortitude, its sense of itself as a society of tangible accomplishment and self-discipline, rested on industrialization. The Age of Acquiescence rests on deindustrialization. In our time, a new system of disaccumulation looted American industry, liquidating its assets or shipping them abroad to reward speculation in "fictitious capital." The rate of investment of new plant, technology, and research and development began declining during the 1970s, a fall-off that accelerated in the gilded eighties and thereafter. For more than a quarter-century the fastest-growing part of the economy, by any measure, has been the FIRE sector. Deindustrialization set off an avalanche whose impact is still being felt in the economy, the country's political culture, its moral priorities, and the warp and woof of everyday life. It set in motion what we might call a process of autocannibalism, in which capital accumulation in one part of the economy rested on devouring the accumulated material wherewithal and standard of living of its own body parts. It is the story of the active underdevelopment of a developed economy: a grim tale of decline, dispossession, and marginalization. Finance capitalism, in hollowing out the industrial heartland, disarmed a whole society.

Deindustrialization laid low the industrial working class and the labor movement. Lamentable, perhaps—but why should it matter, some might ask? That question itself is evidence of how much our world has lost. For a hundred years the labor movement was the bone and sinew of social protest against the iniquities and inequities of industrial capitalism. It is, either solely or in conjunction with other rebellious elements, responsible for the weekend, for the eight-hour day, for the abolition of child labor, for minimum-wage and hour standards, for some semblance of democratic rights in the workplace and civil rights for excluded minorities, for progressive taxation, for protections against the safety and health hazards of industrial work, for old-age pensions, for low-cost public housing, and for health insurance. That is an impressive list of reforms, to be sure: ones that define much that is essential about modern life, a list that could easily be extended.

But the point is more than that list entails. The labor movement's presence in our public life embodied an alternative ethos to the reigning practice of free-market competitive individualism. It held out the prospect of social solidarity, of cooperative endeavor, of moral limits to the pursuit of self-interest. Moreover, when it was most robust—certainly in the decades before the Age of Acquiescence—the labor movement deployed real muscle and was recognized universally, even by its enemies, as a major player in the country's political life, a shaper of public policy, a force of resistance to be reckoned with, champion not only of its paid-up membership but of working people more generally.

Then it was killed, twice over. Labor was mortally wounded by direct assault, beginning with President Reagan's decision in 1981 to fire all the striking air-traffic controllers. His draconian act licensed American business to launch its own all-out attack on the right to organize, which continues to this day. In itself, however, resorting to coercion to deal with opposition hardly distinguishes the behavior of our own gilded elite from that of past ruling circles. If anything, we live in less savage times, at least here in the United States. More fatal by far was the advent of a new mode of capital accumulation starkly different from the industrial economy of the past century and more. Disaccumulation transformed the organized and self-conscious working class into a disaggregated pool of contingent labor, contract labor, temporary labor, and part-time labor, all in the interests of a new "flexible capitalism."

Even sweatshop labor has made a comeback. Back at the turn of the twentieth century, it seemed a noxious aberration. Known

during the first Gilded Age for offering irregular, lawless employment at substandard wages and for interminable hours, sweatshops were ordinarily housed in makeshift workshops: here today,
gone tomorrow. A sweatshop was an underground enterprise that
regularly absconded with its workers' paychecks and made chis-
eling them out of their due into an art form. What once seemed
abnormal no longer does. The planet's top corporations depend on
this system. They have thrived on it. Many of the newly flexible
proletarians working for Walmart, for auto-parts or construction-
company subcontractors, on the phones at direct-mail call centers,
behind the counters at mass-market retailers, and in the hotels and
casinos and restaurants of postindustrial America earn a dwindling
percentage of what they used to—or need to.

"Flexible capitalism" has ushered in a world of double or triple
workloads or, even worse, part-time work always shadowed by
indignity and fear, or worse yet, no work at all.

Ideologues gussied up this floating workforce by anointing it
"free agent" labor, a euphemism designed to flatter the free-market
homunculus in each of us. What a linguistic tour de force! Passions
that once ignited the New Left and the counterculture, their ardent
advocacy of self-empowerment, of "do your own thing," their *cri de
coeur* to stop the leviathan machinery of the corporate and state
bureaucracies purportedly crushing freedom and individualism,
were now a seduction to demobilize.

A rich historical irony indeed! A cold-eyed look suggests instead
that to be a "free agent" today is to be free of health care, pensions,
job security, security in every sense. It is another word for an existential form of downward mobility. Nor does this profile only apply
to workers of color, immigrants, or the less educated and skilled.
White-collar denizens of that Tomorrowland of "free agent" techies,
software engineers, and the like—not to mention a whole endangered species of middle management—live a precarious existence
under intense stress, chronically anticipating the next round of

layoffs. Once members of the "respectable middle class," they find themselves on the down escalator, descending into a despised state no one could mistake for the middle class. But, so far at least, they remain too intimidated by the experience to do much about it. After all, who wants to admit to being coddled? Why be enervated by Social Security, employer-funded pension and health plans, not to mention something as humiliating and infantilizing as national health insurance? Who needs the demeaning assurance of employment when you can, and rightly ought to, be out there on the frontier blazing a path of adventurous self-reliance? Dispossession under the guise of empowerment!

Deindustrialization eviscerated towns, cities, regions, and whole ways of life. It demoralized working people and gutted popular institutions that had mounted resistance (unions certainly, but also fraternal and ethnic associations, churches, and local political and civic alliances). Stripping away the tissues of modern working-class communal life and self-esteem stoked the fires of resentment, racism, and revanchist muscle-flexing. Here was the raw material for mean-spirited division, not solidarity.

Socialism also vanished as the sinews of solidarity atrophied. But why even talk of "socialism," for God's sake, in America of all places? It never amounted to much here even in its heyday. True! But everybody from presidents to sharecroppers, robber barons to radicals, preachers to cartoonists agreed that the "labor question" was the preeminent social question in American life from before the Civil War to the post–World War II era. That's because a whole society underwent two great transformations: the end of unfree labor and the advent of "wage slavery." These were shattering experiences. They raised fundamental questions about the relationship of labor and property, about wealth and poverty, about democracy in the political arena and autocracy in the factory. A slew of answers, some callous and reactionary, some ameliorative, some intransigently confrontational, roiled the currents of public life for generations. Socialism loomed on the far horizon of all these possible solutions to the "labor question." It might serve as a stand-in for a much more generalized yearning for an alternative: not merely an economic one but a way out of the tooth-and-claw way of life, the savagery and degradation industrial capitalism has visited on so many. Which is all to say that once upon a time, people believed in life after capitalism—or, more modestly, life under a domesticated capitalism subjected to the rigors of public scrutiny and collective discipline.

Seventy-five years ago, the universe of political possibility was still expanding. When the Great Depression spread from America to Europe and then back to the United States, many were ready to conclude that capitalism had failed. Socialists, of course, believed that. But what is worth remembering in our own end time is that even in America, a broadly anticapitalist culture—partly socialist, partly antitrust, partly populist—remained vibrant. It was ready to contemplate doing something more daring than rearranging the deck chairs on the Titanic. Even the Soviet Union still seemed an inspiring experiment in labor emancipation. Karl Marx was still a name to reckon with. Mainstream magazines like *The Atlantic*, *Harper's*, and *Scribner's* placed capitalism on trial and seriously contemplated the prospect of revolution. The vocabulary and grammar of the nation's political culture still made room for notions of class conflict, plutocracy, "malefactors of great wealth," and "the money trust." Speculators still gave off a sulfuric aroma. The far side of political debate embraced Upton Sinclair's "production for use" Democratic Party gubernatorial campaign to "End Poverty in California," Farmer-Labor Parties in the Midwest, and much more. In part, that's why Roosevelt and the New Deal even now raise the specter of "socialism" for some. John Maynard Keynes once excoriated money lust as "a somewhat dispiriting morbidity, one of those semi-criminal, semi-pathological propensities which one hands over with a shudder to the specialists in mental disease." Except for an occasional piety uttered in and out of church these days, such an attitude would be treated as embarrassingly muddle-headed by our temporizing techno-economic cognoscenti—or, for that matter, by much of today's popular culture. Back in the day, however, Keynes's moral-ethical criticisms didn't seem so remarkable. Challenges to unadulterated capitalism endured for some time into the postwar era, when the labor movement especially continued to drive the New Deal to the frontiers of social democracy. But then the "labor question" seemed increasingly less urgent, and less interesting, surely, to Americans not themselves involved in organized labor. In the toxic atmosphere created by McCarthyism, economic equality could be made to look like a version of Communism.

To be sure, there was a vigorous revival of egalitarian thinking during the sixties. But whole lines of thought—socialism, Keynesianism, economic populism—became endangered species, living, if at all, on the margins of public life. Losing these languages— the end of socialism in the generic sense—has been disabling, like losing a limb or a vital brain function. This withering away of the political imagination left American society defenseless against the predations of a new gilded elite.

The New World

Every day, at least since the worst of the meltdown crisis ended, the media puts on display the official schizoid thinking about the current predicament. On the one hand, recovery beckons: it's about to start, it's already started, the crisis is over. People in charge, from Obama on down, are quoted to this effect. Evidence accumulates mainly, however, in the financial sector where big banks have so much cash on hand that some have paid back the government its bailout money and others are begging to do so. Profits in the FIRE sector are back; lavish bonuses are back. Can a third Gilded Age be far behind?

But then there's the other kind of story, the one about the spreading misery of joblessness, evictions, homelessness, wage cuts, furloughs, brute amputations of social services in virtually every state and municipality, repossessions, bankruptcies, defaults. A tale of two cities!

It ought to be seen as appalling, arrogant, callous, myopic, credulous, and maybe most of all morally embarrassing to talk with a straight face of recovery amid all this. What can "recovery" possibly mean? Who exactly is recovering? What, after all, is the whole point of an economic recovery if it doesn't mean some improvement in general well-being? What is it that licenses this official complacency?

What allows for this is the long-term financialization of the economy. Among the many lamentable legacies of that profound economic makeover is a kind of moral and cultural numbness. Economic good health, the notion of prosperity itself, has for a long time now been identified with how things are faring for the banks, the insurance companies, the hedge and private-equity funds, and their law firms and legions of satellite enterprises. The ballyhooed prosperity of the second Gilded Age always rested on bubble economies. Inside the bubble an uglier truth lay concealed: shuttered factories and moribund unions; national health and educational indices that left the United States trailing badly behind much of the rest of the industrialized world; grotesque inequities in the distribution of wealth and power; shoddy and sometimes lethally neglected bridges and flood walls and slow-motion trains; a growing dependence on low-wage, sweated labor both immigrant and native born and millions toiling overseas; and, finally, what proved to be an insupportable burden of debt here at home.

Perhaps the greatest gulf separating the Great Depression from the Great Recession is the difference between the political economy born back then and the political economy of the last generation. The New Deal articulated the outlook of a new order based on mass consumption industrial capitalism. It gave birth to a high-wage labor market buoyed by strong unions, an expanding system of social welfare, and a regulatory regime to dismantle the old order's "money trust" and open the sluice gates of private capital and credit, thus "priming the pump" when the business cycle called for it.

Since then—beginning with the Reagan years—finance has triumphed over the New Deal industrial order. Financialization, or what some have called financial mercantilism, won out by gutting the industrial heartland. That is to say, the FIRE sector not only supplanted industry but grew at its expense and at the expense of the unions, high wages, and capital that used to flow into productive investment, as well as of the government regulation that comprised the understructure of New Deal capitalism. Think back to the days of junk bonds, leveraged buyouts, and asset stripping in the 1980s: what was getting bought out and stripped to support the exorbitant interest rates commanded by those high-risk bonds was the flesh and bone of a century and a half of American manufacturing.

Today, and for some long time now, our political economy has been driven by "I-banks," hedge funds, and the downward mobility and exploitation of casual labor. Meanwhile, industrial investment has been exported to the global South. This shift in the balance of power, the preeminence of finance in this new political economy, heavily accounts for (or is itself) the principal expression of the Age of Acquiescence. For decades now, the highest political circles have genuflected (and this has been a bipartisan ritual) to the financial oligarchy and its intellectuals.

Moreover, since at least the days of Michael Milken and Ivan Boesky, cultic admiration for the buccaneering financier and his pin-striped corporate equivalent has dominated our contemporary cultural life. If unromantic, practical-minded bourgeois society has a natural hero, it is the businessman. And when it gave itself over to worshipful fantasies about heroic financiers, the strong and the weak succumbed. For decades—until the recent debacle—the top dogs of business were lavishly celebrated in every highway and byway of popular culture, by our politicians and editorialists, by people of God and our leading academic thinkers, as if they were Napoleons. A whole rag-tag assortment of warrior metaphors drawn helter-skelter from disparate civilizations—from antiquity to medieval Europe, from the Wild West to futuristic, high-tech sci-fi superheroes—became attached to these men.

They were the titans, black knights and white knights, gunslingers, conquistadors, predators, barbarians at the gate. It was psychic-emotional acquiescence with a vengeance. Singled out for special reverence were amoral savagery, unbridled individualism, and, in the words of Theodore Dreiser's Nietzschean "financier," "I satisfy myself" egomania. Yeats put it like this: "We have fed the heart on fantasies/The heart has grown brutal from the fare." Under these cultural conditions, the power to resist diminished inversely with each new addition to the Forbes rich list, with each repeated bending of the knee before our "titans of finance."

Bending the knee suggests something aristocratic, but aristocrats don't exist anymore. And if one is hunting for the seeds of resistance that is not entirely a good thing.

Aristocrats went extinct rather recently, however. FDR was still denouncing "economic royalists" and "Tories of industry" at the height of the New Deal. The immemorial struggle against the counterrevolutionary aristocrat, portrayed as subverting the institutions of democratic life while piling up unearned riches, supplied the energy that powered American rebellion and reform for generations. In real life, the robber-baron industrialists and financiers of

Wall Street were no more aristocrats than my grandma from the shtetl. They were parvenus. But for their own good reasons, they actively conspired in this popular misconception by playing the aristocratic role for all it was worth: performing in *tableaux vivants* at gala balls dressed in aristocratic drag; cavorting in castles and villas they had transported stone by stone from France and Italy; showing off at the weddings of their daughters to the offspring of bankrupt European nobility; parading to New York's Metropolitan Opera in coaches driven by liveried servants and embossed with their family's "coat of arms," complete with hijacked insignia and fake genealogies that concealed their owners' homelier origins, these Social Register arrivistes enacted a great social charade as capitalists to the core camouflaged as aristocrats.

How that world has changed! Minus the oddball exception or two, the new tycoonery of the Age of Acquiescence does not fancy itself an aristocracy. It does not dress up like one or marry off its daughters to fortune-hunting European dukes and earls. On the contrary, its major figures regularly dress down in blue jeans and cowboy hats, affecting a down-home populism or nerdy dishevelment. However addicted to the paraphernalia of flamboyant excess they may be, the new capitalist elite does not pretend these are the insignia of ruling-class entitlement. Once upon a time, the lower orders aped the fashions and manners of their putative betters; today it's the other way around. Indeed, it is no longer even apt to talk of a "leisure class," since our moguls of the moment are workaholics, Olympians of merger-and-acquisition all-nighters.

We are talking here of the withering away and erasure of the very notion of ruling classes. It bears profound consequences, because having an aristocracy to kick around, even an ersatz one, can be politically empowering; lacking one is disorienting and generates anxiety because confronting the realities of power and wealth threatens the understructure of private property—a taboo. To acquiesce is soothing.

Although the economic and political throw-weight of our gilded elite is at least as great as that of its predecessors in the days of Morgan and Rockefeller, an American fear of moneyed aristocracy has subsided. Instead, from the Reagan era on, Americans have been captivated by businessmen who took on the role of rebel against a sclerotic corporate order and an ossified government bureaucracy that, together, they depicted as blocking access to a democracy of the bold. Often from the middling classes, lacking in social pedigree, the overnight elevation of people like Milken, Icahn, or "greed is healthy" Boesky flattered and confirmed a popular faith in the American dream. These irreverent new "revolutionaries," intent on overthrowing capitalism in the interests of capitalism, made fun of the men in suits.

Our corporate elite are much more adept than their Gilded Age predecessors were at playing the democracy game. The old "leisure class" was distinctly averse to politics. If they needed a tariff or tax break, they called upon their kept senator. Otherwise they didn't get much involved in mass party politics, which they saw as too full of uncontrollable ethnic machines, angry farmers, and the like. They relied on the federal judiciary, business-friendly presidents, constitutional lawyers, and public and private militias to protect their interests.

Beginning in the 1970s, our era's business elite became acutely more politically minded and impressively well organized, deeply penetrating all the pores of party and electoral democracy. They've gone so far as to craft strategic alliances with elements of what their predecessors—who might have blanched at the prospect—would have termed the "hoi polloi." Calls to dismantle the federal bureaucracy now carry a certain populist panache, while huffing and puffing about family values has proven a cheap date for a new gilded elite that otherwise couldn't care less. "Populist plutocracy" reconfigures the age-old problem of legitimacy, of the underlying sources of consent on the part of subordinate classes to the rule of tiny, wealthy elites. The plutocrat makes a convincing case that he or she is of the people, expresses their deepest desires and aspirations, and governs in their name. The *Herrenvolk* democracy over which the Bush administration presided epitomized this marriage of plutocratic corporate elitism to blue-collar cowboy populism,

What a wondrous transformation—a vanishing act, really. So disarming, so essential in the Age of Acquiescence. The rise of a populist plutocracy that comes to power with counterfeit credentials of its own manufacture, thereby contributing to its self-erasure as a ruling class: the final nonconfrontation.

South of these rarefied precincts, something similar and indigenously American was afoot, something that helped refresh the social legitimacy of freebooting capitalism. The ascendancy of our faux-revolutionary plutocrats was accompanied by media hosannas to the stock market as an everyday person's Oz. America's long infatuation with its own democratic-egalitarian ethos lent traction to this illusion. Horace Greeley's inspirational admonition to "go West, young man" echoed through all the channels of popular culture, especially in the 1990s—from cable TV and mass-circulation magazines to baseball stadiums and internet chatrooms. Only now Greeley's frontier of limitless opportunity had migrated back east to the stock exchange, across the broad terrain of entrepreneurial startups, and into the ether of virtual reality and the dot-com boom. The culture of money, released from all ancient inhibitions, enveloped the commons. It carried with it its own spiritual élan; freedom and the free market were joined at the hip.

Every sentient citizen is well aware of the triumph of free-market ideology that began during the Reagan era. Indeed, in the realm of ideas there was no more evident or potent sign of acquiescence to the rule of capital than militant hostility to all forms of government regulation and intervention into the economy. Some attribute this remarkable turnabout in the realm of ideas and public policy to the sheer persuasiveness of that bevy of think tanks, foundations, and magazines launched with great fervor and dedication by an ascendant right-wing political establishment. Give credit where credit is due.

To take root, however, ideas must fall on fertile ground. Without doubt that must be so in this case. After all, although free-market thinking and emotions are commonplace in the United States, they had to contest against New Deal–inspired views and sentiments that ran in a different direction: a worldview, so to speak, that had dominated the American political imagination for a half-century. But as the economy of the country shifted in favor of financialization, an older, free-market ideology found itself new constituents.

"Shareholder democracy" and the "ownership society" were admittedly more public-relations slogans than anything tangible. Nevertheless, during the second Gilded Age, half of all American families became investors in the stock market. Dentists and engineers, midlevel bureaucrats and college professors, storekeepers and medical technicians—people, that is, from the broad spectrum of middle-class life who once would have viewed the New York Stock Exchange with a mixture of awe, trepidation, and genuine distaste and warily kept their distance—instead jumped head first into the marketplace, carrying with them all their febrile hopes for social elevation.

"Flexible capitalism," moreover, did in fact open new frontiers of petty entrepreneurship. Indeed, the new "lean and mean" business machine demanded it. Megacorporations offloaded a range of functions once performed internally. Outsourcing, subcontracting, and licensing production, communication, distribution, marketing, and other activities to outside concerns meant that the universe of small and medium-sized businesses expanded considerably. Within the financial sector itself, all sorts of boutique consulting, accounting, legal, research, software, and other essential undertakings nourished free enterprise and its ideological celebration. So too the worlds of retailing and service/entertainment opened up space for smaller-scale specialty businesses, even as the "big-box" capitalism of Walmart loomed over the landscape.

Naturally enough, many have assumed that the triumph of free-market thinking and public policy were the work of our corporate establishment, its financial branch especially. Clearly, there is a great deal of truth to that. The relentless prodding and doling out of oodles of cash by "K Street" lobbyists is well recorded. But however much that world of big business resents this or that form of government regulation, it continues to depend heavily on government assistance—at every level of government—including contracts, tax abatements, subsidies, publicly funded research and development, and above all the advent of the "bailout state." For the country's peak corporations, free-market ideology is a tactic, not a philosophy of life.

Further down the food chain, however, among men and women who've struggled to create their own businesses (or dream of doing so), whose success at doing just that is an affirmation of their self-reliance, ingenuity, discipline, and moral stamina, conflating the free market with individual freedom is instinctive. Together with the popular infatuation with Wall Street, this is the soil in which seeds of counter–New Deal thought, the rebirth of unadulterated capitalism, took root. Here is where the old antitrust movement and other forms of middle-class resistance to big business went to die. Here too, in this social zone, liberty once again prevails only where property is at liberty to do what it will. Back to the future indeed!

Local uproars over the siting of a new Walmart would suggest that, on the contrary, an older antitrust, antimonopoly impulse survives. It does, but barely. Big-box capitalism, so characteristic of our "Age of Acquiescence," actually generates and reflects a very different, dissonant universe of political and cultural desires. The new consumer capitalism appeals first of all to instincts of individual and family material well-being, which may run up against calls for wider social solidarity, especially among the working poor. In the world of Walmart, low prices trump low wages.

Moreover, in its own everyday way, consumer culture channels desire into forms of expressive self-liberation. It feeds an atmosphere of invidious distinction and cravings for immediate gratification, something Tocqueville perceived long ago in its infancy. One casualty of consumer culture is the self-sacrifice and discipline once associated with the work ethic. Repressive that ethic undeniably was. Nonetheless, it once supplied the moral muscle and intellectual acuity that recognized the difference between productive labor and parasitism, between real and fictitious wealth. So too, nothing could be more corrosive of the kinds of social sympathy and connectedness that comprise the emotional infrastructure of collective resistance and rebellion. Instead, consumer culture cultivates a politics of style and identity focused on the rights and inner, psychic freedom of the individual, one not comfortable with an older ethos of social rather than individual liberation.

The financialization of the economy has immeasurably strengthened the syndrome. Perhaps the more profound tragedy ushered in by our highly leveraged economy, which rests on debt, is not the precarious condition of our financial institutions but rather the degree to which ordinary people are implicated in and dependent on what these "masters of the universe" have invented. It would be hard to exaggerate the extent to which the average American has become addicted to debt. Indeed, thanks to the diligence and ingenuity of the FIRE sector, the whole mass-consumption economy, not just the housing market, found itself underwater. And for that same reason, the reach of late twentieth-century consumer culture exceeded anything imagined when it all began. It penetrates the lowest depths of proletarian life: that is, its seductions inveigle even the working poor. Living day to day, one medical emergency, car breakdown, or child-care crisis away from bankruptcy, preyed upon by a vast industry of poverty profiteers (slumlords, check-cashers, loan sharks, and the like), the working poor nonetheless devote a sizeable percentage of their meager income to the fabricated fantasies of consumer culture.

And why not? In a world overrun with quests for psychic identity this is the arena that matters most, the one that promises so much by way of personal liberation and reinvention. It can, after all, ease the pain of an economy eating itself alive.

Consumer culture, leveraged by debt, has helped make the state of permanent wage labor, even a declining, downwardly mobile one, tolerable. Along with deindustrialization and the evisceration of the labor movement, it has left behind a demobilized populace. Grand narratives that tell some story of collective destiny— Redemption perhaps, or Enlightenment and Progress, or that one from the original Gilded Age about the Cooperative Commonwealth, or, later on, Proletarian Revolution—don't play well in this refashioned political theater. The culture of consumption may breed its own discontents. But the dying left, still tethered to the sentiments of social solidarity, cannot feed on these discontents.

Even the native taste for populist insouciance has soured, grown perverse. Populism has always been a house of contradictions, a bewildering network of cross-cutting political emotions, ideas, and institutions. It has oscillated between a desire to transform and so create a new order of things and a desire to restore a yearned-for (or imagined) old order. For decades, stretching from the nineteenth century through the era of the New Deal, it mobilized emphatically, if not exclusively, against corporate capitalism. But during the Age of Acquiescence it drifted rapidly rightward, becoming ever more restorationist and ever less transformative, ever more anticollectivist and ever less anticapitalist, more worried about threats to traditional ways of life, less so about the economic presumptions, power, and privileges of ruling circles. What used to be subordinate themes in an older form of populism—religious orthodoxy, national chauvinism, phobic racism, and the politics of fear and paranoia—have occupied center stage in our time.

Republican strategists have connived at this creation since the days of Richard Nixon's "silent majority" and the carefully orchestrated hard-hat anger directed at the cultural elitism of "limousine liberals" and long-haired, pot-smoking antiwar radicals. The Democratic Party made its contribution to fostering this populism of the right by abandoning its own heritage of economic justice in favor of neoliberalism's worship of the market, the bond market in particular. As the "party of the working man" veered right in the direction of "Republicanism lite," it had less and less to offer a working population wracked by the insecurities as well as the economic and social decline of our disaccumulating, finance-first new order of things. A smoldering sense of dispossession—cultural as well as economic—fed a conservative populism that committed an act of double counterrevolution: against the New Deal welfare state and against the racial, gender, and cultural upheavals that turned the world upside down in the sixties.

Tea Party insurgents are the latest incarnation of these hot-blooded emotions. They remind us that the moral self-righteousness, sense of dispossession, antielitism, revanchist patriotism, racial purity, and "Don't Tread on Me" militancy that were always at least part of the populist admixture are alive and kicking. For all the fantastical paranoia that often accompanies such emotional stances, they speak to real experiences—for some, of economic anxiety, insecurity, and loss; for others, of deeper fears of personal, cultural, political, or even national decline and moral disorientation.

Anticapitalism, however, has receded among partisans of the Tea Party as for its conservative populist predecessors, sounding a muted note now and then but carrying no force. Though outrage at the bank bailout did propel the Tea Party explosion, anti-big-business sentiment is now a pale shadow of what once was a populist staple. Alongside an exalted rhetoric about threats to liberty lies a sour, narrowminded defensiveness against any possible threat to income redistribution or other ways of confronting the brute disproportions of power and wealth. The state, not the corporation, has become the enemy of choice. One might say of this new populism with its angry belligerence that it is hardly acquiescent, but nonetheless serves the larger purposes of the Age of Acquiescence.

After the dolorous 2010 midterm elections, a certain gloomy apprehensiveness about the stunning triumph of Tea Party resentments has settled in. Should it? The capitalism of the "second Gilded Age" may now face a systemic crisis. How long can a society tolerate cannibalizing itself? (It is polite to call this *austerity*.) Arguably, the global economy, including its American branch, is increasingly a sweatshop economy. There is no denying this brute fact in Thailand, Vietnam, Central America, Bangladesh, and dozens of other countries and regions that serve as platforms for primitive forms of capital accumulation.

Here at home, something analogous has been happening, but with an ironic difference and bearing within it a new historic opening. One might call it the unhorsing of the middle classes. "Flexible capitalism" joins the dispossession of the middle class to the superexploitation of millions who never laid claim to that status. Many of these sweated workers are women, laboring away as home health-care aides, in the food-services industry, in meat processing plants, at hotels and restaurants, because the arithmetic of "flexible accumulation" demands two workers rather than one to add up to a livable family wage. Millions more are immigrants, legal as well as undocumented, from all over the world. They live, virtually defenseless, in a twilight underworld of illegality and prejudice.

So too, however powerful they remain, our gilded elites have suffered a severe loss of credibility. Legitimacy is a precious possession: once lost, it's not easily retrieved. Today, the myth of the "ownership society" confronts the reality of the "foreclosure society."

Might these developments augur the end of the Age of Acquiescence? No one can know. Yet anger and resentment over insecurity, downward mobility, exploitation, second-class citizenship, and the ill-gotten gains of our Gilded Age mercenaries and their political enablers rippled the waters during the midterm elections of 2006 and of course since then. As hopes for real recovery dwindle, as the prospect of prolonged decline darkens the horizon, as the good times continue to roll for the "connected," will enough become, finally, enough?

Anger and resentment, however, do not by themselves comprise a visionary alternative. Moreover, nasty competition over diminishing economic opportunities can just as easily inflame simmering racial and ethnic antagonisms. Nor is the Democratic Party, however restive, a likely vehicle (at least as presently constituted) for a new age of collective resistance and responsibility. Much more will have to happen outside the precincts of electoral politics by way of mass movement building to translate today's smoke signals of resistance into something more muscular and enduring. Thus we are talking here as well of a moral reformation to undo the legacy of savage incivility and self-regard that has scarred our Age of Acquiescence.

Those who know the nation's history also know that stranger things have happened. No one alive in 1932 could have reasonably predicted what the country would look like a mere three years later. Will a now unimaginable newness soon take shape again?

Part 3

Populist Plutocracy

9. The Limousine Liberal's Family Tree

What do Glenn Beck, Henry Ford, Father Coughlin, Joseph McCarthy, Barry Goldwater, George Wallace, and Spiro Agnew have in common? They are, or were, all warriors in a peculiarly American version of the class struggle. A motley crew otherwise—a TV and radio shock jock, a Midwestern carmaker, a Detroit priest, an alcoholic senator from Wisconsin, a "maverick" senator from Arizona, a Southern demagogue, a dishonored and deposed vice president—each in his own way took up arms against the ruling class. For the last half-century or so, the representative figure of that ruling class has been widely recognized under a memorable alias: the "limousine liberal."

When the New Deal order first began to fall apart at the seams, a political apparatchik from Brooklyn named Mario Procaccino won the Democratic Party's nomination for New York City mayor in 1969 after a nasty primary campaign. His foe on the Liberal Party line was the sitting mayor, John Lindsay, once upon a time a

---

An earlier version of this chapter appeared in *Raritan*, vol. 31, no. 1, Summer 2011.

congressman representing the "silk-stocking district" on Manhattan's wealthy East Side. Procaccino coined the term "limousine liberal" to characterize what he and his largely white ethnic following from the city's "outer boroughs" considered the repellent hypocrisy of elitists like Lindsay: well-heeled types who championed the cause of the poor, especially the black poor, but had no intention of bearing the cost of doing anything about their plight. They were insulated from any real contact with poverty, crime, and the everyday struggle to get by, living in their exclusive neighborhoods, sending their kids to private schools, sheltering their capital gains and dividends from the taxman, and getting around town in limousines, not subway cars. Not about to change the way they lived, they wanted everybody else to change: to have their kids bused to school, to shoulder the tax burden of an expanding welfare system, to watch the racial and social makeup of their neighborhoods turn upside down. These self-righteous rich folks couldn't care less, Procaccino declaimed, about the "small shopkeeper, the homeowner ... They preach the politics of confrontation and condone violent upheaval." Limousine liberals have been with us ever since. In fact, they were part of the political landscape decades before Procaccino came up with his *bon mot*.

Today, Glenn Beck echoes similar complaints. He excoriates progressive "elitists" who detest, and work to undermine, the protections invented by the Founding Fathers to safeguard "individual natural rights [especially property rights] as the unchangeable purpose of government." Fancying himself an amateur historian, Beck has taken us back to the prehistory of the limousine liberal during the turn-of-the-century Progressive era. Although quick to distance himself from conspiracy-mongers, in describing this original embodiment of the limousine liberal Beck feels compelled to acknowledge that "there's a point when conspiracy is not a conspiracy; it's just true." Beck and Tea Party partisans everywhere have pledged a war to the finish against this strange species of elitism.

Strange indeed! Here in the homeland we don't easily resort to the language of class struggle. Normally it offends true Americans like Beck, who think of class warfare (if they think of it at all) as alien, something they have in Europe or had in Russia but certainly not here in the New World, where it was providentially banned from the beginning. Still, Beck and his forebears do talk this talk, getting their hackles up over an upper-crust claque that has been running the country off the rails for nearly a century. Glenn Beck is more a fabulist than a historian; he makes up stories, omits what is inconvenient, tells half-truths, and specializes in a kind of lachrymose vitriol. Nevertheless, he's onto something—as was Procaccino.

First, limousine liberals comprise a different kind of elite, something new in the long sweep of time. Elites, ruling castes and classes, aristocracies, and the like normally defend the existing order of things. The limousine liberal, on the contrary, is an agent of change. Moreover, the "limousine liberal" epithet has evolved as a peculiarly slippery, elastic category. Over time it has come to embrace a great deal more than wealthy, cosmopolitan elitists like Lindsay. The stigma has attached itself with ever greater force to a heterogeneous milieu of government bureaucrats, social engineers, policy wonks, politically connected Ivy League academics, and mainstream-media savants; a whole "new class," the comfortably situated and socially liberal whose contempt for working- and lower-middle-class folkways and for conventional morality is exceeded only by their own self-regard and appetite for the next new thing. One might call this version of limousine liberalism a ruling class and its entourage. However warped this picture, it resonates with recent history.

Second, this species of elitism arrived on the scene just about when Beck says it did, around the turn of the twentieth century. That was when corporate capitalism supplanted family capitalism and the peculiar form of class struggle Beck alludes to began.

Though they are from the same genus, family and corporate capitalism nonetheless do not possess identical economic and cultural DNA. Once the organic and hallowed connection between private property accumulation and the family is severed, anything is possible. Anonymous, impersonal, and amoral, corporate capital is radical. In the end, nothing, no matter how ancient or revered, can stand in its way in its irresistible quest to accumulate. It may profit from racial segregation or gender discrimination, for example, but it does not depend on those arrangements to exist, and may at any particular historical moment find they get in the way. Its commitment to the family, to religious and traditional moral values, is contingent, subject always to the higher mathematics of the bottom line. As John Maynard Keynes, otherwise a high priest of limousine liberalism, once put it: "Modern capitalism is absolutely irreligious, without internal union, without much public spirit ... a mere congeries of possessors and pursuers."[1]

In family capitalism, by comparison, property and marriage are bound together to make up what we refer to as the bourgeoisie. This union creates conflicting imperatives: family capitalism is eager to grow, but only within the circumscribed confines of the propertied, morally disciplined individual and the dynastic household. At every concrete historical moment, entrepreneurs—or that vast population of people who aspire to entrepreneurship—attach their pecuniary behavior, accomplishments, and desires to distinct local communities, regional connections, family aspirations, ideals of manhood, specific products and forms of workmanship, concrete historical traditions, religious values, comforting racial or ethnic enclaves, and ultimately a whole social universe.

Around the turn of the twentieth century—Beck's primordial moment—the antitrust movement waged war against the new

---

[1] John Maynard Keynes, *Essays in Persuasion* (London: Macmillan, 1931).

corporate order. Hostility to the trust began during the Gilded Age and was part of a group of movements directed against finance and corporate capitalism. Populism was the most celebrated. Like all populism since, it expressed a sense of violation: "Don't Tread on Me." It blanketed rural America from the cotton South to the grain-growing Great Plains and the Rocky Mountain West. The Populist Party indicted high finance and the trusts for destroying the livelihoods and the way of life of independent farmers, handicrafters, and small business owners, the atomic nuclei of family capitalism. It attacked big business as well for subverting the foundations of democracy by capturing all three branches of government and turning them into instruments of rule by a new plutocracy. And it condemned the amorality and decadence of Wall Street, the way the new corporate order encouraged the worship of money for its own sake and corroded the moral and religious armature protecting the family. Tragic uprisings of the dispossessed, the Populists, the anti-trust ferment, and movements of the middling classes in town and cities everywhere yearned to restore a society of independent producers, a world without a proletariat and without trusts. This was a familiar society of Christian virtues, hard work, self-reliance, family continuity, and a rough equality grounded in a smallholder competence. Yet Populists and others also envisioned a new world, something transformative, a "cooperative commonwealth" that would escape the barbaric competitiveness and exploitation of free-market capitalism.

All of that, however, is far from what Beck is alluding to. Still, there is kinship, a real genealogy that joins the animosities, cultural forebodings, and economic anxieties of the Tea Party to this older universe of family capitalism under siege. Henry Ford is that missing link. Beck's bitter antielitism is a distant echo of the car manufacturer's bizarre and enormously popular post–World War I jeremiad against finance capitalism. Its emotional logic is still alive and well today.

Ford, who was well on his way to becoming an American folk hero by World War I, had identified the enemy: limousine liberalism *avant la lettre*. The automobile magnate was the country's iconic family capitalist. That may seem odd. After all, he employed tens of thousands in dozens of sophisticated factories, some the size of several football fields. But the Ford Motor Company was a privately held family firm whose founder meant to keep it that way. Like so many anonymous entrepreneurs before him in midsized cities and towns across Middle America, Ford revered the independent family-owned enterprise as a *point d'honneur* as well as a source of patri-lineal continuity. Amid a society increasingly overtaken by gigantic, impersonal corporations run by faceless men in suits—managers, not owners—Ford stood out as an outsized emblem and champion of an imperiled way of life. He was family capitalism's superhero, as close to a romantic figure as the countinghouse spirit of the bour-geoisie is likely to produce. He was as good as it gets.

Ford hailed from, loved, and in many people's minds personified all the cherished virtues of small-town America. He was a lover, but also a hater. Especially he hated Jews, bankers, and Bolsheviks. This was not a case of serial hatreds. Rather, it was a composite animos-ity in which that trio of Jews, bankers, and Bolsheviks in collabora-tion loomed up, in Ford's eyes, as a singular threat to the continued existence of the American Volk, to that whole integrated universe of private property, the patriarchal family, and God—the bedrocks of bourgeois society.

Starting in 1920, Ford caused to be published a series of articles in the *Dearborn Independent* (a newspaper he controlled) under the general rubric of "The International Jew." The series ran for more than a year and was reissued as a book that became a best seller. Anti-Semitism had always been part of American life; Ford wasn't breaking new ground there. What particularly exercised him was the power of finance capitalism. After all, elite circles of investment bankers had midwifed the birth of the publicly traded giant corporation around the turn of the century, and those great combines were now managed and directed by emissaries from the banks. Nor was their overwhelming influence limited to the continental United States. International finance, which Ford thought to be dominated by, if not exclusively limited to, Jewish investment-banking houses, plotted to overturn all of Western civilization.

Ford's "The International Jew" might be thought of as the folk Marxism of the middling classes. It was a call to arms against a promiscuously composed cabal. Bankers, Bolsheviks, and Jews were all by their natures stateless, owing allegiance to no particular people, nation, or settled way of life. Jews were the world's permanent sojourners, outcasts, and usurers, unloved everywhere, loyal to no one. Bankers were parasites living off the productive enterprise of others. Their loyalty was to money, which knew no homeland. Bolsheviks boasted of their internationalism as well as their atheism and sexual abandon. Moreover, most of the Bolsheviks were, so it was widely rumored, Jews. For the carmaker this was a *ménage à trois* made in hell.

What lent Ford's ravings such grit was the way he managed to connect disparate anxieties about the changing nature of American life to the nefarious doings of this cabal. Now it was hardly news to the heartland that Wall Street bankers were and always had been parasites and speculators, living off the productive labor of others, including small and medium-sized businesses (Ford himself managed for many years to avoid entangling alliances with the banking fraternity he despised). Nor was it a revelation that Jews were, as Ford argued, biologically driven to become moneylenders, and merciless ones at that. Likewise, citizens of Middle America had been experiencing night sweats about communists since the Paris Commune of 1871. The Bolshevik triumph in Russia only confirmed what they already knew: alien forces threatened the basic foundations of bourgeois life, specifically private property, the patriarchal family, and the nation-state.

But how fiendishly clever of these banking conspirators to have enlisted the help of their inveterate class enemies! This was more than a piece of tactical ingenuity or a marriage of convenience; in Ford's eyes, they were soulmates. That was his great discovery and the heart of the matter. It was the moment the limousine liberal was first conceived: the ruling class as subversive. What Ford feared, what he wanted to alert his countrymen about, was a profound existential threat.

Wall Street, in league with a godless Kremlin, was the fount of a pervasive hedonism that mocked all that the heartland held dear while driving it out of existence. Ford's articles ranged widely across the terrain of modern life in a painstaking effort to unearth the hidden pathways linking this satanic conspiracy to every Sodom and Gomorrah of postwar America. Here they were, peddling pornography through their control of the movie business. There they were, extending tentacles into the criminal underworld, running vast stock frauds to loot the innocent. Determined to undermine what was left of the nation's self-discipline, they saturated the country with bootleg gin. Masterminds of the publishing industry, they arranged for an endless flow of sex and sensationalism in newspapers, magazine, and pulp novels. They fed the nation the same titillating diet of cheap thrills and sexual innuendo in one scandalous Broadway production after another, thanks to their backstage domination of the Great White Way. "Jewish jazz," bankrolled by the same circles, was on its way to becoming the national music, its mood and rhythms an open invitation to the lewd and lascivious. Encouraging every form of vanity and self-indulgence, pandering to and promoting an ethos of immediate gratification, the cabal was the incubator of a modernist debauch.

There was something surpassingly odd about Ford's indictment. He was the fabricator of perhaps the single most seductive carrier of the new culture of consumerism, the automobile. Yet he voiced the anxieties of a Victorian middle-class milieu about the inexorable logic of modern life: godless communism plus godless capitalism, ushering in the age of nihilism. This devilish dilemma had always been lurking there. How was it possible to domesticate the desire for individual acquisitiveness without limit that capitalism in any form, after all, encouraged? For a long century the answer had been simple: self-denying accumulation on behalf of the family and its future, combined with a religious faith that sanctioned that behavior. Now that answer seemed to be losing its grip.

The specter of a sinister league of bankers and Bolsheviks would remain an undercurrent of popular political unease from the 1920s forward. Profiles of the leading protagonists changed over time. Jews, bankers, and Bolsheviks slowly receded from view or transformed into pointy-headed corporate and government bureaucrats, effete intellectuals, silk-stocking politicians, social engineers, cultural nihilists, one-worlders, latte-sipping yuppies: in other words, a menagerie of the wellborn and well-bred gone to seed, now acolytes of a way of life in which "all that is solid melts into air." They were running (and ruining) the country.

Ford's conspiratorial sense of history—an active element of populist cosmology long before the automaker arrived on the scene—has remained a live idea ever since. But during the 1930s a portentous shift began in Conspiracy Central, from Wall Street and the City of London to Moscow ... and even New Deal Washington. Anticommunism, already a vital element of Ford's politics of fear and paranoia, was an especially toxic ingredient in the populist politics of family capitalism.

Demagogues like Father Coughlin, the "radio priest" from the Church of the Little Flower outside Detroit, invoked Ford-like images of fat-cat parasites, gold-obsessed Eastern bankers, usurious Wall Street Jews, and their red revolutionary allies. Coughlin won legions of impassioned followers among small-town business owners and farmers, the working and "lace-curtain" Irish-Catholic lower middle classes, aspiring entrepreneurs, and others who resented "the high priests of finance," as he called them. What these middling classes feared and resented was the disruption of local economies and traditional social mores by intrusive outsiders: giant corporations and a self-aggrandizing big government, poking its nose into matters like education, race, and family relations. Theatrical and bombastic, Coughlin likened the New Deal to "a broken-down Colossus straddling the harbor of Rhodes, its left leg standing on ancient Capitalism and its right mired in the red mud of communism."[1]

Like Ford, the radio priest ranted about an incongruous conspiracy of Bolsheviks and bankers whose aim was to betray America. He would eventually add a tincture of anti-Semitism to his jeremiads against this Wall Street cabal. Moreover, his growing sympathy for Nazism was not so shocking. Fascism, after all, had its roots partly in a European version of populism, nurtured by a post–World War I disgust with the selfishness, incompetence, and decadence of cosmopolitan elites as well as a bellicose racial nationalism. Coughlin's followers loathed big business and big government, even though big government (back then, anyway) was taking on big business. For these middling folks, "Don't Tread on Me" meant a defense of local economies, traditional moral codes, and established ways of life that seemed endangered by national corporations as well as by the state bureaucracies that began to proliferate under the New Deal. Coughlin's radio addresses (many millions listened, spellbound) and his newspaper *Social Justice* were filled with references to the "forgotten man," an image first invoked by FDR on behalf of the working poor.

Kindred images would resurface in the years ahead, especially during the tumultuous 1960s in Nixon's appeals to "the silent majority," and more recently in the Tea Party's wounded sense of

---

1 Coughlin quoted by David H. Bennett, *Demagogues in the Depression* (New Brunswick, NJ: Rutgers University Press, 1969), p. 40.

exclusion. From its inception, "forgotten man" populism positioned the middling classes against the organized power blocs of modern industrial society: big business, big labor, and big government. But in the era following World War II, the movement's center of gravity shifted decisively away from the world of business and finance, away from matters of economic justice, and instead directed its ire at the cultural pretensions and moral perfidy of the nation's new elite. This distinctive form of populism became ever more restorationist and ever less transformative, even more anticollectivist and ever less anticapitalist. What were subordinate themes in the old-style populism—religious rectitude, racial and ethnic homogeneity, national chauvinism, and the politics of paranoia—now sounded the dominant note.

Wisconsin's senator Joseph McCarthy, who found much of his following among the same social groupings attracted to Coughlin, came within a whisker of baptizing this peculiar elite with the epithet invented twenty years later by Mario Procaccino. McCarthyism and the Cold War marked a decisive turning point in the transmigration of economic to cultural populism. In the global war against Communism, after all, hostile talk about capitalism was virtually verboten. McCarthy emphasized instead the mortal dangers of the New Deal state, infected at its root with Communist-inflected collectivism. The archetypal enemy looked the same—Anglo-Saxon Ivy League financiers, bankers with "grouse-hunting estates in Scotland," and New Deal government commissars: an aristocracy of destruction. It was the grouse-hunting, however, not the economic overlordship, that aroused McCarthyite resentment. The domestic Cold War, whose real enemy was the New Deal much more than it was the Soviet Union, left many casualties. It committed a kind of cultural genocide, purging and proscribing whole families of languages—not only populism—whose deep grammar had once interrogated capitalist injustice, exploitation, and amorality.

Here was a colossal irony. Those sites, which more than any others had for generations inflamed the anticapitalist and populist emotions of millions, those bastions of good order and reaction— Wall Street, Harvard, the corporate boardroom, and the white-shoe law firm—now incited a feverish uproar over the threat of revolutionary upheaval, of Communism abroad and subversion at home. McCarthy went right for the heart of the WASP "establishment." How galling that these traitors who hailed from the most privileged precincts of American society, beneficiaries of the country's great wealth, best education, highest social honors, and most eminent public offices, worked to undermine the country that had treated them so well.

McCarthyism was no marginal persuasion. It gripped the Republican Party's political imagination. Republicans denounced the Marshall Plan as a "bold socialist blueprint." Robert Taft, leader of its Midwest conservative wing, vented his general resentment against those eastern Wall Street internationalists in control of the party, claiming, "Every Republican candidate for president since 1936 has been nominated by Chase Bank." McCarthy referred to Secretary of State Dean Acheson as "this pompous diplomat in striped pants" with his "phony British accent," parading about with his "cane, spats, and tea-sipping little finger." Warnings went out that men like John McCloy, US High Commissioner for Germany, "with a top hat and silk handkerchief" (who would indeed later go on to run Chase Manhattan Bank), were ill-equipped to deal with the worldwide Communist conspiracy because they belonged to it.

Thus, long before Mario Procaccino penned his one claim to fame, the transmutation of America's ruling class was well under way—at least in the realm of popular fantasy. And, increasingly, that class's most inflammatory features were defined by its social and cultural attributes. Its economic privileges and superordinate positions atop the country's peak corporations and government departments were now taken for granted.

Barry Goldwater's insurgency inside the Republican Party legitimated what had, up to the 1960s, remained a marginal politics. Was the Arizona senator a rebel? Yes, if you keep in mind his condemnation of the too-liberal elite running the Republican Party. In his eyes they represented a clubby world of Ivy League bankers, media lords, and "one-worlders." Above all, Goldwater was an avatar of today's politics of limited government. He was an inveterate foe of all forms of collectivism, including unions and the welfare state—not to mention his opposition to civil rights legislation. He might be called the original "tenther"—that is, a serial quoter of the Tenth Amendment to the Constitution, which reserves for the states all powers not expressly granted to the federal government. For Goldwater and others after him, such federal intrusions simultaneously upset the racial order and transgressed the rights of private property.

As the Goldwater opposition sank its grassroots into the lush soil of the Sunbelt and the South, its desire to restore an older order of things was palpable. The senator's followers were quintessentially middle-class congregants of the church of family capitalism. Yet they were oddly positioned rebels. Unlike the declining middling sorts attracted to Coughlin and others in the 1930s, they came mainly from a newly rising middle class, nourished by the mushrooming military-industrial complex: technicians and engineers, real-estate developers, middle managers, and midlevel entrepreneurs who resented the heavy hand of big government while remaining remarkably dependent on it. They could be described as reactionary modernists for whom liberalism had become the new Communism. How shocking when this Arizona "maverick" won the Republican nomination in a knock-down brawl with the party's presidium, led by New York governor Nelson Rockefeller, which had run the party until then.

During the late 1960s, Alabama's segregationist governor, George Wallace, and President Nixon's ambassador to America's "silent majority," Vice President Spiro Agnew, accelerated this transformation of economic populism into cultural populism. They ratcheted up the invective against what the alliterative Agnew labeled the "nattering nabobs of negativism" and "pusillanimous pussyfooters," who challenged the American war in Vietnam. Wallace inveighed against gilded know-it-alls using their levers of power over the government, media, judicial system, universities, and philanthropic foundations to upset the prevailing order of things: "Do we have an elitist government?" he asked. "They've decreed it's good for the people to do certain things. And even though the people don't like to do it, they must do it because this superelite group is so determined." The governor was addressing, as he put it, "the man in the textile mill," the "barber and beautician," "the little businessman."

Patricians like William Buckley denounced this kind of politics as "country-and-Western Marxism," creeping in from the hinterland. Buckley had a point. Wallace was all at once an antielitist, a populist, a racist, a chauvinist, and tribune of the politics of revenge and resentment. He appealed to an expanded universe of family capitalism that embraced the upper reaches of the white working class. He defended the hard-hit American heartland more by hailing its ethos of hard work and "family values" than by proposing concrete measures to assure its economic well-being. Wallace railed against the arrogance of "pointy-headed" Washington bureaucrats, the indolence of "welfare queens," and the impiety, immorality, and disloyalty of privileged, pot-smoking college students—all the camp followers of limousine liberalism.

Precariously positioned blue-collar workers felt beleaguered by taxes, inflation, and the apparent collapse of the existing order of things. They hunkered down to defend the value of their mortgaged homes, the autonomy of their local schools, and their ethnically and racially familiar neighborhoods. This was a proletarian version of family capitalism that enlisted race as another medium of class struggle. When Wallace ran in the Democratic Party primaries in 1968, he polled big numbers not only in the South but also in industrial states like Michigan, Indiana, and Wisconsin. At the height of the 1968 campaign, a crowd of 20,000 attended a Wallace rally at a sold-out Madison Square Garden in New York City.

"Country-and-Western Marxism," Buckley's dismissal notwithstanding, showed up elsewhere in the ranks of conservative populism. Procaccino's paisanos from Brooklyn's Italian-American Civil Rights League believed that "oil, steel, insurance, and the banks run this country." Around the same time, Louise Day Hicks, the heroine of the antibusing movement in Boston, explained that she was engaged in a struggle between "rich people in the suburbs" on the one hand, and "the working man and woman, the rent payer, the homeowner, the law-abiding, tax-paying, decent-living, hard-working, forgotten American" on the other. In the late 1970s Paul Weyrich, a godfather of the populist right, observed, "Big corporations are as bad as Big Government ... They are in bed together."[1] Weyrich was right, of course. But by this late date no conservative rebel was seriously proposing an assault on Wall Street and the Fortune 500. Instead, by the 1980s, the most intimate matters were at stake in electoral politics: the raising of children, relations between men and women, neighborhood turf, God, and the racial status quo. What was once a marginally suspect language of opposition, periodically surfacing and submerging, has become a vital part of our political grammar and vocabulary in the decades since the Reagan Revolution.

Tea Party leaders communicate this message of elite deceit, disloyalty, and decadence to their heartland constituents today in ways that were first enunciated nearly a century ago—as Glenn Beck and others suggest. So, for example, the Obama

---

1 Paul Weyrich quoted in Alan Pell Crawford, *Thunder on the Right* (New York: Pantheon, 1980), pp. 213–14.

administration, infested from head to toe with investment bankers and corporate CEOs, is alleged to be hellbent on cooking up some version of redistributive "socialism." Rand Paul's explicit, if fleeting, opposition to the Civil Rights Act of 1964 was simultaneously about the inviolability of smallholder property and about race.

A potent emotional logic is offered up to explain this penchant for subversion on the part of the privileged classes. Their pampered lives sap their wills and cut them off from the grassroots patriotism of more common folks. Their cosmopolitan lifestyle exposes them to an armada of cultural viruses that eat away at that bedrock individualism that made the country strong. Their urbanity implies a kind of impiety, a social and psychological dissipation, and a loss of frontier vigor. Concealed behind the impersonal exterior of the bureaucratic welfare state, this new mandarinate of upheaval cultivates a primal urge to make the free but self-disciplined individual, the hero of family capitalism, dependent on the lockstep rhythms of the leviathan state.

Oddly enough, actually existing specimens of the limousine liberal have become scarcer and scarcer. Precious few "captains of industry" or "titans of finance" show up on the barricades of social and cultural upheaval. Indeed, the core of American big business and finance has, for a generation, tended (although not invariably) to line up on the side of conservative fiscal and monetary policy and deregulation. But liberal capitalism, which is really a bipartisan persuasion, has no objection to the social and cultural reforms of the 1960s—racial and gender equality, for example. The modern American corporation, as a matter of sound business policy, is among the more politically correct institutions in the country. The capitalism of the *Volk* holds no intrinsic appeal for the avowedly multicultural corporation (except perhaps as a marketing strategy). Capital's logic is strictly commercial, an arithmetic of cold cash, not morals.

But corporate political correctness resonates with the self-righteous and social liberalism of what John Kenneth Galbraith characterized as the "New Class"—deracinated, upwardly mobile professionals, technocrats, midlevel "financial engineers," new-media makers, and liberal academics. They don't drive around town in limousines or make strategic decisions for corporate America. They may not even be shareholders. But they share a meritocratic worldview and a disdain for all those traditions and vestigial institutions standing in the way of individual self-empowerment and self-gratification. Partisans of political correctness, this "New Class" doesn't think of challenging the foundations of the political economy. Rather, they themselves become the target of the morally appalled populism, arising from the cultural terrain of family capitalism.

Limousine liberalism has lived a long time in the American imagination—from Ford to Beck. It has risen and subsided without any inherent connection to the ups and downs of the economy, although it may be inflamed by either. Many once assumed that after the great antitrust movement was defeated in the earlier part of the twentieth century, family capitalism had breathed its last. This turned out not to be the case. During World War II, the war economy incubated new industries and new companies in such newly industrialized regions as Texas, California, and the Southwest. New entrepreneurial fortunes piled up but did not necessarily carry with them political access or social prestige. This stoked resentment among a milieu of midsized-business owners who, in style, language, and emotional tone, were much closer to their plebian roots than they were to the transatlantic mores of upper-class professionals. These new adventures into the free market hated the snobbish exclusivity, the air of Eastern sophistication, and the gratuitous, self-serving, tax-laden sympathies for the lower orders evinced by liberal mandarins of change.

Is the Tea Party the latest expression of this family capitalism at the barricades? Its preoccupation with fiscal probity and especially its obsession with minimizing its own tax burden and starving the welfare state are certainly suggestive. When they get their dander up about the Wall Street bailout, Tea Party partisans are angrier about the government interfering with the remorseless but irreproachably just operations of the free market than they are with the felonious greed of financiers. Moreover, it is noteworthy that heavyweight funders of Tea Party organizations tend to come from the ranks of newly minted robber-baron family dynasties—the Koch brothers are a prime example. But things are messier than that. The movement is too protean and chaotic and fed by too many cultural, social, and religious subcurrents to be reduced to family-capitalism redux.

For the country's Fortune 500, free-market ideology and the conflation of freedom with limited government is a tactic, not a philosophy of life. That elite circle depends heavily on government assistance, including contracts, tax abatement, subsidies, publicly funded research, and above all a robust "bailout state."

Further down the food chain, however, among men and women who have struggled to create their own businesses (or dream of doing so) and whose success at doing just that is an affirmation of their self-reliance, ingenuity, discipline, and stamina, conflating the free market with individual freedom is instinctive. They too, in perhaps less direct ways, are deeply dependent on an array of local, state, and federal government programs and bureaucracies. But this dependence doesn't enter into their calculus. Nor can they any longer face up to the disorienting fact that the "permissiveness" they condemn originates, first of all, in the corporate boardroom, the headquarters of consumer capitalism. Instead, they scout the landscape for enemies that threaten their way of life. There are many: "illegal" immigrants, perhaps, or the morally dissolute, or those living on the dole—including the "dole" of public employment. All of these and more may be enlisted in the army captained by "limousine liberals." And to that foe, before all others, Glenn Beck says: "Don't tread on me."

Our native taste for populist insouciance has soured, grown perverse. Tea Party insurgents remind us that the moral self-righteousness, sense of dispossession, antielitism, revanchist patriotism, and desire for racial purity that were always present in populism's house of contradictions are alive and kicking. For all the fantastical paranoia that often accompanies such emotional stances, they speak to real experiences—for some, of economic anxiety, insecurity, and loss; for others, of deep feelings of personal, cultural, political, and even national decline and moral disorientation. For a half-century now, Republican strategists have connived to deflect these feelings away from the understructures of power and wealth in America. One might say that this new cultural populism, with its angry belligerence, is hardly acquiescent, but it nonetheless serves the larger purposes of our own age of acquiescence.

10. The Genie Grown Monstrous: How Donald Trump, the All-American Frankenstein, Devoured the GOP

There is something all-American about Donald Trump—late-vintage all-American perhaps, but in the American grain. At the same time, there is something profoundly scary about him. Philip Roth once referred to "the indigenous American berserk." Roth was talking about a sixties suburban radical gone over to the dark side of nihilism and terror in his novel *American Pastoral*. Nonetheless, Trump belongs inside that aperçu, only he is more frightening, more alien.

Looked at from one angle, Trump is hardly unique; he shares the traits common to the tribe of jumbo-size businessmen. He is smug, cocksure, in love with money, semieducated, rough around the edges, inclined to pontificate, fond of trophies (wives, houses, hotels,

An earlier version of this chapter appeared in *Salon* on January 24, 2016.

girlfriends, the mansion *du jour*). Indeed, The Donald, by his larger-than-life presence, has helped to burnish that image, like a living advertisement for living large.

An aura of the Confidence Man also hovers around The Donald. His braggadocio pumps up grandiose, if iffy, projects that rise and fall on the tides of speculation and sometimes require bank bailouts to keep things afloat. But what could be more all-American than that?

The confidence man is a national archetype invented early in the nineteenth century that comes in relatively benign and more malignant versions. The nastier kind we are all familiar with at least since the debacle of 2008, Goldman Sachs, Bernie Madoff, and the gang. "Yankee Jonathan"—who amused the multitudes, especially men on the make, back in the early nineteenth century—was a kinder type and more fetching. Imagine a peddler roaming from village to village; he might seem a comic country bumpkin but turn out to be shrewder than that image suggests: a clever, versatile wheeler-and-dealer adept at getting people to "buy a pig in a poke." He was fast-talking, inventive, and seductive, never totally honest, always sexually notorious—all in all, someone it was dangerous to be near but hard to stay away from. It's hard to picture The Donald as an itinerant village peddler. Still, if he and Yankee Jonathan are not twins, they clearly share a genotype.

The Donald, then, is a piece of Americana: maybe not the most edifying or appealing, but part of the family. He embodies that well-worn, if still stinging, observation that "America is the only country that went from barbarism to decadence without passing through civilization." He is his own caricature. Self-parodying, easy to laugh at, so why worry? Because we sense that he also hails from the land of the berserk, that for all his familiarity we may never before have seen his like, and that the last laugh may be his.

After all, he is enormously popular. He has been for decades. Qualities that might repel some attract others: megalomania, narcissism, sociopathy, chest-thumping self-promotion, theatrical excess, bullying, moral elasticity, an insouciant penchant for the outlandish. These are the attributes of the wannabe Great Man as irreverent pathfinder. Although these might read like a roster of epithets, they are not meant that way. Market society nurtures these traits in people preoccupied with mastering it, and having done so they offer that up as their credential for superhero status. That they might also be thought of as symptoms, and the person presenting them as clinically diseased, is cold comfort. Because if Trump suffers—or, rather, indulges—a Napoleon complex, that too appeals to legions who have grown weary and cynical about the shadow-boxing that passes for democracy in twenty-first-century America. They are beguiled by someone unafraid to talk outside the box, to scoff at the propriety that camouflages the disconnect between the people and their governors. They imagine Trump as the Force that is with them. Moreover, scratch most tycoons anytime over the last two centuries and you're likely to uncover a latent Alexander the Great, a Caesar of the countinghouse, a conquistador of the marketplace. It comes with the territory—and The Donald walks well-trodden paths.

Still, he is more than that. He is the leading candidate to become the nominee for president of one of the country's two main political parties. That brute fact sets him apart. From its earliest days, the nation has witnessed its fair share of demagogues—some from the left, some from the right, even some from an elusive zone that overlaps left and right but is neither. Some have aspired to high office; others have even managed to get there (Huey Long and Joseph McCarthy, for example). But none of them—except one—shared Trump's profile. None of them—except one—rested their claim to political preeminence on their previous careers as titans of industry and finance. None of them—except one—threatened to breach the borders of conventional political protocols and established hierarchies to seek approval instead from the streets.

William Randolph Hearst is that exception. He was the media king of his day, commanding an armada of newspapers, the Rupert

Murdoch of turn-of-the-twentieth-century America. What he shared with Trump—and what he emphatically did not—can tell us something about that American road to decadence and where it might terminate.

Hearst evinced all those attributes of Napoleonic command, certitude, and delusion for which Trump is famous. The most unforgettable record of that psychological state is Orson Welles's masterpiece, *Citizen Kane*. The movie is fiction, of course, and without any pretense to being factually faithful to the events of Hearst's life, purely speculative when it comes to suggesting the childhood sources of his megalomania. But the film nonetheless captures Hearst's peculiar forms of commercial cunning and his insatiable, imperial business ambition. This combined with a vainglorious, evangelical zeal about himself as a kind of popular messiah to make him a figure that loomed over American public life, not just its economic affairs, for the first several decades of the twentieth century.

Like Trump, Hearst was born wealthy. Like Trump, he was a ruthless competitor in the industry he came to dominate: newspaper publishing in Hearst's case, real estate for The Donald. Like Trump, Hearst did not have to chase after publicity; he was the story. He made sure of that by owning newspapers in cities all over the country; if there happened to be a city without a Hearst paper, he bought one or started one. Garnering the lion's share of attention has never been a problem for Trump, who benefits from living in the age of the journalism of the picaresque, of reality masquerades, of news as entertainment. Known as "The Chief," Hearst, like Trump, was a seasoned practitioner of the Great Lie. Both men lived large. Hearst was a sport, liked to party, married a showgirl, dressed brashly, spent lavishly (one thinks immediately of San Simeon, his grotesque palace in California, where the haunting final scenes of *Citizen Kane* are set). Despite his enormous fortune, the establishment of that era frowned on all this. Like Trump at a different moment, Hearst was their bad boy.

Patrician enemies first laughed, then grew alarmed. They deplored him as a "low voluptuary," called him a "degraded, unclean thing." As his political ambitions surfaced, they spied "a new horror in American politics." And that was what really rankled. So long as he thumbed his nose at the social protocols of the Social Register elite, he was considered noxious, not dangerous. Once his more grandiose yearnings to run the country became clear, matters grew more serious.

Hearst, like Trump, had nurtured those desires for years before acting on them. When he did, he let loose with a wild, bilious rhetoric that only The Donald could match. Historians credit the jingoism of his newspapers with helping incite the Spanish-American War. He accused the secretary of war of poisoning American soldiers with "ancient" and "diseased" beef. But what really bothered the country's elites was his fulsome assault on the plutocracy.

How strange! He belonged to that plutocracy. Here is just where "The Chief" and "The Donald" converge and radically diverge. On the one hand, both held in contempt the sachems who ran the two major political parties: in Hearst's case the Democrats, in Trump's the Republicans. Neither held any elective or appointive office before reaching for the top. Both had the resources and chutzpah to stage their own campaigns, dealing with and bulldozing party hierarchs when they had to—or because they enjoyed doing it.

Like Trump, Hearst showed total confidence he could realize his ambitions with or without an established political machine, boasted that for that reason he couldn't be bought, and set out to create a political machine for himself. He had his own media megaphone, after all, and used it to tap into something then new in American political culture. One of his closest advisers commented, "The American people—like all people—are interested in PERSONALITY ... Hearst appeals to the people—not to a boss or corporation." The Chief represented, according to one observer, "a strange new element. He is the first one-man party to have gained anything like national headway in the history of our democracy ... His power has been gained purely by advertising himself ... He is a celebrity who is guaranteed four million readers every day." Sounds familiar.

Hearst tried his hand first at the vice-presidential nomination in 1900, assuming he'd be William Jennings Bryan's running mate, even though his connections to the inner circles of the Democratic Party were thin to nonexistent. He was rejected. Then he initiated a ten-year plan to become president. Along the way he secured a congressional seat (the Democrats hoped they'd bury him there) that became his platform for provocative attacks on the power elite. Then he ran for mayor of New York, creating his own independent party, and probably would have won except for undercover machinations by Tammany Hall—the municipal machine that ran the Democratic Party—to steal the necessary votes. The Hall was notorious for just this. Fearing his power, the party nominated Hearst to be governor in 1906. He lost. Even after the defeat, he kept his eyes trained on the White House.

Despite these striking similarities, The Chief and The Donald didn't really speak the same language, even if both were masters of political invective and the Great Lie. What they didn't have in common is a commentary on the evolution of American public life over the last century.

Hearst rose to the surface on a tidal wave of populist anticapitalist sentiment. The Populist Party and its call for a cooperative commonwealth preceded him. So did a vast labor insurgency that faced off against the armed might of the nation's mightiest industrialists. Those often violent confrontations continued as Hearst established his media empire. So too did a nationwide antitrust movement that captured the imaginations of millions of working- and middle-class people and even influenced the country's political establishment. Immigrants toiling in the nation's sweatshops made common cause with middle-class reformers to expose the scandal capitalism had become in urban ghettoes from coast to coast. The Socialist Party elected local officials all over the country, including some congressmen. The Chief tried, and to some considerable degree succeeded in, convincing all these foes of the new order of industrial and financial capitalism that he was their champion, their "chief."

Relentlessly, Hearst denounced the trusts: local monopolies that dominated New York's economy and national ones that lorded it over the country and preyed on workers, consumers, and small businesses alike. He talked about the "Trust Frankenstein." He loathed Teddy Roosevelt (who hated him in return) for his "preening, bombastic, and aristocratic airs." Like many populists and progressives of the day, he called for the direct election of senators, an income tax, and public ownership of public services. He was staunchly pro-union, arguing that without unions the country would be like "China and India, where rich mandarins and rajahs lord it over starving populations." He campaigned for shorter hours and higher pay and portrayed himself as a hero of the immigrant working classes. He came so close to becoming New York's mayor precisely because he did so well among those immigrant workers, as well as the emerging white-collar proletariat and small-business people. Not only did Tammany lose the loyalty of its immigrant base, but Hearst took away votes from the Socialists, a party of real weight in the city.

Was The Chief a populist? He was, after all, a warmonger, called for the annexation of the Philippines, indulged in anti-Semitism, and traded in sensationalism as much as or more than he did information. Later he became the bitterest foe of the New Deal. He lived in that interstitial zone between left and right—but not in the middle. There would be others like him who would haunt the American imagination in novels like Sinclair Lewis's *It Can't Happen Here* and movies like Frank Capra's *Meet John Doe*. But in real life there was no one from the same prepossessing background, no plutocrat gone native. Call him what you want, his political dreams and delusions and his extraordinary political ascendancy rested entirely on a fierce culture of anticapitalist resistance abroad in the land. Did he mean it? What might he have done in power? We will never know.

One thing is certain, however. For The Donald, this is terra incognito (think immigrants, for starters). If Hearst was the inheritor and master manipulator of a widespread left-leaning populism, the prodigal son of Jefferson, Jackson, Bryan, and Debs, then Trump is the bastard son of Richard Nixon. Himself a maestro of political choreography (until it did him in), Nixon invoked something he famously anointed "the silent majority" to grease the wheels that landed him in the White House. What nearly got Hearst there was the polar opposite; we might call it the "vociferous majority." (There is, of course, no mathematical reality behind either of these "majorities.") It is the silent one of which Trump now speaks and which makes him a salient component of our public life.

Silence can be dangerous. What, after all, is it saying, who is it speaking for, how do you break its vow of silence? What does it want? The "vociferous majority" was loud and clear about all that. The "silent majority" required a ventriloquist ... or, rather, a translator.

"Tricky Dick" Nixon sensed that a converging series of discontents among "the people" might be steered in the direction of the Republican Party, which had always seemed an unlikely haven for them. White "ethnic" blue-collar and lower-middle-class white-collar workers were anxious about their own economic decline, suffering the early onset of deindustrialization and the long regression in the standard of living for ordinary folk. They were also scandalized by the sexual and gender and cultural revolutions of the time. Above all, they were angry that the racial status quo was being overturned, and at what they not wrongly considered their expense. More maddening still was that much of this was happening with the connivance of elites, most of them affiliated with the Democratic

Party, that onetime party of the New Deal, which they had long thought of as their true haven and which now seemed traitorous. Thus was born the incendiary image of the "limousine liberal," which remains part of our political lingua franca to this day.

Americans experienced a seismic cultural revolution. Issues that had once been treated as matters of economic equality and social justice, as face-offs between the forces of organized power and wealth and those they exploited and disempowered, were deftly translated into cultural antipathies. The struggle over "family values" and all that that rubric evokes about sex, patriotism, religion, education, race, masculinity, and the specter of the "nanny state" followed on. It was a brilliant piece of political invention. Nixon won not only in the South and Sunbelt but across broad stretches of the working class in the Northeast and Midwestern heartland. The Republican high command therefore remained committed to the genie of the "silent majority" he had conjured. But genies have a way of misbehaving.

Donald Trump is the genie grown monstrous and no longer silent. His arrival has caused enormous consternation among the party's old guard, which itself is not that old but still accustomed to the conventions of the Beltway. Those whom these wise elders once controlled now vie to control them as the party drifts inexorably to the outlands of the right. The official leadership trails behind the ideological fervor that animates the rank and file, and it's no longer clear who's converting whom. The populist right evinces serial animosities toward immigrants, big banks, secularists, "sexual deviants" and the politically correct corporations that pander to them, the racially suspect, bureaucrats of every rank and order, and anything that can be identified as an establishment—even their own Republican one. The Donald can thumb his nose at party honchos because it is in his nature to do so, but also because that natural inclination is buoyed up by a new "vociferous majority" that has turned on its creator.

What is scary is that the new "vociferous majority" has been so formless and fractured. Until the formation of the Tea Party it was without organizational definition and easily steered. Unlike the old "vociferous majority," for a long time there was "no there there." One is reminded of the shadowy people's hero in the film *Nashville*— but that character was far too vague and softy contoured, if nonetheless worryingly mysterious. Trump has more than enough edge to suit the edgier times we live in. So too, the old "vociferous majority" had offered a set of reasonably clear propositions and programs about an alternative future. If the new insurgency has a program for the future, that program should be called "The Past."

While they share with Hearst's earlier "vociferous majority" economic and cultural suspicions about the corporate powers that be, today's right-wing populists are hardly about to invoke the anti-capitalism that impassioned the people Hearst counted on. On the contrary, part of what draws them to The Donald is that he is an übermensch risen atop the capitalist order, whose Darwinian ruthlessness as a moneymaker presumably fits him to command outside that realm. For some in a generation saturated in the romantic heroics of the free market and that idolizes those who triumph over its daunting risk, that elixir is hard to resist. Notwithstanding the financial debacle of 2008, the free market remains a compelling realm where people supposedly self-invent, prove their mettle, light out for the territories.

Moreover, this oddly composed milieu of upwardly mobile Sunbelt professionals and techies and downwardly mobile working people, small-town evangelicals and billionaire dynastic entrepreneurs, lives in emotional ambivalence. It resents being told what to do but wants a tough guy to command it. This is what happens when the myth of the free market meets the myth of the enemy alien.

As the unthinkable becomes at least thinkable, if not probable, the auguries are not reassuring. What used to be largely confined to the dark corners of the American imagination at a time when fascists and Nazis controlled large portions of the planet now may be prefigured in this yearning for a Great Man: someone rude and muscular, trading in half-truths and bald prevarications, preying on the fears and anxieties that a predatory capitalism he so well embodies has visited on us all. Hearst and Trump, two übermenschen from the plutocracy but somehow not of it, the first promising to dethrone it, ours promising ... we know not what.

11. Playing God: The Rebirth of Family Capitalism, or, How the Koch Brothers, Sheldon Adelson, Sam Walton, Bill Gates, and Other Billionaires Are Undermining America

George Baer was a railroad and coal-mining magnate at the turn of the twentieth century. Amid a violent and protracted strike that shut down much of the country's anthracite coal industry, Baer defied President Teddy Roosevelt's appeal to arbitrate the issues at stake, saying, "The rights and interests of the laboring man will be protected and cared for ... not by the labor agitators, but by the Christian men of property to whom God has given control of the property rights of the country." To the Anthracite Coal Commission investigating the uproar, Baer insisted, "These men don't suffer. Why, hell, half of them don't even speak English."

An earlier version was published in *TomDispatch* on September 11, 2014.

We might call that adopting the imperial position. Titans of industry and finance back then often assumed that they had the right to supersede the law and tutor the rest of America on how best to order its affairs. They liked to play God. It's a habit that's returned with a vengeance in our own time.

The Koch brothers are only the most conspicuous among a whole tribe of "self-made" billionaires who imagine themselves architects or master builders of a revamped, rehabilitated America. The resurgence of what might be called dynastic or family capitalism, as opposed to the more impersonal managerial capitalism many of us grew up with, is changing the nation's political chemistry.

Our own masters of the universe, like the "robber barons" of old, are inordinately impressed with their ascendancy to the summit of economic power. Add their personal triumphs to American culture's perennial love affair with business—President Calvin Coolidge, for instance, is remembered today only for proclaiming that "the business of America is business"—and you have a formula for megalomania.

Take Jeff Greene, otherwise known as the "Meltdown Mogul." Back in 2010, he had the chutzpah to campaign in the Democratic primary for a Florida Senate seat in a Miami neighborhood ravaged by the subprime-mortgage debacle—precisely the arena in which he had grown fabulously rich. In the process, he rallied locals against Washington insiders and regaled them with stories of his life as a busboy at the Breakers hotel in Palm Beach. Protected from the Florida sun by his Prada shades, he alluded to his wealth as evidence that, as a maestro of collateralized debt obligations, no one knew better than he how to run the economy he had helped to pulverize. He put an exclamation point on his campaign by flying off in his private jet only after securely strapping himself in with gold-plated seat buckles.

Olympian entrepreneurs like Greene regularly end up seeing themselves as tycoons-*cum*-savants. When they run for office, they do so as if they were trying to get elected to the board of directors of America, Inc. Some will brook no interference with their will. Property, lots of it, in a society given over to its worship, becomes a blank check: everything is permitted to those who have it.

Dream and Nightmare

This, then, is the indigenous romance of American capitalism. The man from nowhere becomes a Napoleon of business and so a hero because he confirms a cherished legend: that it's the primordial birthright of those lucky enough to live in the New World to rise out of obscurity to unimaginable heights. All of this, so the legend tells us, comes through the application of disciplined effort, commercial cunning and foresight, a take-no-prisoners competitive instinct, and a gambler's sangfroid in the face of the unforgiving riskiness of the marketplace. Master all of that and you deserve to be a master of our universe. (Conversely, this is the dark fairy tale that Gilded Age anticapitalist rebels knew as the "Property Beast.")

What makes the creation of the titan particularly confounding is that it seems as if it shouldn't be so. Inside the colorless warrens of the countinghouse and the factory workshop, a pedestrian preoccupation with profit and loss might be expected to smother all those instincts we associate with the warrior, the statesman, and the visionary, not to mention the tyrant. As Joseph Schumpeter, the mid-twentieth-century political economist, once observed, "There is surely no trace of any mystic glamour" about the sober-minded bourgeois. He is not likely to "say boo to a goose."

Yet the titan of capitalism overcomes that propensity. As Schumpeter put it, he transforms himself into the sort of person who can "bend a nation to his will" and use his "extraordinary physical and nervous energy" to become "a leading man." Something happens through the experience of commercial conquest so intoxicating that it breeds a willful arrogance and a lust for absolute power of the sort for which George Baer hankered. Call it the absolutism of self-righteous money.

Sheldon Adelson, Charles and David Koch, Sam Walton, Rupert Murdoch, Linda McMahon, John Paulson, and Steven Cohen all conform in one way or another to this historic profile. Powers to be reckoned with, they presume to know best what we should teach our kids and how we should do it; how to defend the country's borders against "alien" invasion, revitalize international trade, cure what ails the health-care delivery system, create jobs where there are none, rejigger the tax code, balance the national budget, put truculent labor unions in their place, and keep the country on the moral and racial straight and narrow.

All this purported wisdom and self-assurance is home bred: that is to say, these people are first of all family or dynastic capitalists, not faceless suits who shimmy their way up the greased pole that configures the managerial hierarchies of corporate America. Functionaries at the highest levels of the modern corporation may be just as wealthy, but they are a fungible bunch whose loyalty to any particular outfit may expire whenever a more attractive stock option from another firm comes their way.

In addition, in our age of megamergers and acquisitions, corporations go in and out of existence with remarkable frequency, morphing into a shifting array of abstract acronyms. They are carriers of great power, but without an organic attachment to distinct individuals or family lineages.

Instead, the dynasts of yesteryear and today have created family businesses—or, as in the case of the Koch brothers and Murdoch, taken over those launched by their fathers, to which they are fiercely devoted. They guard their business sanctuaries by keeping them private, wary of becoming dependent on outside capital resources that might interfere with their freedom to do what they please with what they've amassed.

They think of what they've built up not so much as a pile of cash but as a patrimony, to which they are bound by ties of blood, religion, region, and race. These attachments turn ordinary business into something more transcendent. They represent the tissues of a way of life, even a philosophy of life. Its moral precepts about work, individual freedom, family relations, sexual correctness, meritocracy, equality, and social responsibility are formed out of the same process of self-invention that gave birth to the family business. Habits of methodical self-discipline and the nurturing and prudential stewardship that occasionally turns a modest competency into a propertied goliath encourage the instinct to instruct and command.

There is no Tycoon Party in the United States to impose ideological uniformity on a group of billionaires who, by their very nature as übermensch, march to their own drummers and differ on many matters. Some are philanthropically minded, others parsimonious; some are pietistic, others indifferent. Wall Street hedge-fund creators may donate to Obama and be card-carrying social liberals on matters of love and marriage, while heartland types like the Koch brothers obviously take another tack politically. But all of them subscribe to one thing: a belief in their own omniscience and irresistible will.

There at the Creation

Business dynasts have enacted this imperial drama since the dawn of American capitalism—indeed, especially then, before the publicly traded corporation and managerial capitalism began supplanting their family-capitalist predecessors at the turn of the twentieth century. John Jacob Astor, America's first millionaire, whose offices were once located on Manhattan island where Zuccotti Park now stands, was the most literal sort of empire builder. In league with

Thomas Jefferson, he attempted to extend that president's "empire for liberty" all the way to the western edge of the continent and push out the British. There, on the Oregon coast, he established the fur-trading colony of Astoria to consolidate his global control of the luxury fur trade.

In this joint venture, president and tycoon both failed. Astor, however, was perfectly ready to defy the highest authority in the land and deal with the British when it mattered most. So when Jefferson embargoed trade with that country in the run-up to the War of 1812, the founder of one of the country's most luminous dynasties simply ran the blockade. An unapologetic elitist, Astor admired Napoleon, assumed the masses were not to be left to their own devices, and believed deeply that property ought to be the prerequisite for both social position and political power.

Traits like Astor's willfulness and self-sufficiency cropped up frequently in the founding generation of America's "captains of industry." Often they were accompanied by chest-thumping braggadocio and thumb-in-your eye irreverence. Cornelius Vanderbilt, called by his latest biographer "the first tycoon," was known in his day as "the Commodore." Supposedly, he warned someone foolish enough to challenge his supremacy in the steamboat business that "I won't sue you, I'll ruin you."

Or take "Jubilee Jim" Fisk. He fancied himself an admiral but wasn't one, and after the Civil War, when caught plundering the Erie Railroad, boasted that he was "born to be bad." Later on, when a plot he hatched to corner the nation's supply of gold left him running from the law, Jim classically summed up the scandal this way: "Nothing lost save honor."

More than a century before Mitt Romney and Bain Capital came along, Jay Gould, a champion railroad speculator and buccaneering capitalist, scoured the country for companies to buy, loot, and sell. Known by his many detractors as "the Mephistopheles of Wall Street," he once remarked, when faced with a strike against one of his railroads, that he could "hire one-half of the working class to kill the other half."

George Pullman, nicknamed "the Duke" in America's world of self-made royalty, wasn't shy about dealing roughly with the rowdy "mob" either. As a rising industrialist in Chicago in the 1870s, he—along with other young men from the city's new manufacturing elite—took up arms to put down a labor insurgency and financed the building of urban armories, stocked with the latest artillery, including a new machine gun marketed as the "Tramp Terror." (This was but one instance among many of terrorism from above by the forces of "law and order.")

However, Pullman was better known for displaying his overlordship in quite a different fashion. Cultivating his sense of dynastic noblesse oblige, he erected a model town, which he aptly named Pullman, just outside Chicago. There, residents not only labored to manufacture sleeping cars for the nation's trains but were also tutored in how to live respectable lives—no drinking, no gambling, proper dress and deportment—while living in company-owned houses, shopping at company-owned stores, worshiping at company churches, playing in company parks, reading company-approved books in the company library, and learning the "three Rs" from company schoolmarms. Think of it as a Potemkin working-class village, a commercialized idyll of feudal harmony—until it wasn't. The dream morphed into a nightmare when the Duke suddenly began to slash wages and evict his "subjects" amid the worst depression of the nineteenth century. This in turn provoked a nationwide strike and boycott, eventually crushed by federal troops.

The business autocrats of the Gilded Age could be rude and crude, like Gould, Vanderbilt, and Fisk, or adopt the veneer of civilization, like Pullman. Some of these "geniuses" of big business belonged to what Americans used to call the "shoddy aristocracy." Fisk had, after all, started out as a confidence man in circuses, and Gould accumulated his "startup capital" by bilking a business partner. "Uncle" Daniel Drew, top dog on Wall Street around the time of the Civil War (and a pious one at that: he founded Drew Theological Seminary), had once been a cattle drover. Before bringing his cows to the New York market, he would feed them salt licks to make sure they were thirsty and then fill them with water so they would make it to the auction block weighing far more than their mere flesh and bones could account for. He bequeathed to America the practice of "watered stock."

Not all the Founding Fathers of our original tycoonery, however, were social invisibles or refugees from the commercial badlands. They could also hail from the highest precincts of the Social Register. The Morgans were a distinguished banking and insurance clan going all the way back to colonial days. J. P. Morgan was therefore to the manor born. At the turn of the twentieth century he functioned as the country's unofficial central banker, meaning he had the power to allocate much of the capital on which American society depended. Nonetheless, when asked about bearing such a heavy social responsibility, he bluntly responded, "I owe the public nothing."

This sort of unabashed indifference to the general welfare was typical—and didn't end in the twentieth century. During the Great Depression of the 1930s, the managements of some major publicly owned corporations felt compelled by a newly militant labor movement and the shift in the political atmosphere that accompanied Roosevelt's New Deal to recognize and bargain with the unions formed by their employees. Not so long before, some of these corporations, in particular US Steel, had left a trail of blood on the streets of the steel towns of Pennsylvania and Ohio when they crushed the Great Steel Strike of 1919. Times had changed.

Not so, however, for the adamantine patriarchs who still owned and ran the nation's "little steel" companies (which were hardly little). Men like Tom Girdler of Republic Steel resented any interference with their right to rule over what happened on their premises and hated the New Deal, as well as its allies in the labor movement, because they challenged that absolutism. So it was that, on Memorial Day 1937, ten strikers were shot in the back and killed by the Chicago Police Department while picketing Girdler's Chicago factory.

The Great U-Turn

By and large, however, the middle decades of the twentieth century were dominated by modern concerns like US Steel, General Motors, and General Electric, whose corporate CEOs were more sensitive to the pressures of their multiple constituencies. These included not only workers but legions of shareholders, customers, suppliers, and local and regional public officials.

Publicly held corporations are, for the most part, owned not by a family, a dynasty, or even a handful of business partners but by a vast sea of shareholders. Those "owners" have little if anything to do with running "their" complex companies. This is left to a managerial cadre captained by lavishly rewarded chief executives. Their concerns are inherently political but not necessarily ideological. They worry about their brand's reputation, have multiple dealings with a broad array of government agencies, look to curry favor with politicians from both parties, and are generally reasonably vigilant about being politically correct when it comes to matters of race, gender, and other socially sensitive issues. Behaving in this way is, after all, a marketing strategy that shows up where it matters most—on the bottom line.

Over the last several decades, however, history has done a U-turn. Old-style private enterprises of enormous size have made a remarkable comeback. Partly, this is a consequence of the way the federal government has encouraged private enterprise through the tax code, land-use policy, and subsidized finance. It is also the outcome of a new system of decentralized, flexible capitalism in which large, complex corporations have offloaded functions once performed internally onto an array of outside, independent firms.

Family capitalism has experienced a renaissance. Even giant firms are now often controlled by their owners the way Andrew Carnegie once captained his steel works or Henry Ford his car company. Some of these new family firms were previously publicly traded corporations that went private. A buyout craze initiated by private equity firms hungry for quick-turnaround profits, like Mitt Romney's infamous Bain Capital, lent the process a major hand. This might be thought of as entrepreneurial capitalism for the short term, a strictly finance-driven strategy.

But family-based firms in it for the long haul have also proliferated and flourished in this era of economic turbulence. These are no longer stodgy, technologically antiquated outfits, narrowly dedicated to churning out a single time-tested product. They are often remarkably adept at responding to shifts in the market and highly diversified in what they make and sell, and—thanks to the expansion of capital markets—they now enjoy a degree of financial independence not unlike that of their dynastic forebears of the nineteenth century, who relied on internally generated resources to keep free of the banks. They have been cropping up in newer-growth sectors of the economy, including retail, entertainment, energy, finance, and tech. Nor are they necessarily small-fry mom-and-pop operations. One-third of the Fortune 500 now falls into the category of family-controlled.

Feet firmly anchored in their business fiefdoms, family patriarchs loom over the twenty-first-century landscape, lending it a back-to-the-future air. They exercise enormous political influence. They talk loudly and carry big sticks. Their money elects officials, finances their own campaigns for public office, and is reconfiguring our political culture by fertilizing a rain forest of think tanks, journals, and political action committees. A nation that, a generation ago, largely abandoned its historic resistance to organized wealth and power has allowed this newest version of the "robber baron" to dominate the public arena to a degree that might have astonished even John Jacob Astor and Cornelius Vanderbilt.

The Political Imperative

That ancestral generation, living in an era when the state was weak and kept on short rations, didn't need to be as immersed in political affairs. Contacting a kept senator or federal judge when needed was enough. The modern regulatory and bureaucratic welfare state has extended its reach so far and wide that it needs to be steered, if not dismantled.

Some of our new tycoons try doing one or the other from offstage, through a bevy of front organizations and hand-selected candidates for public office. Others dive right into the electoral arena themselves. Linda McMahon, who with her husband created the World Wrestling Entertainment empire, is a two-time loser in Senate races in Connecticut. Rick Scott, a pharmaceutical entrepreneur, did better, becoming Florida's governor. Such figures, and other triumphalist types like them, claim their rise to business supremacy as their chief—often their only—credential when running for office or simply telling those holding office what to do.

Our entrepreneurial maestros come in a remarkable range of sizes and shapes. On style points, Donald Trump looms largest. Like so many nineteenth-century dynasts, his family origins are modest. A German grandfather arriving here in 1885 was a wine maker, a barber, and a saloonkeeper in California; father Fred became the Henry Ford of homebuilding, helped along by New Deal low-cost housing subsidies. His son went after splashier, flashier enterprises like casinos, luxury resorts, high-end hotels, and domiciles for the 1 percent. In all of this, the family name, splashed on towers of every sort, and The Donald's image—laminated hairdo and all— became his company's chief assets.

Famous for nothing other than being very rich, Trump feels free to hold forth on every conceivable subject of public import from same-sex marriage to the geopolitics of the Middle East. Periodically he tosses his hat into the electoral arena, but he comports himself like a clown. He even has a game named after himself, whose play currency bears Donald's face and whose lowest denomination is $10 million. No wonder no one takes his right-wing bluster too seriously. A modern day "Jubilee Jim" Fisk, craving attention so much he's willing to make himself ridiculous, The Donald is his own reality TV show.

Rupert Murdoch, on the other hand, looks and dresses like an accountant and lives mainly in the shadows. Like Trump, he inherited a family business. Unlike Trump, his family pedigree was auspicious. His father was Sir Keith, a media magnate from Melbourne, Australia, and Rupert went to Oxford. Now the family's media influence straddles continents, as Rupert attempts—sometimes with great success—to make or break political careers and steer whole political parties to the right.

The News Corporation is a dynastic institution of the modern kind, in which Murdoch uses relatively little capital and a complex company structure to maintain and vigorously exercise the family's control. When the Ford Motor Company finally went public in 1956, it did something similar to retain the Ford family's dominant position. So did Google, whose "dual-class share structure" allowed its founders, Larry Page and Sergey Brin, to continue calling the shots. Murdoch's empire may, at first glance, seem to conform to American-style managerial corporate capitalism: apparently rootless, cosmopolitan, fixed on the bottom line. In fact, it is tightly tethered to Murdoch's personality and conservative political inclinations and to the rocky dynamics of the Murdoch succession. That is invariably the case with our new breed of dynastic capitalists.

Sheldon Adelson, the CEO of the Las Vegas Sands Corporation and sugar daddy to right-wing political wannabes from City Hall to the White House, lacks Murdoch's finesse but shares his convictions and his outsized ambition to command the political arena. He's the eighth-richest man in the world, but grew up poor as a Ukrainian Jew living in the Dorchester neighborhood of Boston. His father was a cab driver and his mother ran a knitting shop. He went to trade school to become a court reporter and dropped out of college. He started several small businesses that failed, winning and losing fortunes. Then he gambled and hit the jackpot, establishing lavish hotels and casinos around the world. When he again lost big-time during the global financial implosion of 2007 and 2008, he responded the way any nineteenth-century sea-dog capitalist might have: "So I lost 25 billion dollars. I started out with zero ... [There is] no such thing as fear, not to any entrepreneur. Concern, yes. Fear, no."

A committed Zionist, Adelson was once a Democrat. But he jumped ship over Israel and because he believed the party's economic policies were ruining the country. (He's described Obama's goal as "a socialist-style economy.") He established the Freedom Watch, a dark-money group, as a counterweight to MoveOn.org and George Soros's Open Society. According to one account, Adelson "seeks to dominate politics and public policy through the raw power of money." That has, for instance, meant backing Newt Gingrich in the Republican presidential primaries of 2012 against Mitt Romney, whom Adelson denounced as a "predatory capitalist" (talk about the pot calling the kettle black!) and, not long after, funneling cash to Romney's presidential candidacy.

Free Markets and the Almighty

Charles and David Koch are perfect specimens of this new breed of family capitalists on steroids. Koch Industries is a gigantic conglomerate headquartered in the heartland city of Wichita, Kansas. Charles, who really runs the company, lives there. David, the social and philanthropic half of this fraternal duopoly, resides in New York City. Not unlike George "the Duke" Pullman, Charles has converted Wichita into something like a company city, where criticism of Koch Industries is muted at best.

The firm's annual revenue is in the neighborhood of $10 billion, generated by oil refineries, thousands of miles of pipelines, paper towels, Dixie cups, Georgia-Pacific lumber, Lycra, and Stainmaster Carpet, among other businesses. It is the second-largest privately owned company in the United States. (Cargill, the international food conglomerate, comes first.) The brothers are inordinately wealthy, even for our "new tycoonery." Only Warren Buffett and Bill Gates are richer.

While the average business owner or corporate executive is unlikely to be ideological, the Koch brothers are dedicated libertarians. Their free-market orthodoxy makes them adamant opponents of all forms of government regulation. Since their companies are among the top ten air polluters in the United States, that also comports well with their material interests—and the Kochs come by their beliefs naturally, so to speak.

Their father, Fred, was the son of a Dutch printer who settled in Texas and started a newspaper. He later became a chemical engineer and invented a better method for converting oil into gasoline. In one of history's little jokes, he was driven out of the industry by the oil giants, who saw him as a threat. Today, Koch Industries is sometimes labeled "the Standard Oil of our time," an irony it's not clear the family would appreciate. After a sojourn in Joseph Stalin's Soviet Union (of all places), helping train oil engineers, Fred returned stateside to set up his own oil-refinery business in Wichita. There he joined the John Birch Society and ranted about the imminent Communist takeover of the government. He was particularly worried that "the colored man looms large in the Communist plan to take over America."

Father Fred raised his sons in the stern regimen of the work ethic and instructed them in the libertarian catechism. This left them life-long foes of the New Deal and every social and economic reform since. That included not only predictable measures like government health insurance, Social Security, and corporate taxes, but anything connected to the leviathan state. Even the CIA and the FBI are on the Koch chopping block.

Dynastic conservatism of this sort has sometimes taken a genera-tion to mature. Sam Walton, like many of his nineteenth-century analogs, was not a political animal. He just wanted to be left alone to do his thing and deploy his power over the marketplace. So he stayed clear of electoral and party politics, although he implicitly relied on the racial, gender, and political order of the old South, which kept wages low and unions out, to build his business in the Ozarks. After his death in 1992, however, Sam's heirs entered the political arena in a big way.

In other respects, Walton conformed to type. He was impressed with himself, noting that "capital isn't scarce; vision is" (although his "one-stop shopping" concept was part of the retail industry before he started Walmart). His origins were humble. He was born on a farm in Kingfisher, Oklahoma. His father left farming for a while to become a mortgage broker, which in the Great Depression meant he was a farm repossessor for Metropolitan Life Insurance. Sam did farm chores, then worked his way through college and started his retail career with a small operation partly funded by his father-in-law.

At every juncture, the firm's expansion depended on a network of family relations. Soon enough, his stores blanketed rural and small-town America. Through all the glory years, Sam's day began before dawn, as he woke up in the same house he'd lived in for more than thirty years. Then, dressed in clothes from one of his discount stores, off he went to work in his red Ford pickup truck.

Some dynasts are pietistic; some infuse their business with religion. Sam Walton did a bit of both. In his studiously modest lifestyle there was a kind of outward piety. Living without pretension, nose to the grindstone, and methodically building up the family patrimony has for centuries carried a sacerdotal significance, leaving aside any specific Protestant profession of religious faith. But there was professing as well. Though not a fundamentalist, he was a loyal member of the First Presbyterian Church in Bentonville, Arkansas, where he was a "ruling elder" and occasionally taught Sunday school (something he had also done in college as president of the Burall Bible Class Club).

Christianity would play a formative role in Walton's labor-relations strategy at Walmart. His employees—"associates," he dubbed them—were drawn from an Ozark world of Christian fraternity that Walmart management cultivated. "Servant leadership" was a concept designed to encourage workers to undertake their duties serving the company's customers in the same spirit as Jesus, who saw himself as a "servant leader."

This helped discourage animosities in the workforce, as well as blunting the dangerous—to Walton—desire to do something about them through unionizing or responding in any other way to the company's decidedly subpar working conditions and wages. An aura of Christian spiritualism, plus company-scripted songs and cheers focused on instilling company loyalty, profit-sharing schemes, and performance bonuses constituted a twentieth-century version of Pullman's town idyll.

All of this remained in place after Sam's passing. What changed was the decision of his fabulously wealthy relatives to enter the political arena. Walton family lobbying operations now cover a broad range of issues, including lowering corporate taxes and getting rid of the estate tax entirely; his heirs subsidize mainly Republican candidates and causes. Most prominent of all have been their efforts to privatize education through vouchers or by other means, often turning public institutions into religiously affiliated schools.

Wall Street has never been known for its piety. But the tycoons who founded the Street's most lucrative hedge funds—men like John Paulson, Paul Tudor Jones II, and Steve Cohen, among others—are also determined to upend the public school system. They are among the country's most powerful proponents of charter schools. Like J. P. Morgan, these men grew up in privilege, went to prep schools and the Ivy League, and have zero experience with public education or the minorities who tend to make up a large proportion of charter schools' student bodies.

No matter. After all, some of these people make several million dollars a day. What an elixir! They are joined in this educational crusade by fellow business conquistadors of less imposing social backgrounds, like Mark Zuckerberg, who has ensured that Facebook will remain a family domain even while "going public." Another example is Bill Gates, the most celebrated of a brace of techno-pioneers who—legend would have it—did their pioneering in homely garages, even though the wonders they invented would have been inconceivable without decades of government investment in military-related science and technology. What can't these people do? What don't they know? They are empire builders and liberal with their advice and money when it comes to managing the educational affairs of the nation. They also benefit handsomely from a provision in the tax code passed during the Clinton years that rewards them for investing in "businesses" like charter schools.

Our imperial tycoons are a mixed lot. They range from hip technologists like Zuckerberg to heroic nerds like Bill Gates, and include yesteryear traditionalists like Walton and the Koch brothers. What they share with each other and their robber-baron ancestors is a godlike desire to create the world in their image.

Watching someone play God may amuse us, as The Donald can do in an appalling sort of way. It is, however, a dangerous game, with potentially deadly consequences for a democratic way of life already on life support.

Afterword: The Priest, the Commissar, and The Donald

The year 2017 seems filled with portents, omens, and forebodings. In an eerie coincidence, it is the occasion of a double anniversary: the five-hundredth of the Protestant Reformation and the hundredth of the Bolshevik Revolution. In October 1517, Martin Luther nailed his Ninety-Five Theses to the door of the cathedral in Wittenberg, Germany. In October 1917, Vladimir Ilyich Ulyanov, better known as Lenin, proclaimed the Union of Soviet Socialist Republics. In January 2017, a Moloch became the most powerful human on earth. Is this year one of a new Dark Age?

Moloch was a Biblical-age god of the Canaanites, often depicted with a goat's head wearing a royal crown. He devoured children offered as sacrifices. He makes an appearance in John Milton's *Paradise Lost*, where he's saturated in a mother's tears and children's blood. Allen Ginsberg's *Howl* invokes the "nightmare of

An earlier version of this chapter appeared in *Salmagundi*, no. 195/196, Summer–Fall 2017.

Moloch, Moloch the loveless ... Moloch whose eyes are a thousand blind windows."

There is a kind of thunder in the name Trump which echoes that menace. The point, however, is not to raise up horrific premonitions or melodramatically exaggerate what is imminent. Year one, after all, may not even last a year. Something else is worth pondering: Just how, on the double anniversary of these seminal moments in Western civilization, did we get here? (*Here* being the lower depths.) Is there some winding passage that leads from visions of sacred liberation to secular emancipation and from there to hell on Earth (speaking metaphorically)?

Whatever else might be said about the Reformation and the Russian Revolution, they bracket a span in Western history during which dreams of a "new humanity" abide. At first blush this sounds Pollyannaish, at best. Those centuries also embrace mayhem and bloody misery, some of it tied directly to those watershed moments.

Still, when we think of the making of the modern world, these moments (and others) stand out as emblematic. No matter their messier, ground-level reality, they lent a distinctive meaning to the human experience, a narrative logic that had something to do with freedom, with throwing off shackles, with doing away with inner and outer forms of subordination, with enlightenment, with creating heavenly and earthbound utopias. Even now they might be viewed as promissory notes, never redeemed.

In contrast, the age of the Moloch invites nihilism. Trump comes on the scene as some grotesque variation of capitalism as moral idiot. He is the offspring not of an ideology (even if now and then he bowdlerizes a conservative one for effect). He believes in nothing beyond his own self-interest, as he pathologically pursues it. He is an empty vessel into which have poured all the toxins produced by decades of callous indifference and social anomie, the cynicism corroding all conviction, the brute wisdom of winner-take-all jungle ethics. This is the spirit of a political economy that has, in Moloch fashion, cannibalized its innards like so many sacrifices to a deity of destruction.

Trump stares into the abyss and the abyss smiles back at him. His ascension punctuates the looming end of a long era in which belief in something more edifying, more socially capacious and liberating, has grown increasingly anemic.

The Double Anniversary

Often mortal enemies, the Reformation and socialism nonetheless imparted a profound significance and trajectory to everyday life that has long since become next to impossible to take seriously. They laid down a challenge to hierarchy in human affairs.

Beginning with Luther's audacity and ending with Lenin's trip to the Finland station, one compelling way to tell the story of "the West" has been to recount it as a struggle for liberation. Uglier tales about imperialism, for example, or racial oppression, or the intertwined relations between freedom and slavery, are equally germane. Arguably, there would be no story of liberation without the counterstory of domination. Still, this double anniversary coincides with the rise to power of something inimical to what might be considered the best inherent in those historic moments. That makes it worthwhile to emphasize their promise. Doing so can be a measure of how far we've come. It might, as well, inspire an alternate future.

Luther's reputation as a liberator usually attaches to the spiritual realm. By criticizing, ridiculing, even damning the ecclesiastical authority of the Catholic Church, he made possible a direct relationship between the worshiping individual and his or her God. Stripped of their role as intercessors in that sacred encounter, the spiritual raison d'être of priestly hierarchs was called into question.

More was at stake, however. The Church exerted enormous secular power. All were compelled to tithe to support its operations and physical infrastructure. It was a continental landowner, land speculator, and rent collector. It relied on the sale of indulgences— promoted as passes to absolution and heavenly rest—and even high offices to the wealthier laity. So it was impossible to separate the spiritual and social dimensions of the institution's overlordship. And Martin Luther did not try.

Even while the Wittenberg theologian and priest enunciated his vision of an intimate, direct relationship to God that dispensed with officially sanctioned go-betweens, he denounced that same hierarchy as corrupt. It had turned its spiritual coup d'état into a lucrative business. Indulgences were traded like commodities. Church potentates, often in collaboration with secular authorities—kings and princes and feudal lords—battened onto the populace like an incubus, indulging their own appetites while plundering those they were supposed to safeguard.

Spiritual rebellion could therefore spill over into social upheaval. It was bound to, whatever Luther might have desired. And so it did, in sixteenth-century Germany and elsewhere. Thousands of irate peasants, urban guild members, even impoverished aristocrats and others enlisted in the "Peasants' War" of 1525 and other uprisings against the Holy Roman Empire. Their aims were as much directed at social leveling as sacral freedom.

Thomas Müntzer, a well-educated pastor from a family of burghers, led an uprising of miners and others against the upper classes of Mühlhausen. He called on "the inner light" available to everyone, not Scripture, to justify what they were doing. Common people were instruments of God, and their lack of property left them pure in intent. The "Twelve Points" of the Memmingen Charter, which established an "eternal council," called for the abolition of serfdom and feudal dues and the preservation of the commons. Ten years after the Mühlhausen revolt, a Dutch tailor's apprentice in the town of Münster led an insurgency of Anabaptists that established a commune and waited for the Day of Judgment.

Luther, who had been excommunicated by the Pope, was nonetheless appalled and denounced the Mühlhausen rising and similar upheavals elsewhere: "Gospel does not make goods common." Peasant rebels were "insane" in their "raging." He called for their ruthless suppression. Brutally suppressed they were: The leaders were tortured to death and many thousands were slaughtered.

The cat was out of the bag, however. From this time forward, one version of the story of the West would connect the struggle for inner freedom and self-determination to the quest for social emancipation. The great liberal and democratic revolutions that midwifed the modern West would subscribe to this belief. The English Revolution of the seventeenth century drew on the springs of radical Protestantism to rationalize regicide. Moreover, its notions of democracy and equality and civil liberties—nurtured then and given further sustenance by the American Revolution— became the foundation stones of the West's civil religion. The Enlightenment and the French Revolution it helped inspire a century and half later had no patience for the obscurantism or the political and social privileges of the Church.

Religious toleration became an essential component of the liberal tradition. So did the separation of church and state, even though Luther himself ended his life deferring to secular authority, settling into a political quietism that would be characteristic of the denomination for a long time to come. All through the nineteenth century, recalling Luther's Ninety-Five Theses was part of ritual celebrations of the victory over absolutism in both the secular and sacred realms.

Socialism and the "Sigh of the Oppressed"

Socialism too recognized a kinship. Marx's famous aphorisms about the social role of religion anticipate that bond. In the same literary breath in which he described religion as the "opium of the people" (for which he has been forever condemned), he likened it to the "sigh of the oppressed creature, the heart of a heartless world, the soul of soulless conditions." For Marx, "religious suffering is at the same time an expression of real suffering and a protest against real suffering." A sigh, a protest, a utopia; we might call it a yearning to breathe free, expressed as the collective dream of the species.

Marx, his acolytes, and his disciples to follow acknowledged the genetic link between what Luther had set afoot and what socialism promised to finish. Marx valued Luther's critique of usury as a precursor of his own criticism of capital as a threat to the commonweal. For Luther, as for Marx, capital accumulation was first of all the accumulation of power in the hands of a grasping few; the soul, in Luther's mind (society, in Marx's), was in jeopardy for that reason.

Both Marx and Engels interpreted the Reformation, in particular the social upheavals it provoked, as premonitions auguring the fateful transition from feudal society to capitalism. As a spiritual undertaking, it was halfway there: "Germany's revolution," Marx concluded, "is theoretical, it is the Reformation ... But if Protestantism was not the true solution it was at least the true setting of the problem." Loosening "the shackles of the medieval Church" was a vital development in that larger story. Luther and Marx belong to a fraternity of transcendence, share an apocalyptic promise of transfiguration and redemption.

However, the great consequence of Luther's revolt was not social emancipation but the creation of the self-disciplined, self-motivated individual as a universal possibility, rather than the prerogative of a privileged caste. That was a profoundly liberating accomplishment—but one that carried with it a new kind of enslavement.

Unlocking "the shackles of the medieval church" also liberated the animal appetites of self-interest. The pursuit of individual advantage became the characterological undercarriage of capitalism. It became the new normal: mastering what might be called "the art of the deal." Those who became masters, however, tethered the individual to a regime in which they had no choice but to live at the sufferance of those in possession of the means of life.

Whether Protestantism gave rise to capitalism or the other way around is still debated. In either case, the "new man" that the Reformation helped create was simultaneously free and self-possessed, yet subject to a system of capital accumulation that undermined that apparent freedom. Socialism offered an ascent from individual to social emancipation. The individual freedom promised by the Reformation would remain illusory so long as capital retained its power to dictate.

Moloch in the Modern World

Martin Luther, of course, knew of Moloch as well as Mammon. Mammon, like Moloch, played a central role in the Church's dramaturgy of evil and was often identified as one of the seven princes of Hell. For Luther, Moloch belonged in that company, a dreadful version of the sin built into the spiritual DNA of mankind. Citing Jeremiah, Luther recalled how the sinful "built the high places of Baal and burned their sons and daughters to Moloch." For the father of the Reformation, Moloch captured the venality of the self-indulgence and parasitism of the Church: "The worshiping of idols was in Popedom very frequent in my time."

Marx too invoked the ancient god, but not to indict greed. Rather the opposite; he was after the chilling logic of accumulation that both prized the rationalism of individual self-denial and kept hidden its social enslavement. He described capitalism as the religion of daily life and capital as a Moloch that "requires the whole world as a due sacrifice." Capitalism turned progress into a "monstrous pagan god that only wanted to drink the nectar in the skulls of the dead."

For Marx, Moloch's ravenous appetite functioned as a metaphor for capitalism. It is at the very least suggestive that what many scientists now date as the onset of the Anthropocene—when human beings became a material cause of climate and environmental change thanks to the advent of capitalism and eventually the Industrial Revolution—roughly coincides with the Reformation. To stay alive, the new world needed to ingest its human and natural surroundings; its cravings were insatiable.

That was both a moral judgment and a social-science one, in Marx's view. Capital must conform to a logic of endless expansion, no matter in whom or in what (the family enterprise or the impersonal corporation) it may be embodied, or else die. It is demonic in that modern sense: not immoral but amoral.

The Moloch of capitalism is as deadly and merciless as its Canaanite ancestor. But its altars are everywhere, virtually invisible yet part of the warp and woof of everyday life: at one moment prayed to on Wall Street, at another configuring the most hidden desires and anxieties of everyone's emotional life.

By liberating the individual from feudal restraints, Luther's Reformation had helped make capitalism possible. But critics of capitalism, socialists especially, saw that new way of life as a finely reticulated system of production without social coherence or purpose. The Enlightenment honored Luther for helping free people from mental enslavement. Socialism vowed to do something greater: take the truth of religion as a protest against real suffering and translate its yearnings into real life. Abolishing capitalism would in that sense redeem the mission enunciated by Luther. In this grand historical narrative, Luther had midwifed capitalism, which would midwife socialism.

Lenin, and all the authors of the socialist movement from Marx's death until the *summa* of the Russian Revolution (and past that time as well), would inherit this view. Karl Kautsky, "the Pope of Marxism" and leader of the German Social Democratic Party in the early decades of the twentieth century, penned an appreciation of the Reformation in the spirit first enunciated by Marx and Engels. He cogently noted that the most popular part of the Bible at the time of the Reformation was the Apocalypse, the Fifth Monarchy prophesized by Daniel, with its forecast of the downfall of the existing order of things.

It is customary to depict religion and socialism as irreconcilable; one believes, the other doesn't. No one could doubt the atheism of the socialist movement and of the October Revolution, so relentlessly were they stigmatized with that transgression and so often did they embrace it. But the atheism implicit in the normal operations of a society given over to worship of the commodity has been unmentionable. Capitalism's fealty to God is a charade, its supplications more in the nature of a call for a heavenly gendarme when social turmoil threatens to get out of hand.

If socialism gave up faith in God, it nonetheless carried the torch for what one social commentator called the "secular sacred." So, for example, Rosa Luxemburg, like Lenin, took on the Church but not the religious instinct; a true Christian was a premature socialist, in her view. Antonio Gramsci, the imprisoned leader of the Italian Communist Party under Mussolini, characterized religion as "the most gigantic utopia, that is, the most gigantic metaphysics that history has ever known ... and is therefore the brother of other men, equal to other men." The Reformation might function as "a model of moral and intellectual reform."

None of this was to be. No need to rehearse the failures and appalling denouement of the Russian Revolution or the more profound dying away of the socialist moment. The proletarian metaphysic that was supposed to redeem the promissory note issued by the Reformation and the secular revolutions that followed remains unredeemed. The fable of emancipation entertained for centuries lacks credibility. Because of that, Moloch grows more fearsome.

The Clown Prince of Darkness

Is Donald Trump a fitting avatar of Moloch? In some sense, no; he's too ridiculous. If he wasn't himself so humorless, he might have borrowed this apt Marxism (not Karl's, but the brothers'): "Who do you believe, me or your lying eyes?" Yet his presence is nonetheless spectral. There is about him an essential brute narcissism and cruelty of sensibility that conduces to despair. In his mouth, everything turns to ash, including five hundred years of dreams deferred.

The Donald is not the author of that destruction but rather its outcome. A pervasive atmosphere of cynicism is his oxygen. Everything is a lie, a put-on, a false front, a way of getting over. Trump didn't invent that conviction about a world without convictions. That's a Wall Street state of mind. That's the moral refuse of a world given over to the capitalist Moloch. Decades of dispossession, of fixes in the highest sanctums of political and economic power, of intellectual genuflections at the altar of the bottom line, of death as collateral damage, bred Trumpism in the bone and sinew of American life. He's not Doctor Frankenstein; he's the good doctor's experiment gone awry.

Trump is also the vessel of soured fantasies. Invest enough psychological and emotional energy exalting the businessman as an übermensch—an ardently held element of our civic faith for many years now—and you get a facsimile to run things. Only a facsimile, however.

The Donald comports himself like a Mafia don—and, as a matter of fact, has maintained close relations with that criminal underground, as Sidney Blumenthal's essay in the *London Review of Books* recently reminded us. Trump's real-estate deals, construction projects, casinos, and hotels have left his retinue populated with "made men." What could be more fitting to our age when all gods are dead? Even Moloch reappears as a warped burgher–*cum*–Tony Soprano. Nonetheless, the titan of finance as Napoleonic strongman has lived in the American imagination since the robber-baron days. Trump passes as its latest incarnation.

Another fantasy powers Trump's ascendancy. Two generations have lived under the reign of a capitalism less and less encumbered by social restraint, more and more tone-deaf to its social responsibilities. Consequently, so much resentment of the political class and the business elite has piled up over the last half-century. It was bound to find an outlet—or several.

Trump was one. His utter fecklessness, his capricious relationship with his own social surroundings, allowed him to step forward not only as a generalissimo but as a Hero of the People, its knight errant against the "establishment." Here the point is not that he doesn't mean it. In a sense, he doesn't mean anything. What's important is that the capitalism of the "postindustrial" era has devoured, Moloch-like, the lives of so many and left them angry and vengeful. A savage savior with a taste for blood beckoned.

Trump is Moloch's messenger. What is the message? That the dreams transported from Wittenberg to Saint Petersburg are dead. There are no human universals, only bloodlines. There is no enlightenment, only nightmares. There is no truth or seeking after truth, only "alternative facts." There is no transcendence, only vengeance. There is no Mother Earth, only a slag heap. There is no storyline, just an impromptu moment-to-moment.

It's not so much what Trump stands for that is to be feared, but that he stands for nothing. He ad libs and oscillates wildly, because he changes not so much his mind but rather his mood. He latches on to and discards political positions at will, moves hither and yon driven by the whimsies of polls, his adolescent temper, and an insatiable craving for adulation.

Whatever works: xenophobic today, sentimentalizing "the Dreamers" tomorrow; the billionaire's buddy in one tweet, godfather of the working stiff in the next. This is not merely garden-variety political hypocrisy, always in plentiful supply. It is that, but also more. His incoherence expresses the hidden logic of what works—and what works in the land of capital is inherently ephemeral.

Is there, then, "no there there"? First, last, and always a dynastic businessman, Trump has filled his government with similar types, family capitalists writ large. If there is a center of gravity to his administration, that's it. Dynasts who have come of age running their own affairs, Wall Street sea-dog speculators not accustomed to accommodating the views or interests of others, anti-bureaucrats, men and women of imperial will for whom the state is an annoyance and impediment, something they are not familiar with and don't care to be. Policy in these circles roughly approximates the raw desires of men and women on the make, especially those who've already made it.

A bulldog provocateur, Trump seems to bite himself in the ass with remarkable frequency. While this might be diagnosed as a form of political stupidity, it's more than that. It is a learned instinct. This inbred authoritarian willfulness is a social character trait that belongs to the genus and species *Capitalist patriarchus*. In Trump's case and for many of the dynastic capitalists that now occupy cabinet posts, it's a trait that has metastasized, invaded other elements of the social organism, and now attempts to trample over a strange terrain full of political obstacles. They are maddened by the encounter.

Rumors to the contrary, Trump is not a fascist, even if in the course of his mental perambulations he stumbles or ventures onto terrain littered with fascist incendiaries. But to be that real McCoy takes some thought, more commitment, and at least a normal attention span, which The Donald has in very short supply. While he performs the politics of fear, Trump has never been inclined to do the gritty work of organizing a movement; when he makes gestures in that direction, the turnout of his troops is pathetic. He hasn't done the spade work. All is theater.

Moreover, his haplessness as a manager and commander of a complex bureaucracy produces disarray so massive as to undo or paralyze the regime, which is harassed by opposition from within and from without. His rump government is furthermore undermined by the "hidden state"; it already has been in the realm of foreign affairs, where the national security state deploys its polished dark arts to thwart his most parochial, self-interested impulses.

Damage has been and will be done more without regard to Trump than because of him. What is most alarming, on this double anniversary of the West's best hopes of the last half-millennium, is that there is abroad in the world the spirit of Moloch, luridly lighting up the abyss out of which Trump has emerged.

What is most heartening is the remarkable, massive, and largely spontaneous eruption responding to the threat. Trump may not last long. Moloch will, however. Recovering the capacity to dream again of social emancipation and to undertake the ground-level work to make that into flesh and blood has become the urgent task of today and tomorrow.

Index